WHISPERS OF BETRAYAL

Whispers of Betrayal: Love Letters That Changed Everything. A Memoir

Library of Congress Control Number: 2024933961

ISBN (paperback): 978-1-963271-15-7
ISBN (ebook): 978-1-963271-16-4

ARMINLEAR

Armin Lear Press, Inc.
215 W Riverside Drive, #4362
Estes Park, CO 80517

WHISPERS OF BETRAYAL

Love Letters That Changed Everything

Adela Edgecombe

Adela Edgecombe

This book is dedicated to my dad.
Can you hear me, Dad? I can hear you so much clearer than I ever did before. You are my hero and I'm so sorry I didn't see it sooner. Your loving daughter.

Nina and her Uncle Giro arriving at San Salvatore Church in Passiano

PART ONE

ONE

"Bella! Bella!" chanted the crowd.

Flowers flew from a bomb-damaged balcony, landing on the cobblestones at her feet as she and her uncle Giro led the press of people past shops that had closed in anticipation of the day.

It was March 29, 1951, the day before her 17th birthday and, somehow, her wedding day. But the only thing she wanted was her mother.

She tightened her grip on Giro's arm as they continued towards the church. Her father was not far behind, but he'd felt his clothes were not refined enough to escort her. He wanted everything perfect for her wedding. But why couldn't she have her sisters there? They didn't have proper clothes either, but why was that so important to him? Her sisters meant more to her than anything in the world since her mother was gone, and she wanted them with her. She searched the crowd, even though she knew they weren't there.

"Viva Nina!" The crowd started a new chant. Security pushed them back as cameras flashed.

At least her dress was beautiful. Her groom had brought it from America, and her aunt had taken it in to fit her tiny frame. Layers of white silk transformed her into a princess, with a veil and train stretching behind her.

Despite her confusion and fear, she couldn't help but smile shyly at the hordes of people there to see her and wish her well. Children laughed and dashed through the crowd. Everyone wanted a glimpse of her as she floated down the cobblestone road to her destiny. The cameras kept flashing in front of her. She swallowed her fear as she continued to put one foot in front of the other.

If only her father had allowed her to visit her mother's grave this morning. Her mother shouldn't have died; she was the only one who could have explained all this to her. She blinked back tears as she thought of her mother. Would her mother have wanted her to go to America with a man she didn't know and leave her sisters? But there was no way to stop it now. Her father had made that clear.

More flowers flew through the air. There were so many flowers they lined the streets. After the wedding, she'd have them put in a wagon and brought to her mother's grave. Visualizing her mother's resting place piled high with flowers strengthened her as she walked to the church.

She lifted her chin and waved at the crowd. She didn't understand why this frenzy surrounded her or why the paparazzi were determined to take so many pictures of her.

But if they wanted her to feel like a movie star, she would try to enjoy the journey, even if it led to a man she hardly knew and certainly didn't love.

* * *

I'd always felt my parents' story deserved to be told. However, it took me decades to realize it was me who had to tell it. Some say it resembled a fairytale with my father, the handsome American Soldier, in the role of the prince, who saved Cinderella, my mother, from never-ending poverty. After her mother died, she'd been like Cinderella. Cooking and cleaning for her father and older brother, while her little sisters, ages 12, 10, 5, and 3, needed her constant care. At times, it was overwhelming. But did she want to be the Princess carried away by her prince charming to a better life?

The accurate tale, I found, was far from a fairy tale. The truth revealed itself as I researched my parents' experiences of life and love: the startling histories I unearthed, the romance I tried to uncover, and the drama I wished I could run from.

In 2005, my father died, and in 2007, my husband, Mark, and I settled my mom into a lovely house in Fallbrook, California, so that she would be close to us. Fallbrook is known for its avocados, with groves and nurseries dotting the hills. Mom was not enthusiastic. She protested that Fallbrook lay too far out in the country and there was no place for her to wear her heels or dress-up, as she loved to do. Even though she'd been raised in rural Italy raising chickens and growing vegetables, Mom didn't like country life. I couldn't imagine my mother tending to chickens, and she had no interest in growing vegetables. The woman my mom had become was so different from the girl she related in her stories from war-torn Italy. I often wondered how she could've changed so much.

Her wedding pictures, taken by *Life Magazine* photographer David Lee, were some of her most treasured possessions. I had them framed and matted and hung them for her in the hallway of her new home. I also took the *Life Magazine* article and created a collage, which I hung in her stairway. So now she had her walk of fame, which she loved and enjoyed sharing with others. Dad's recliner sat in the family room, where she could sit with a throw wrapped around herself and tell her stories. From the recliner, a beautiful view of the sunset and hillsides spread beyond the windows. I was glad I could find my mother a home she could love, even if she didn't love Fallbrook itself.

True to my mother's nature, after getting settled, she first called the local Village News to share her story in their newspaper. Their journalist came to her house, and with my mother explaining every picture, took the walk of fame. The resulting article in the Village News had a beautiful picture of her and a lovely story of how my parents met during the war, highlighting how closely the media followed her marriage. She'd never discovered how Life Magazine found out about the wedding or how she ended up on the cover of many European magazines. That's a mystery I wish I could solve. Her story was her claim to fame, even after all these years, and she enjoyed telling it over and over again.

After she got more comfortable with her new surroundings, she and I established a weekly tradition of a shopping trip to the Oceanside Mall followed by lunch at a nearby restaurant, often our favorite Asian buffet. Then, on the way home, we would stop at Trader Joe's for groceries. The love of shopping was one of the things I shared with my mother, even if I had to hear her tell her story to the salesclerk at Macy's or the waitress at the restaurant.

These trips were usually a mix of mother/daughter camaraderie and mother/daughter frustration. Mom had comments about everything: her dislike of Fallbrook, my brothers' choices, my friends, and whatever was causing the newscasters to go into a frenzy on that particular day. Some days, I could navigate the conversation, but other times, her negativity wore on my soul. Over the years, I'd finally developed the skill to sometimes direct these tedious discussions in more positive directions, but I still often found the outings exhausting.

Putting her groceries away after one such trip on a blazing October day in 2013, I tried to ignore my weariness. Mom had fixated on her unhappy relationship with Dad all day. Repeatedly, she'd told me, "He never loved me. We never had a conversation." I'd heard this litany of complaints so many times it hardly phased me, but today, I paused to wonder why their relationship had been so dysfunctional. True, they had little in common. At home, I remembered them fighting some when I was young, but Dad worked so much that Mom was often just home alone. Then, socially, Mom had always been the chattering one, the butterfly who drew people to her like a pot of honey. Quiet in the background, Dad was easy to overlook: before he retired, because he was always at work, and after he retired, because he was content with simple pleasures like gardening and cooking. They never went anywhere together before he died, probably because he embarrassed her. She was fifteen years his junior and looked even younger. She enjoyed displaying her shapely legs and dressing to the nines; while in his retirement, Dad wore slippers and frumpy clothes everywhere he went. Were those shallow reasons enough to explain her discontent, or was there more?

The phone rang. I was staying for dinner, so while she took the call, I pulled out the vegetables I knew she intended for the meal and started chopping as I listened to her chattering away to some friend. She was twisting her wedding ring around her finger and gazing into the distance. "He was so handsome when he came back to Italy. His eyes were so blue. All the girls stared at him and me for being with him."

I marveled at her comments. Was this the same man she'd been complaining about all day? But I'd heard these positive statements a few times since Dad had died. It dawned on me that now that he was gone, she could sometimes forget the frumpy, older man in embarrassing slippers and remember the handsome Prince Charming who had come for her in Italy.

After she hung up, she turned to me, "Oh Adela, I need you to help me. Put that down, let me cook," she said as she took over her kitchen. She looked at me, and I knew what she would ask before the words left her mouth. "Please, Adela. I want people to know about my life. Won't you tell my story?" Mom had just turned 79. Seeing her story in print had become increasingly more important to her.

I sighed. With my sixtieth birthday looming imminently around the corner, it felt like it was finally time to find out the truth, time to unlock the mystery surrounding my mother and father's marriage.

"Okay, Mom,"I agreed with a wave of anxiety, "I'll do it."

TWO

What was this story Mom wanted me to share? It was a tale woven into my life since my earliest memories. It was my mom's moment of glory, and as a child, it had always been mine as well.

One autumn morning, when I was nine years old, I awoke full of anxiety thinking of the presentation I would make that day. To distract myself, I propped up my current book on my pillow to catch the morning light and lost myself in the world of Peter Pan. Then, just as Tinker Bell met the ageless boy, I was sure a shadow glided down the hallway outside my room in the murky morning light. The hair on the back of my neck stood at attention. Could it be an intruder or, worse, a ghost? I dog-eared the page and scooted off the bed to peek around the doorway. A loud bang erupted from the kitchen.

It was just my mom getting things ready for the day. Now that I'd been jolted from the story by my imagined ghost, the anxiety I'd woken up with flooded my mind again.

Today was the first Sharing Day of 4th grade, and I would have to stand up in front of a whole classroom full of kids who thought I was shy and stupid and talk. I took a deep breath. It was going to be okay. Maybe what I had to share was impressive enough to change their opinion of me.

I'd begged and pleaded with my mom to let me take our treasured copy of the April 23, 1951, Life magazine as my sharing item, and she had finally agreed. Last night, she'd slipped it in a plastic bag, inserted a piece of cardboard, and laid it on the kitchen table with a look that made it very clear she didn't know if I could be trusted. But I knew how much it meant to her and how much it could mean to me. After all, how many kids have parents who have a whole article in Life Magazine? And it was such a good story, too. Right in the middle of the magazine, between an essay about the movie An American in Paris and an advertisement for Carling's Red Cap beer, showcasing Lucille Ball holding up a full, bubbly glass, was the beautiful story of my parents' fairytale wedding.

I made my way into the kitchen. The magazine was still on the table, right between the two bowls of cereal Mom had set out for my brother and me. At least she hadn't changed her mind. She was scrubbing away at the sink, which looked perfectly clean to me.

My younger brother George came out of his room. He eyed the magazine on the table.

"Adela's gunna stand up in class, and everybody's gunna laugh." He sing-sang.

Mom hushed him and gave me a warning glare before I could lunge at him. I dropped to my chair with a thud while she added milk to our bowls of Cheerios.

Centering the Cheerio box between us so George was out of my line of sight, I slid the magazine to my side and gently pulled it out of its sleeve. It was eleven years old, two years older than me, but it was already fragile. I turned the pages, being careful not to tear the delicate paper.

I'd heard Mom share her story more times than I could count. With her light Italian accent, she told the tale to everyone she met. As a child, it became my tale of fame, as the offspring of the parents I thought of as celebrities.

I ran my finger over the title, A Wedding in Passiano. An Italian Girl Marries the GI Who Really Came Back for Her. The wedding pictures were beautiful. Surrounded by the graceful architecture of an old Italian village, my mother appeared shy and sweet in her luminous wedding dress that my dad had brought all the way from the United States. Despite the thronging crowds that surrounded them and filled the streets, my dad only had eyes for her. At the top of the article was a picture of my mom at her first communion and another of my dad looking young and handsome in his army uniform. That is when the story really started. The magazine said my mom was 10 when she met my dad, but Mom always insisted she was only nine.

I was nine. How could she know she would marry Dad when she was so young and he was so old? I looked at her now, at the counter, wiping down the coffee pot and sliding it to its spot next to the toaster. Nothing about my parents' existence resembled the beautiful life those pictures promised. My dad worked nights, and we barely saw him. Mom was always busy scrubbing, mopping, and dusting. When my parents interacted, there was either an uncomfortable silence, mom nagging, or the two arguing.

Would she marry my dad again? I watched her open a cupboard and shift the glasses into a perfect line. The question was just on the tip of my tongue, but my mom didn't talk about things like that, especially with me, so there was no point in asking her. She was like Cinderella. In fact, they called her that in some of the magazine articles. After her mother died, she took care of her four young sisters and made meals for her father, brother, and the whole family. I'm sure many saw her as a Cinderella and my father as the handsome prince who saved her from a life of drudgery.

I stopped my daydream as Mom rushed me to my room. She pulled my favorite dress from the closet, a white one with pink stripes.

"Adela, you have to look your best today," she said as she pulled the bow tight in the back. Then, she transferred her energy to my hair, brushing out each knot and pulling it into a tight ponytail, and continued with her instructions, "Teacher conferences are next week. Mr. Jackson better have a good report."

Mom and Mr. Jackson would probably talk more about her story than me. Maybe that would be good; if they were talking about her story, then Mr. Jackson wouldn't have time to tell her that I never paid attention in class and was always daydreaming.

Today, I would stay focused. I had a mission to get to school on time without damaging my mother's magazine and do a good job telling her story.

Mom gave my hair one last tug, and I was out the door.

I ran past the rest of the houses on my street. The ponytail mom had just finished started slipping right away. But that was normal. I couldn't keep it the way she liked it.

La Mirada, CA, was a lovely, friendly town, which was a good thing because I had a mile of neighborhood streets to make it through to get to La Pluma Elementary. It was a warm fall day, so I slowed and skipped a little. I tried to think about the words I would use when I showed my class the magazine. My mom loved to put me on the spot even when she knew I hated it. When I was struggling with telling time in third grade, she would stand me in front of her friends and say, "Adela, tell everybody what time it is." I'd always freeze and mumble as I stared at the clock and tried to decide the correct answer. I couldn't do that today. The kids would laugh, and my mom might find out. I just wanted to make her proud.

I had just turned on La Pluma Drive when I realized I needed to hurry or I'd be late. I started running and felt the rest of my hair slip from my ponytail. I rushed into Mr. Jackson's classroom. He was frowning at me. I tried to catch my breath as I pushed my hair out of my eyes.

I dropped to my desk and checked the magazine. With

relief, I saw that I'd gotten it there in one piece without a dent or fold. I glanced around the classroom; maybe by the end of the day, one of these kids would want to be my friend, and I could stop being so shy and scared. But right now, fear was all I felt. The other students laid out their things to share on their desks: model airplanes, picture books, and artwork. The boy next to me was going to share his potato plant. Everyone was quiet and seemed worried that their items weren't good enough. Maybe I wasn't the only one that was afraid to get up in front of the class.

It was almost my turn. My stomach started to hurt, but I wasn't going to cry. I would be brave. I tried wishing my shyness away, but that never worked. A month ago, when school started, I told myself that I wouldn't be shy this year but would be wise and make friends. But that was easy to say and harder to do. To distract my worry, I thought about my dream from the night before, where I'd imagined I could fly. I could still feel the air as I leaped from rooftop to rooftop.

"Adela, it's your turn." I jerked my head up. Mr. Jackson was pointing at me. I'd daydreamed right through the middle of Sharing Day. A boy was sitting down with a handful of baseball cards that he must've just been talking about.

More than ever, I wished I really could fly away. But everyone was looking at me, so I gathered up my magazine. I had to walk to the front of the class without tripping, turn around and face the class. I carefully took the magazine out of the bag and held it up. The Dahil Lama was on the cover, and

I knew most had never seen anything like him here in Southern California. My hands were shaking a little, and I tried to make them stop.

Everyone was watching me as I flipped to the correct pages. I took a deep breath and started, "This is my parents' story. They met in Italy when my dad was a soldier, and my mom was only nine years old," I pointed to her communion picture, then continued, "even though the magazine says she was ten." One of the girls in the front row silently mouthed the word 'Wow," and my voice stopped shaking as I continued, "My dad gave her chocolate and promised that when the war was over, he would come back and marry her."

I took a deep breath. My classmates were all paying attention now. Maybe, like me, they were interested because we were the same age my mom had been, and none of us had any idea who we would marry.

"My mom didn't speak any English, and my dad didn't speak any Italian, but they wrote letters back and forth with a translator for four years after the war was over. Then my dad went all the way to Italy and married my mom the day before her 17th birthday."

I flipped through the following pages, showing my classmates the rest of the pictures, the wedding with my mom looking so beautiful in the dress my dad had brought for her, then one of them cutting the cake. Another photo showed my parents leading crowds of people through the village streets. I told the class, "They were like movie stars. So many camerapeople were taking pictures, and people yelled congratulations and threw flowers. They were in Life Magazine, so they were famous."

My classmates clapped. After all, who doesn't love a good fairytale?

Through the years of my childhood, I cherished the fact that I was the result of such a unique beginning. And just like my mother held on to those days of fame, I ran behind, grabbing at the virtual wedding streamers.

THREE

I had one requirement when I agreed to tell my mother's story. I'd heard my mother's story for years, and I knew I didn't want her to be my only source of information. My dad had been a buttoned-up, non-expressive man, and now he was gone. But he had left something behind. Something I hadn't seen since I was a teen. Something my mom had kept hidden. That was precisely what I needed to start putting together this puzzle. I needed my father's letters.

The first time I saw my father's letters, my mother was sitting on the floor surrounded by photos, newspaper clippings, and magazine articles documenting her wedding day and the whirlwind weeks and months following her marriage to my father. Titles written in Italian scrawled across faded pages, my parent's faces smiled at me from the shiny covers of magazines, and black-and-white photos recorded the crowds that had surrounded them that day. On one cover, my father stared pensively into the distance while my young mother studied him as if she were trying to discern who he was.

At the time, I was 16. I don't think my mother had any intention of showing the letters to me, and at that age, quite honestly, I didn't have much interest. Still, I needed to distract her from a poor report card. The thick manila envelope sitting on the floor, among other scattered memorabilia surrounding her, served that purpose very well.

I pointed at the envelope. "What are those?" I asked instead of answering her angry question about my grades.

"Your father's letters from after the war," she answered.

I'd known letters were exchanged after they met in Italy during World War II, when she was a young Italian teenager, and he'd returned from the army to New Bedford, Massachusetts. Still, I was surprised my parents had kept all the correspondence.

"What do they say?" I asked.

"I don't know." Mom shrugged and picked up a picture of herself as a little girl, "I never read them."

Startled by her strange answer, I silently congratulated myself on distracting her, but then I was curious. I picked up the envelope and opened it. With one eye open and one shut, I peered inside and fingered through its contents. I marveled at the well-written script; Dad had such beautiful handwriting. I pulled one of the letters away from its neighbors and scanned a few lines. "You have nice teeth, Nina, so take good care of them. Brush them at least twice a day."

Brush her teeth, really? He talked to her like she was a child. I supposed she had been compared to him. I didn't think of their age discrepancy often, but he was fifteen years older than her. Now, it didn't seem like that big of a deal, but how could he have wanted to marry someone young enough that you had to tell them to brush their teeth?

I shoved the letter back into the envelope, feeling oddly disgusted and confused. Why had Mom just said she didn't know what the letters said? Did she even know Dad had told her to brush her teeth? I had so many questions, but I had just calmed Mom down, and I thought I would just quit while I was ahead.

Decades would pass before I got to ask those questions.

* * *

When Dad passed away in 2005, I was almost 52. We never talked about his correspondence back and forth to Italy. The simple reason that I didn't read his letters, much less discuss them with him, was that I never saw them again after that quick glimpse when I was sixteen.

But the more complex reality was that we didn't have the type of rapport where those conversations occurred. I never felt moved to talk with him about anything pertaining to his life in the past. I can't picture us chatting about his choice to wait for his bride in Italy to grow up, what he'd given up waiting for that to happen, or what his thoughts were when he discovered things were completely different than he expected. We certainly wouldn't have talked about whether or not he was disappointed with his life. He was a quiet, reserved man, and our relationship didn't involve the kind of exchanges that revealed emotions or explored feelings. He did what he needed to do without complaint.

My mom had plenty of complaints about him, however. From an adult perspective, I tried to analyze her criticism. As a child, we did little together as a family, but the few outings I remember didn't go well. In those days, you could go to Knott's Berry Farm, which was close to our house, and walk around for free. I have little recollection of enjoying the outings. My parents didn't talk to each other or us. It was like we were going through the motions, trying to be a happy family but not knowing how. My parents were so dispirited it never took much for one of them to get mad at one of us, prompting the return to the car and a drive home in complete silence.

Dad worked hard standing on his damaged feet all day. It must have been hard on him having a young wife who wanted to do things, and he didn't want to because he was tired. My mom related a rare day when Dad announced, "Let's go to the beach." With great excitement, she packed a picnic lunch and grabbed a blanket. Dad rented an umbrella, and we played in the sand. But my mom remembered Dad abruptly getting up and saying that he would wait in the car. Mom was heartbroken that he ruined the day. I don't understand. I could make excuses for him, but that isn't right. Could he have been so tired? Or was it that he was just so unhappy?

I spent a generous portion of my youth and even my adulthood wishing that my father would be more open, but it wasn't until I was much older that I started to think about why he was that way. During combat in World War II, he received injuries, but maybe the mental wounds he suffered really caused more damage. Over recent years, the subject of PTSD has become widely accepted and readily acknowledged. Considering all that my father endured, there was no doubt he suffered from his war experience, and one of the most prevalent symptoms of PTSD is avoidance.

We might not have had a sentimental relationship, but Dad was always there for me. When I was a newly divorced, single mom in the 80s, I was grateful to Dad for helping me as much as he could. He used to pick up my son, Andrey, from preschool and keep him until I was off work. When I left my boyfriend a few years later, he came and helped me move. It was a quick move. All my stuff went into my parents' garage, and I had to live with them for a month. He went through all my disorganized boxes and repacked and labeled them while I was at work. He then moved me to Palm Springs when I found a job there. After the move, I fondly remember him sitting in a chair in front of my apartment, cutting down the boxes as I tossed them out to him. A few years later, after I had moved into my condo in Rancho Mirage, he came over and painted the entire place.

He was so wonderful, working so hard, physically giving all that he could, but his emotions were locked up tight behind a brick wall with extra rebar. He never talked to me about anything but the mundane. We had no discussions that week he painted my condo. I'd come home from work; we'd have dinner and watch TV.

But my biggest regret is that I never realized it didn't

have to be that way. Why didn't I try to pick away at that wall? Why didn't I push? I made no effort to get to know my dad. I never considered there was so much more to this quiet man. His life must have been so different from what he had dreamed of when he waited all those years for his wife. Indeed, he had hopes that were dashed and loneliness he never expected.

It brings tears to my eyes to think about what could have been. I've asked myself why I didn't ask my dad questions back when he could have responded, but I have no answers

lack of curiosity. Maybe I did try, and when he

it discouraged me from any continuing efforts.

is perspective on their story would remain a

only try to piece together.

FOUR

Before their marriage, my parents suffered levels of trauma that most of us could never truly comprehend. Growing up in war-torn Italy, my mom endured all the horrific deprivations of war, starvation, sickness, and fear. When she was nine years old, right before her eyes, a bomb struck her favorite teacher and blew him to pieces. Meanwhile, my dad knew his war-time agony and, true to his stoic generation, never spoke of his trauma. He was involved in several significant invasions and all the death and suffering that came with such maneuvers. Toward the war's end, his tank ran over a land mine in France. He received his life-changing injury and witnessed his commanding officer's head blown off. I don't know if my dad had ongoing nightmares about that. I know I can't talk to my mom about the war without her weeping.

The war ended, and my mother grew up. Meanwhile, my father, the American Soldier, as her family called him, was waiting to come for her.

When she was 17, and he was 32, their wedding was an image of hope and joy, the opposite of everything the war had thrown at them. After years of traumatic news, the media was ready for their happy story. They were inundated with 1950s paparazzi, who documented their wedding and continued to follow them around for the following eight months that they were in Italy. They were on the cover of numerous European magazines and newspapers such as Tempo and La Settimana Incom. The American press jumped on board, documenting their story in "Life" magazine with a five-page spread. In the 1950s, "Life" magazine had made a name for itself as the leading magazine in the country, and its photographers were respected as some of the best photojournalists in history.

This period became the cornerstone of my mother's story. It was a moment of fame that overshadowed all the suffering and loss that preceded it and eclipsed the reality of what her life would become in the United States.

Many years later, in 1989, the retired managing editor of "Life" magazine, Philip B. Kunhardt Jr., remembered my parents' story. He republished it in a book called *The Joy of Life*. He put it in the chapter called Miracles as one of his favorite stories. There, alongside the story of a man regaining his sight, people surviving a plane crash in the middle of the ocean, and other unbelievable events, was the story of "The G.I. Who Really Did Come Back." It's incredible to me that the managing editor of one of the most prominent magazines in history picked my parents' story to highlight out of thousands and thousands of Life magazine stories. I believed in miracles, and this discovery made it clear to me that it was time for me to delve into this history to see what else I could find.

Thinking about all of this, I wondered who my mother would've been if her fairytale moment had never occurred. She would have never left Italy; I wouldn't have had her for a mother. But on the other hand, I'd always considered her story such an integral part of who she was as a person that I couldn't imagine her without it. As children and then adults, my brothers and I heard her story so often all we could do was roll our eyes when she started in on her tale with some unsuspecting person. It was her claim to fame; it was who she was, and it was a part of her soul.

I don't think Mom had ever considered me as a potential scripter of her story. In her eyes, I was still an awkward little girl. But I had grown in more ways than one, and I had a miracle of my own. I found my soulmate, Mark, on March 29, 2001, after 18 years of being single. The day was stuck in my mind because it was my parents' 50th wedding anniversary. While they did nothing to honor the day because they never went anywhere together in public, it obviously struck me as an impressive accomplishment.

On May 24, 2003, Mark and I were married. My mom always said I was lucky to have found Mark, but she didn't see that it had taken years for me to transform myself from the uncertain, insecure girl I'd been into a woman who was a perfect match for my husband. I wasn't just fortunate; I'd solved my issues with poor self-esteem. I'd grown spiritually.

I needed to have faith; without it, I was nothing. I had a list of what I wanted in a man, and spirituality was at the top. All those changes and growth remade me into someone who could connect with a man like Mark. Our love has helped us grow into who we are today. Without his understanding and encouragement, I doubt I would have considered embarking on the journey to explore the saga of my family and uncover the secrets to enable me to put the past to rest.

Maybe Mom finally saw that growth and realized I was happy in my shoes and my place in life, ready to handle her powerful story, or else she had just run out of others to ask, but after Dad died, she finally made the request.

Her desire touched my heart. She was aging, and the opportunity to meet her desire was drifting away. In my mind, her story was a fairy tale without a happily ever after. Everything I knew about the story never added up. What if I uncovered something that would change how I saw our family forever? I'd heard my mother's version so many times I'd become numb to the story's uniqueness. It wouldn't hurt to do a little research to see what I could uncover.

I googled "war brides" because that is what she called herself, even though it was years after the war when my parents got married. More than 60,000 war brides came to America after World War II. All of them had a story to tell, and many did just that. I explained to my mother the most unique thing about her marriage was how the media loved it and her eight months of fame in Italy, but was that enough? I didn't know how I could write an entire book on the stories I had heard thus far. Even though mom's stories were extraordinary, were they enough for a whole book?

As I mentioned, my mother had stacks of newspaper and magazine articles that featured her and Dad. First, I had to find some order in all these pieces, and I worked to file them all into a scrapbook. Many articles were in Italian, some were in English, and the rest were from journalists she had met over the years. I studied them, trying to decide if I could come up with enough material for a book.

They were such a beautiful couple. As I took in their young faces, I wondered what they were thinking on those days before and after the big wedding day. I smoothed the articles down with my fingers, wishing they could talk to me and tell me what was really going on.

First, I made a trial run of what I knew so far. At my mother's insistence, I agreed to write a summary of her story to send to Oprah and Good Morning America, her two favorite shows. She felt convinced that if she could get her story into the hands of someone famous, they would feel the value and help her. But those endeavors fell into the same category as my mother's previous efforts, and we never received a response. But nothing was going to discourage my mother. I needed to unearth and dig deeper to discover more about their story, or there was no point in going further.

But there was one more resource. Four years of letters were sent between my father and Italy. Could there be some revelations in those letters? I could hardly wait to read them.

FIVE

My mom didn't respond right away when I requested the letters. She looked at me, then looked away with just the slightest hesitation. Obviously, she wasn't thrilled with the prospect of me reading them. I made it clear I couldn't start anything until I had a look at them. I had reviewed all the magazine articles and newspaper clippings, but there just needed to be more to warrant an entire book. When I left her house, she promised she would bring them.

Why was she hesitating? It felt like there was something she didn't want me to find out, and I had no idea what that could be. Decades ago, Mom had told me that she never even read the letters, so why would she care if I read them? What could be hidden in those pages that apparently only my grandparents and my dad had read? Either way, it made me more determined to ensure I read them, too. Something was missing from my parents' tale. Before I could move forward with Mom's request to tell her story, I needed to delve into my father's perspective as well.

Three nights later she appeared at my house with the same large, manilla envelope I remembered from so many years ago. She seemed optimistic that I could do something with her story. I could see that glimmer of hope in her eyes that I might finally put her story in print, realizing her lifelong dream. I set the letters on the coffee table and promised her I would read them as soon as possible. She seemed enthusiastic at this point, and there was no sign of her earlier hesitation. She probably decided she wanted her story in print no matter what I might discover.

After she left, my husband headed for bed. I told him I'd take a stab at the letters, and then I'd turn in as well.

The envelope seemed heavier than it had been when I was 16. I settled on the living room couch, opened the clasp, and tilted the opening toward my lap. The letters spewed out onto my flowered pajama pants like a solid brick, as if the pages had melded together after so many years of not being touched. I gingerly flipped through them. My father's elegantly scribed handwriting stood out starkly on the yellowing pages, almost glowing in the dim lighting. They seemed to be in random order, and scattered among them were letters from Italy, written in Italian.

I paused as I noticed each of my father's letters was addressed only to Nina, my mother. From my mother's comments, I would have thought the rest of the family would have been included in the greetings.

I cleared books off the coffee table and began arranging the letters chronologically.

They spanned just over four years, from the autumn of 1946 until weeks before my parent's wedding in March 1951. My dad had shared his thoughts and the details of his daily life with the little Italian girl for whom he professed more and more fondness as time progressed. But how could that be?

My questions grew as my dad's life unfolded on the pages before me, and yet I was fascinated with this young man I didn't know existed. He liked to read and play cards with his family. He loved his dog Dixie and seemed to be such a good son and brother. He was so skilled at expressing himself in his letters. As I discovered when I was young, writing was a much more effective format for communication than trying to express myself verbally. I saw other startling similarities to myself. How could that be? Why didn't we have a stronger bond? I was very much like my dad, yet we hadn't been close. The tears started to pour as I continued to read.

The man I knew as my father worked hard and provided for his family, but he had been quiet and closed. He didn't share hopes and dreams like he did in these letters. Yet, he didn't express disappointment or loss either. He hadn't even protested when my mother had moved him out of her room into a small room down the hall for the last few decades of their marriage. As I mentioned, he had helped me with projects and such when I was on my own with my boys, but I'd had no clue that the emotion these letters revealed even existed inside my father.

Where had this man gone? What had changed him? The man in these letters was someone I could relate to. His letters vividly reflected the same fears and awkwardness I had always struggled with throughout my lifetime. I could have gone to him as I tried to find my place in the world. He would have understood. But I never did, and he never gave me a reason to think I could. My heart ached for the quiet man I had so misunderstood. I continued reading through broken translations and missing letters when the truth kicked me in the gut: I had never truly known my father.

But there was another confusion revealed in the letters. A repeated detail that didn't make sense. Who was my dad sharing all these intimate details with? Just as Dad's letters were all addressed to Nina, the letters from Italy, both the Italian and the English ones, were all signed by Nina.

But my mother, Nina, couldn't have written those letters. First of all, neither the Italian letters nor the English ones were in her handwriting. Secondly, according to her, she hadn't even read them.

I rescanned the letters from Italy that I could read. One line caught my eye, "All I can send to you is all my love and a big kiss." And then a few letters later, "You make me very happy that you still love me and have trust in me." Had my mother actually had the translator write those lines? I could hardly imagine it.

So that meant either my mother was lying, or the letters were all the fabrication of my grandmother, Agnese. But that scenario brought even more questions. My grandmother died two years before my parents were married. So, who wrote the later letters? I paged back through the Italian correspondence; my grandmother could have easily written the letters in Italian, but the English ones were all in the handwriting of the interpreter, so that revealed nothing. Had the interpreter continued the farce on his own after my grandmother died? Or was my grandfather somehow involved? Or, back to my original thought, was my mother lying?

I slid to the floor and dropped my head to my knees. Between discovering a side to my father, whom I never knew existed, and the confusion about who was writing the letters, I was overwhelmed. A sob shuddered through me. I had never really known my dad, and now he was gone. The content of these letters didn't make any sense with what I knew of my parents' relationship. The words reflected a tender love that built over the years. But that was impossible if I confirmed that my mother never read the letters. So, was that true? My mother had also constantly claimed that my father never loved her. Had their relationship eroded so far that she was denying the truth? But my mother had been so young; how much could she have even understood?

So then, was the actual truth that the letters were from my grandmother, with one additional, glaring, shocking detail: she was impersonating her daughter? Could that be possible? How could she? What kind of mother could do that to her daughter? And then there was my unsuspecting father. Nothing in his letters indicated he thought he was writing to anybody but his future wife. If my grandmother had actually written the responses, then he'd been purposely misled for years. A chill rolled over me. He had banked his whole life on a lie.

Everything I knew about my parents' dysfunctional relationship pointed directly to the possibility that it had started with a big giant lie. Shuddering, I rubbed my eyes and cried for both my parents. The house was silent around me. The stillness of the night and my discovery engulfed me. The questions kept circling in my mind as my head started to pound. Was this why my dad was always so quiet? When had he realized what had happened? My parents didn't even speak the same language when they got married. So why did he go through with it? Why did my mother? What did my grandfather think of all this? Indeed, grandfather must have been a part of it. Did anyone else know? Why had they kept it a secret all these years? Did my mother even understand what actually happened if she had never read the letters? Was this why she'd hesitated when I asked her for the letters? Was she suspicious as to what her mother had done?

It was 3:00 in the morning. I thought about waking my husband and sharing the pain of my discoveries, but I just continued leafing through the pages. There was no way I could sleep. I needed desperately to talk to my mother.

SIX

My mind raced faster than the clock while what was left of the night ticked by with painful slowness. After finishing my father's letters, I was awake the rest of the night with a growing headache, waiting to call my mother at 8:00 a.m. on the dot. All those years, all those news outlets, even Life magazine, not one of them got the truth? It hadn't been a love story; it'd been a lie, outright fraud, a betrayal.

As the grandfather clock chimed eight o'clock, I took a deep breath and called my mom.

"Mom, I'm coming over."

When I arrived, letters in hand, my mom sat in the front room, staring out the window. Her fingers were twisted in a locket that had hung around her neck for as long as I could remember. Tension lined her voice as she greeted me. She couldn't quite meet my eyes. She must have known that I'd made a discovery.

I didn't waste any time with niceties. I was exhausted and angry. I dropped the manilla envelope on the coffee table in front of her. "Mom, did you know all those letters are addressed to you? And that all the letters from Italy appear to be written by you? I thought you had an arranged marriage, and all the correspondence went between Grandmother Agnese and Dad. Did you ever read the letters?"

"No." she said, "I never read them. I was afraid to give them to you. I thought you might find out something."

"Mom, how could you never read them?"

Had she not known the truth even though the answers were right in front of her? But maybe it made sense. Perhaps she couldn't bear to place any blame on her beloved mother. My mom had an incredible bond with my grandmother. The two of them had been through immense pressure together, the devastation and struggles of war, sickness, and care for the younger children. All of that was then compounded by the fact that her mother died when she was 15. At that point, I think she placed her mother's memory on a pedestal to be cherished and revered. She would never believe her mother had done anything wrong. I backed down as I saw the anguish on my mother's face.

A silent tear rolled down her cheek, and she fidgeted with her short dark brown hair, apparently trying to mask her emotion. The locket fell open, and I noticed she had switched the photo from my grandmother's image to my dad in his army uniform. Maybe just like she had placed my grandmother on a pedestal, perhaps now, after his death, she'd done the same thing with my father.

"Well, I was young, and I never thought he would come," she explained, "After we got married, there never seemed a point to reading them."

Did my mom know more than she was sharing, or in her mind, was it always just an arranged marriage? When their marriage was struggling, she could have read those letters to understand her husband. But apparently, she never had.

But my thoughts went back to my grandmother Agnese. I sat for a moment and tried to process what she had done. I needed to understand what would drive a mother to impersonate her child and dishonestly represent that child. She'd painted a path for my parents' future without giving them any input or telling them the whole story.

"Mom, I need you to explain this all to me. Start at the beginning."

"Adela, you just don't understand how hard things were."

"Then you need to explain it to me."

Without hesitation, she said, "It started with my mother's life."

SEVEN

I sat across from my mother on the couch as she drew me into the past. Growing up, I had heard glowing stories of her long-suffering mother. Mom had held her up as a shining example, but she had never given me details of her life. Now, she attempted to fill in some of those holes.

"My mother was only two when her mother, Anna Maria, died of tuberculosis."

Mom's eyes had already filled with tears. My anger at my grandmother was still too high to feel any tenderness. But Mom continued, "The great war changed my grandfather."

She explained how her Grandfather Giuseppe had returned from the war as a sullen and morose man. He'd received a burn on his right eye that gave him a ghostly cornea, but along with that injury came good fortune from the government, the right to sell regulated goods, like salt and tobacco. If he hadn't been able to sell those regulated goods through the Great Depression, my grandmother Agnese's family would have been just as poor as most of the population in their town. So instead, they had a three-bedroom apartment above their little store named Sale e Tabacco (Salt and Tobacco) in Cava de' Tirreni. Cava de' Tirreni is in the province of Salerno, region Campania, just south of Naples, on the ankle of Italy's boot.

Life was challenging for Agnese. Her father remarried, and his new wife, Antoinetta, brought two children from her first marriage with her.

Mom stopped and rubbed her chest, "At the time, tuberculosis was a scary disease that no one knew much about. It was a mystery how it spread." Mom scowled. "Since Grandmother Anna Maria had died from it, Antoinetta used that fear to isolate my mother. For most of her childhood, she wasn't allowed to eat with the others and had to play alone."

A little compassion for my grandmother stirred in my heart.

Lonely was a feeling I knew all too well. At least when I was a child, we ate together as a family, but dinners were usually silent and uncomfortable. Conversations that did occur often turned into unhappy arguments. Many nights, I'd end up in my room, sitting in the dark, staring out the window, wondering how to improve my life. Did my grandmother do the same thing with her pain? My life had never been nearly as bad, but listening to her story, I found myself relating to her suffering. I wonder if she fantasized the same way I did that a boy would come along and swoop me up like Prince Charming and make everything better. The more I listened to her sad story, the more I felt strangely close to this woman I had never known. Perhaps, like me, she needed to move on and escape from her family, who didn't demonstrate value for her.

Limited options presented my Grandmother Agnese with twenty-three-year-old Giovanni Farano, a talented woodworker only four years her senior.

I remembered my Grandfather Giovanni during the years he lived in California. He was kind to me, but because of the language barrier, we couldn't speak to one another, and my relationship with him was limited.

Giovanni didn't meet the expectations of Agnese's father, but she felt she had no choice but to marry. She no longer belonged in her childhood home, and Giovanni treated her well. As I listened to my mother, I wondered if my grandmother even loved my grandfather or if she married him out of necessity.

I'm sure she felt hopeful as she was leaving the family home for a new life, the same way I did when I walked down the aisle in June of 1974 when I was 21. The freedom from her childhood prison must have given her a sense of hope as it did me. I got goosebumps as I thought of the similarities between my grandmother's marriage and my first marriage.

That feeling of being alone with no allies must have been Grandmother Agnese's experience, just like it'd been mine. Initially, my first husband made me forget how insecure I always felt by teasing me and making me laugh. Maybe my grandfather did the same for my grandmother. I sighed as I remembered my grandfather and imagined him laughing and teasing my grandmother, as I'm sure he did. Finally, I was starting to understand who she was, taking a moment to slip into her skin. I got chills as I thought of my grandmother; it was like she was right there with me.

On the couch, my mother reached for a Kleenex. "Adela, her father told her that he wouldn't even come to her wedding." I sighed as my mother broke the time-traveling spell I'd been under.

My grandmother and grandfather were married on October 9, 1926. She was just 19 years old, and he was 23. They tied the knot a mile from Cava de'Terrini, in the lovely little village of Passiano, where they would raise their family.

I tried to imagine what my grandmother's wedding must have been like. There would've been no fancy wedding outfits, few gifts, and probably no wedding cake. She didn't know if her brother and sister would defy their father and come to wish her well. It could not have been a very happy day. She would have watched and waited, hoping her family would come. Happily for her, some did. Antoinetta, Agnese's stepmother, even sent a bridal basket with Agnese's stepsister, who arrived at the wedding along with her brother. But its contents were almost laughable, just a few sheets and towels. It must have been such a shadow on what should have been a joyful day. Antonietta had basically raised my grandmother. How could she and my great-grandfather have been so cruel? I found myself hoping that Grandmother had some joy that day.

My mother proceeded to tell me how Grandmother

Agnese ran into her father weeks after the wedding. She was walking along the road near the church on the other side of town, wearing her Sunday best, when she spotted him. Agnese waved but was apprehensive as she hadn't seen him since before her wedding. The scowl on his face pierced through the distance, and she wondered what she could have possibly done wrong now. He approached her and grumbled, "You should have married someone better who could buy you lovely clothes and hats." Her smile faded as she realized she didn't look as presentable as she had imagined. My grandmother walked away with a sense of dread washing over her. Not being able to please my parents was a feeling I knew all too well, and that realization offered one more window into my grandmother's reality to which I could relate.

It was so ironic to hear the sadness in my mother's voice when so often she was the one who made me feel those same insecurities. Even as an adult, if I had gained weight or chose to wear jeans instead of a dress, she'd always been quick to criticize me. She decided my breasts weren't big enough and bought me dozens of padded bras. I happened to like my body just the way it was, but I couldn't do or say anything right. Despite her criticism, I was happy with how I looked, and a larger bust was something I had never longed for. I tried to put those thoughts out of my head as I continued to write and ask questions of my mother.

"Mom, if her life was so hard, how could she risk you having an unhappy life by marrying you to a stranger?" I asked.

"Their life was so hard," She repeated.

I took a deep breath. I needed to acknowledge Grandmother Agnese had more to worry about than just some harsh words. Not enough food, not enough medicine, and poor living conditions. Poverty would push people to extremes I wouldn't understand.

My mother continued explaining how arduous my grandmother's day-to-day life was. In Agnese and Giovanni's apartment, the concrete was cracked in a few places along the walls, and the tall wooden double doors hung just a few centimeters too high off the ground, allowing drafts of cold air to whistle through the space. Grandmother had an oversized iron key that she used to get into their home. The key was big enough that she could use it as a weapon if needed. Which was good because she was alone a lot as her husband would go off drinking and sometimes wouldn't come home for days. I imagined her clutching that giant iron key to her chest when she was home alone, fearing intruders.

Her kitchen had a giant concrete stove in the center. She did her laundry on a jagged stone ledge beside a large, deep, ominous well just outside their building. They shared a bathroom with six other families. Usually, there was a line of at least three people to use the bathroom, which was just an outhouse, not anything we would recognize as a modern bathroom. There was no running water, just a ledge over a hole in the concrete, which led to a holding tank below. Each family in the building took turns emptying the tanks into the farmer's fields to fertilize the rocky soil. When she became pregnant, she had to use a chamber pot at night and dump it in the morning. Toilet paper was scarce, so everyone saved any paper or even rags.

The First World War had ravaged the village of Passiano, where my grandparents lived. When the Depression hit major cities hard, life was even worse in the little villages. My grandmother had been lucky that her father could sell tobacco and salt. It's what kept them out of poverty. I'm sure she missed that apartment she grew up in. Her husband was a carpenter, and I can't imagine many could afford to buy the new furniture he built. Grandfather Giovanni's parents had no money at all and lived in the streets. It must have pained my grandparents that there wasn't anything they could do to help them. Grandfather occasionally brought them food, but now he had his own family to consider.

My grandmother constantly worked at the sewing machine that her father had given to her when she was young. She made clothes for her family and did fancy work that she could sell. Perhaps that was her one freedom. As she worked on her sewing, I imagined her thinking about her short visit with her father and hearing him say, "You should have married someone better who could buy you lovely clothes and hats." Maybe that was when she became determined to give her children a better life.

But how did the desire for her children to have a better life morph into her plan for her young daughter to marry a grown man entirely unknown to them? Did it worry my grandmother that she would send her daughter to live with a man in a different country? My mind drifted to my first marriage when I was young. My husband was born in Iran and moved here to go to college, where we met when he was 23 and I was barely 20. He made me laugh, and that felt like freedom. My parents didn't want me to marry him, but I was an adult and could make my own decisions, whether good or bad. But my Grandmother Agnese set my mom's life on a trajectory where Mom had no say at all.

But thinking of my first marriage, I found compassion for my grandmother. When she married my grandfather, she'd been searching for an escape from her hard life, but her marriage hadn't lived up to her hope. I came to this same realization with my first husband. The man who made me laugh turned into someone else, one who was cruel and even occasionally hit me. It wasn't until I was twenty-nine that I finally found true freedom after divorce. My poor grandmother never had the opportunity to escape her disappointing marriage. With the standards of the times, where divorce was virtually unknown, and with World War II looming around the corner, she was stuck in her marriage. Her prison was built to last a lifetime.

But I was still puzzled about why my grandmother would plan for my mother to marry a stranger. He must have impressed her so much that she thought he would be good to her daughter, unlike her husband. My first husband, at one point, got a job offer in Iran. He had become a mechanical engineer during our marriage and got an offer from a big company in Iran. I refused to go, afraid I would never be able to come home with my boys. I couldn't imagine the struggle my grandmother had gone through plotting to send away her daughter. Poverty would have colored everything with a different perspective. How could I judge my grandmother when I could barely conceive of the details of their life?

I left my mom's house in a daze, trying to make sense of everything she'd told me. Driving home, I couldn't stop thinking about my grandmother and everything she had gone through. She didn't have a mother, only a stepmother who had been a classic fit for the evil fairytale version, and on top of that, her father treated her like she couldn't do anything right.

Grandmother Agnese must have felt so alone.

My earlier anger at my grandmother dissolved as I realized she must have made the choices she did to give her daughter a better life, a life without poverty. I'm sure she wanted that for her whole family and thought the American Soldier could help her realize that goal. I was beginning to understand more and more what she must have been feeling and why she did what she did, but I needed to know more. I needed to learn more about everything to grasp how my parents became who they were and how I became who I was.

I spent the afternoon organizing my notes on what my mother had shared with me, my thoughts, and all the questions this new information suggested.

I called her to clarify some of the details about my grandmother. It was apparent she had been reliving her days with her mom since our conversation as she jumped right into a monologue about how much she missed her mom and what a special rapport they had.

She said, "She always talked about everything with me, just like I was an adult. We were best friends."

A wave of emptiness flowed through me. We'd never had a connection where I considered my mother my friend.

I asked, "Why didn't we have a relationship like that?"

She had no answer for me, and we ended the conversation.

A couple of days later, she called.

"Do you remember what you asked me a few days ago?"

I knew right what she was talking about because I had been thinking about it constantly. "About our relationship?" I asked. Maybe it wasn't too late; maybe we could work toward that friendship now.

"Yes, I was thinking about it," she said, "You were the reason we didn't have that kind of friendship, like Mom and me. You were different than me. I always did everything my mom asked of me."

Her words sucked the life out of me. I felt like an eight-year-old child trying to defend myself as I answered her, "Mom, I was a really good girl."

She ignored my response.

After the call, I couldn't stop thinking about her words, which could only be described as a cruel accusation. Her words bothered me, and my reaction morphed from hurt to anger. Was it really my fault? It was hard to remember all those years ago, but in my heart, I knew the blame wasn't mine. I'd been eager to please, to the extent I often froze in the indecision of the proper action or words. I lived in fear of disappointing her.

Ultimately, I'd been a child, and she was the adult. She should have been the one to direct our relationship. But I knew there would be no convincing her of that. Would we have had a closer relationship if we'd suffered together through a war and its traumas rather than the stable existence I had known as a child? Interviewing my mom brought up feelings I didn't want to have and childhood memories I didn't want to remember.

EIGHT

The sunshine streamed through my mother's living room window as I anticipated another day of history. As soon as I arrived, she took a seat in her favorite chair. Her brow was dramatically furrowed, a look I recognized well from each time she'd shared her story with someone. But she was silent for a moment. I waited; she was thinking hard about something.

Finally, she turned to me and looked at me very seriously. "Adela, I want to make sure you understand the importance of everything I have been telling you."

I nodded.

With a stern look in her eye, she leaned forward and said, "You know, I'm lucky to be sitting here talking to you today. I should be dead."

"I know, mom. The war was hard on everyone."

"No, Adela. You don't understand. Before the war even started, life was tough for us Italians in Passiano. My mother worked hard, but there was just nothing—nothing—she could do to make it better."

I could see she was going somewhere with this now, so I remained silent and let her continue.

"Children, they died all the time. There was no food. Mothers had no milk. My mother nursed her neighbors' children when they couldn't." She wrung her hands as she struggled with her emotions, "That was before the war; when the war started, everything just became that much worse."

I got up to make tea while she continued her story about herself as a young child. My mother was born with the name Anna Maria, but even as a baby, everyone called her Nina, a name that stuck with her for her whole life.

She told me about the morning she awoke with her head hitting the floor. The two wooden chairs she slept on had separated under her again. This was a nightly battle she often lost. I remember hearing about her makeshift bed back when I was a child. It sounded so much worse now when I could understand it from an adult perspective.

"On the opposite side of the room, my baby sister, Amelia, popped her head up from the crib." My mom said, smiling as she remembered her little sister, whom she now called weekly in Italy. "Her fuzzy dark brown hair was all messed up. She peeked at me, and then she laid back down." My mom shook her head. "How I'd wished I was back in that crib. But, instead, I rolled over on the floor and gathered my father's wool coat around me to try and sleep a little longer."

I sipped my tea and was swept into that cold, little home in Passiano as she continued her story.

EIGHT

The prayer card of the Blessed Maria Fortunata Viti pressed against her cheek on the cool ground. It must have fallen off her forehead when she fell. Her mom placed it on her head each night after tweezing through infected hair follicles while she slept. It was the least painful route to get rid of her dreaded head disease. Her scalp always got infected in the spring and itched through fall.

Minutes later, the church bells next door startled Nina out of her dreamy stupor. She caught the last three chimes. Counting the one that woke her up, the time must have been four in the morning. Her brother Joseph's boots hit the floor in the other room. He was getting up to start fetching water from the well. She stood up and went to join him, rubbing the sleep from her eyes. No matter how tired she was, she wouldn't go back to sleep now anyway. Her mom would be up any minute, and the whole cortile would start stirring soon afterward.

Nina felt her way through the darkness into the front room where Joseph slept. "Peppino," she whispered her brother's nickname, fumbling through the pitch black of the early moonless morning like a bat making its way out of a cave. She had only the sounds of her brother's movements to guide her. There was no electricity in the entire village of Passiano, and they had no candles in their flat. Light was a luxury they couldn't afford. "Peppino," she called again when she couldn't hear him moving anymore. Her hands crept along the wall until she found the corner of the room where she kept her handmade wooden clogs.

"Nina, it's my turn. You can go back to sleep," Joseph replied.

"I don't feel well," She said, "I need air."

"Nina, I'm only going to the well downstairs."

She hated going to their well. There was always a cold breeze drifting from it. She was sure a ghost lived in the well. Maybe it was La Signora del Pozzo. She asked, "Can we just go to the one in the village? It's not that far."

"No, Nina. Papa needs me at work early today," he sighed. "You still coming?"

"Si." Nina followed in defeat, hoping they would need to go to the village well anyway. They felt along the walls on the way down the stairs to avoid the crumbling center. "Peppino, I'm scared," Nina whispered as they approached the bottom of the stairwell. She peered into the darkness in vain; the sun wouldn't bring light for another hour.

"It will be fine. I won't let La Signora del Pozzo get you," he said. She could hear the grin in his voice.

They rounded the corner to the laundry area and squinted their way through the gloom toward an even darker round spot in the corner of the room. Nina paused behind her brother, peeking around him at the rim. He grabbed a wooden handle attached to a long rope. He began pulling up the bucket at the end.

"Throw a rock in first. What if it's mud anyway?" Nina said.

She was sure something would jump out and grab them while he was trying to find a rock. Finally, Joseph located a small pebble and tossed it in. The stone landed with a "clunk" in the distinctly too-thick-to-be-water liquid. Nina breathed a deep sigh of relief. The sooner they could get away from that well, the better.

As they exited to the street, the early morning twilight finally started to illuminate their path, and Joseph asked, "Why does the well scare you so much?"

"The ghost who died there."

"You're silly. That's just a myth," he said.

"No, it's true. Mom told me about her."

"It's just a scary story to make you behave," he said with one eyebrow raised.

"La Signora del Pozzo isn't a myth. I've seen other ghosts, too," she said, looking down at her feet. They began walking again, and she shrugged, "I don't see them as much now."

"You were young. You don't know what you saw."

"Joseph," she said as sternly as she could for a six-year-old.

He tried to keep a straight face.

She continued, "There were priests and lights and things with big heads walking in the middle of the room!"

"Big heads?"

"Big heads," she insisted, vigorously nodding her head. She thought he was starting to believe her.

"How come I never saw them?" he asked with another wide grin.

Her shoulders slumped lower when she realized he was making fun of her. "How do you explain Mama then? She hears tapping," she pouted her rebuttal.

"Tapping? On the window? You mean when she hears the rats and gets up at night?"

"It's not rats!" Nina nearly screamed.

"Alright, alright," he said, putting his hands up in defense. Thankfully, they'd just reached the back of the line at the closest of Passiano's two water pumps. Unfortunately, it was already ten people long. By the time they got their water, the line was at least twice as long, and the light from the still-sleeping sun grew slowly brighter.

They'd barely gotten halfway back when they heard two short clangs of the church bells. Joseph sighed heavily and picked up his pace. "Papa's going to be angry. I'm late."

They entered the kitchen downstairs. Wood was stacked and ready for Nina's mother to light a fire. The water sloshed over the edges of the buckets, leaving a small puddle of water next to a large copper pot. Last night, the pot held their spaghetti, but in the morning, it was their clean water supply. All water needed to be sterilized to make sure no one got sick. Often, the children did get worms from the well water. They had a neighbor who'd massage the stomachs of the neighborhood children and pray over them. Eventually, the worms would come out, sometimes with Agnes pulling them out of her children's rectums. Nina asked her mother where the worms came from. Her mother responded that inside the stomach was a pouch of worms, and sometimes, the worms would escape the pouch. She probably told them that so they'd still drink water.

Nina and Joseph finished setting up the water to boil just as Agnese rounded the corner. Joseph leaped across the room to take the heavy pile of coal from her arms. Nina emptied the stove's ash catch, stuffing the ashes into a sack by the stove. Her brother brought the coals and piled them underneath the stone cooking ledge.

Their mother slumped into a small handcrafted wooden chair in the corner with a heavy sigh. The sun wasn't even up yet, and she was already sweating with her left hand resting on her lower back. "Did you save the ashes, Nina?" she panted. Her other arm was wrapped around her tiny belly. There was no bump yet, but she was pregnant again.

"Si, Mama." The ashes were used to clean everything—the dishes, clothes, and even their hair. They would be mixed with lemon, violets, and other flowers found in the woods to make a version of soap.

Three more short church bells rang, and Joseph started pacing by the door. "I need to go, Mama."

"One moment, Peppino. I need to check your heads," his mother replied.

"My head is just fine. Take a look for yourself." He tilted his head downward and pointed, saying, "See?"

"Except you have bald spots," Nina snickered as

Mother began sifting through her hair like a chimpanzee looking for bugs.

"Tsk," her mother made a clicking noise of disapproval. "Nina, you didn't sleep with the Blessed Maria."

"Si, mama. I did," Nina protested.

"We don't have time for this, mama," Joseph said. He paced faster.

"Fine," Agnese said. She quickly wiped Nina's head with alcohol and then wrapped it in a cloth. When done, she secured a little white bonnet and put both hands on her daughter's cheeks. "Bella," Agnese smiled.

Before they could both get out the door, the church bells rang once more. The wood door slammed back, revealing their fuming father, Giovanni. "I said I wanted to leave by five, Joseph," he grunted. His fists gripped the back of a chair so tightly they turned white.

"I'm sorry, Papa. We had to go into the village for water. Our well is mud today."

Giovanni sighed and shook his head. Nina and Joseph remained apprehensive. Giovanni was still agitated, and it was clearly not just because they were late. They stayed glued to the floor until he began again. "I need to talk to you two. Sit down." He gestured toward the beautiful little table in the center of the room. He'd made it himself, just as he'd made all the other furniture in the flat.

"What is it, Papa?" Nina asked, pulling on his coat sleeves.

"Something has happened. Life is going to get worse.

Italy is at war," he paused to search his children's faces, "Do you know what war is?" Nina shook her head in confusion, but her brother's eyes widened. He nodded and tried not to look afraid. Joseph had heard stories of the Great War, but Nina was too young. All he knew was that men came back angry or in boxes to be buried. Some never came back at all.

"War is when countries fight each other. Many people die, and fighting takes a lot of money and materials. Nina, other countries want to hurt us. Our leader, Mussolini, sends soldiers around to gather supplies to help them fight our enemies. People are going to get desperate. They'll steal more, so keep an eye on your things. We work hard to give you everything we possibly can. Don't let anyone take your things from you, understand?"

Giovanni's eyes darted back and forth between his two children intently. Nina looked at Joseph, who was twelve, and thought he looked like an adult for the first time. Nina looked back and forth between her brother and her Papa, slowly feeling the weight of what was happening- even if she didn't grasp the whole meaning. Life was already hard. How could it get more complex?

"Do you understand?" their father asked.

"Yes, Papa," his children said in unison.

He stood to his feet. "We're already late, Joseph. Take your sister to her class and meet me in Cava."

Joseph nodded, and Nina gathered her school supplies. She grabbed her tattered old baby blanket. Its frayed edges and hole-filled fuzzy softness wouldn't really keep her warm.

She didn't need it, but it was all she had to soothe herself. The wool itched her nose when she pulled it tight around her shoulders, but the smell of ash and flowers comforted her. Joseph chuckled softly at his little blue teddy bear of a sister.

"Ready?" he asked. Nina nodded, and they started their journey to the schoolhouse.

When they turned to go up the hillside, Nina said, "What did Papa mean that Mussolini wants to take our things?"

Joseph's eyebrows scrunched up when he answered, "To fight in a war, our country needs our help."

Nina asked, "How does what we have help?"

"I don't know," he said honestly. He'd only learned a little about war, himself.

"But we have nothing!" she protested. Her eyes started to water.

"They don't know that, Nina. Don't worry. Mama and Papa will think of something." Joseph stayed by her side until she reached the doors of the little house where classes were held. Before he went, he said, "Listen, Nina, everything will be okay. Just keep an eye on your things." He looked around suspiciously at the other little six and seven-year-olds piling into the room.

"Si, Peppino," Nina said. Joseph walked away, and Nina stood there for a moment, puzzled. Then, she felt a tap on her shoulder and turned quickly. At the same time, somebody else grabbed her bonnet string to loosen it. She turned back the other way, hoping to catch her attacker. But her tormentor had planned for that. Her bonnet slipped off her head, and she turned toward the erupting laughter and spotted two little boys sprinting away. In seconds, Nina dropped her book bag on the floor and had her wooden shoe in her hand before she even started running. She caught the boys and began beating them with the shoe. Caving to her rage, they tossed the bonnet back to her and continued laughing with fingers pointed at her. Steaming, red, and burning with anger, Nina ran back to pick up her bag. Next to it, her blanket was in three pieces, a casualty of The Battle of the Bonnet. She stuffed the pieces into her bag and ran toward her teacher's desk with her head down so no one could see that she was about to cry.

Insegnante Papalo looked up from his book as Nina approached her seat and smiled at her frantic little face. He took one look at the scruffy pile of hair on top of her head and laughed.

"Why don't you sit up here with me today, Nina?" he asked.

"Can I?" she almost cried. Her teacher, Insegnante Papalo, was always so nice to her. It made school much more bearable, especially on days like that one. She sat at the teacher's desk and reached into her book bag for a pencil and paper. When her hand found nothing but tattered blanket pieces, she picked up the bag and began frantically digging with both hands.

Insegnante Papalo, who had been busy writing on the chalkboard, looked down at her and raised an eyebrow. Nina stood and held the bag upside-down in both hands above her head. She knew nothing was there but hoped it might fall out anyway. Nothing did, and she began crying. Insegnante Papalo bent down to wipe away her tears and handed her his pencil and a piece of paper from his book bag. Nina sniffed a little and tried not to make eye contact with anyone else in the room as she pretended to write down the day's lesson through tear-blurred vision.

She left school that day, dreading what would happen next. Things couldn't get much worse. On her way home, one of their neighbors frantically ran down the stairs and whispered harshly, "Move! Out of the way!" His arms were piled high with pots and pans, pillows, and blankets.

Nina ran up the stairs to find their mother pacing next to the crib, muttering to herself. Joseph was in the background, darting around the house just as panicked as the neighbor.

Her mother turned to her. "Gather pots, pans, blankets, and anything else of value!" Confused and slightly terrified, Nina joined Joseph in sprinting around their flat, grabbing their most valued possessions. She followed him outside and dumped her items in the shallow hole Joseph had already dug.

Nina's mother peered through the curtains at the window when Nina ran back inside. Stopping to catch her breath, Nina asked, "What are we doing? Why do you keep looking out the window?"

"Keep moving, Nina," her mother replied. "I'm looking

for soldiers and your father." Then, contemplating what her father had warned them about that morning, Nina decided to bury her pillows in the yard.

"Where is your father?" her mother complained when Nina returned from her pillow-saving mission.

"I don't know, Mama. What do you want us to do with the linen?"

"We must have something left, or they'll be suspicious. Bury your school things, too, Nina," she said, turning back to the window. Nina had turned to pretend to get them from her book bag just as they heard steps in the hallway. Was that the soldiers? They all froze as the door handle turned.

Her father walked in. His eyes widened, and he demanded, "What are you doing?"

"Hurry, Giovanni, they're coming," Agnese explained. The soldiers had started their supplies search in Cava earlier that day. She'd come from her sister's house where the raids began.

"You're going to get us thrown in jail!"

"No, they will never find out." She looked outside again and hissed in a voice that made the children freeze, "They're coming."

After a hard knock, three soldiers marched in, searching their home for anything they could use. Nina's parents stood in the corner, watching as one of the soldiers took their wool mattress. The soldier said apologetically, "We need warmer uniforms," and carried it out on his shoulder. He knew his actions would hurt the family, but he had to do it anyway. Nina couldn't understand it. Why did they need a mattress?

Her mother grabbed her husband's hand, and her ring flashed in the afternoon sunlight streaming in from a tiny window. Another of the soldiers caught sight of it and stopped.

He approached her and said, "Let me see that ring."

She looked to her husband for guidance, but he just shrugged and kept his eyes downcast. Then, not knowing what else to do, she handed it over, fixating her vision on the soldier's muddy boots.

The soldier in charge walked up behind him and peered over his shoulder. "It's too small," he said, grabbing it and handing it back to Agnese.

Her eyes filled with tears, and she slipped it back onto her finger. She held her ring finger to her chest and stood straighter as they all watched the soldiers tromp away.

There'd been no time for Nina to bury her school things even if she'd had them. Could she blame the school supplies on the soldiers? Maybe her parents wouldn't even ask why she needed more. She went to find her pillows in the yard. After digging them up and brushing as much dirt away as possible, she curled up with her face buried into the soft, grimy surface. Dirt gritted between her teeth as its earthy scent overwhelmed her, but she didn't care. They were the only soft things she'd have to sleep on that night.

Things would only get worse for the little family.

Later that summer, a warm breeze blew through the

village, rustling the leaves along the dirt road where Nina lived. Grapevines trailed along the short white concrete wall that surrounded their cortile. Nina perched on the wall and watched her father play horseshoes with some of the neighbors. Her mother was inside somewhere, cooling off with her little sister, Amelia.

Another horseshoe hit the pole with a large ping that rang across the gravelly parking lot. It dropped to the ground just as a low rumble spread from under the church. It came from down the hill. Her father ran to the road to see what it was and stopped dead in his tracks. The blood drained from his face. Whatever it was, it was big and headed toward them. Her father turned and sprinted back toward the group. "Tedeschi!" her Papa yelled over the rumble, Germans. Nina's attention was captured by the large vehicles turning at the corner, followed by a brigade of trucks full of men and weapons.

Motorcycles with machine-gun-mounted sidecars flanked the sides of a parade of armed soldiers marching down the road. Nina had never seen anything like it before. When they got closer, she could see the faces of the men marching behind the trucks. They weren't men at all. They were boys. She guessed most were hardly older than her brother.

Over the next few days, the Germans set up camp directly behind their little church. Surprisingly, it took them little time to set up a perimeter with anti-aircraft guns pointed at the sky. Every day until they were done setting up, Nina sat on the wall watching, shaded by the grape leaves from her father's vineyard. The men shouted in harsh tones. Nina couldn't understand, but they were smiling and laughing, so they couldn't have been angry.

Their language was strange and almost as fascinating as their behavior. Seeing all the giant guns frightened Nina, but she couldn't stop watching.

Some neighbors stopped to watch as the soldiers moved cannons to the back of the church building. Once they were in place, the church looked like a fortress with two rows of German tanks watched over by Italian-made anti-aircraft artillery. However, the Germans weren't as scary as Nina initially thought. She expected monsters from the stories she'd heard, but these were boys. Still, she kept her distance and often observed them from afar, hiding in the bushes in the garden or playing with Amelia outside.

As they played, she kept one eye on the Germans. Her sister, Amelia, was too young to pay attention to the soldiers' antics. On hot days, the wall around their garden was lined with German soldiers hoping for refuge from the sun under the grape leaves.

One day, one of the soldiers hopped down and walked toward the chicken coop, where Nina's mother was sprinkling food for the hens. She failed to hear him approach, so he cleared his throat loudly, and she jumped in surprise. Her eyes widened, and she looked around for her husband or a neighbor. The giant iron key she usually had with her was sitting upstairs on the table. Nina grabbed Amelia's hand, and they crept to the corner of the yard behind a large squash plant so that they could hide and watch.

Through the leaves, they saw the man point at the coop, but her mother stood frozen, afraid to look. When he pointed again, she finally looked up, and he made a gesture as if he were eating food. She slowly backed up without turning, grabbed an egg, and raised it in question. He nodded and held his hands out in front of him.

All he wanted was an egg, Nina realized. She had time to look at him more closely with the threat level back to a minimum. He was one of the prettiest men she'd ever seen. His blonde hair glimmered in the sun, and when he smiled, his baby blue eyes flashed with a genuine gleam, warm and inviting. From that moment on, he became her favorite German. Every day, he'd walk up to their gate and politely wait for Nina's mother to take notice of him. They'd exchange a series of awkward gestures to communicate in their made-up version of sign language before he left with his egg.

Nina couldn't understand anything they said, but they seemed to smile a lot together. On days he didn't come to them, her mother brought an egg to him. She'd walk the rows of German tents and tanks until she found him. Sometimes, when her mother asked, Nina was brave enough to take the egg to him. The chance to see his exotic features up close was intriguing. She'd approach slowly with her head tilted slightly down, bonnet shading her eyes just enough so she could peek at him from under it. The moment he took the egg from her outreached hand, she would turn and walk straight home, her adrenaline rush slowly seeping away.

The following January, life changed completely. The Germans were tenser. Occasional air raids disrupted the lives of Nina and her family. Nothing was ever peaceful. Nina was only six, almost seven when things started escalating to a state of extreme violence. Bombs were dropping, and people were dying; it seemed nothing was ever going to be the same.

My mom was finished telling her story for the day. Her face was almost gray with weariness after reliving those overwhelming days. The most influential years of her life were spent in constant fear of death or loss.

I can only imagine the anxiety my mother must have felt. To this day, she is sometimes anxious when she doesn't know where my brothers and I are. She will call and fret constantly until she knows we are safe. Her fear was annoying at times, but it's totally understandable now that I know her history.

NINE

For weeks, I'd been working with my mother, listening to the tales of her early life. I knew she had much, much more to say, but I decided to give her a break from dredging up all those memories. I'd gained a new perspective on her life, but now I wanted to do the same with my dad. But unfortunately, the opportunity to do that in person was gone. The guilt ravaged me again as I looked at his picture and tried to write. Ever since I'd read his letters, I couldn't stop thinking about him. It was like I had never really seen him or known him. Did my children really know me? What did they think of me? Would they have questions when I was gone?

While I didn't have Dad, at least I had his letters. By this time, I'd organized them carefully into plastic sheet protectors in a binder. Again, I appreciated how much my dad's letters were a gift to me, allowing me a clearer vision of who my dad truly was.

After reading my dad's letters, I was hungry to learn more about him. He was constantly on my mind, and researching his war experience made me feel he was near. So, I joined several World War II groups on Facebook.

A member of one of those groups talked about how trauma could alter our DNA. I was curious and quickly googled it to see what I could find. I read that trauma can leave a chemical mark on a person's genes, which can then be passed down to future generations. This idea would have seemed unbelievable 20 years ago, but now it is a field of study. We now know a person's experiences could alter the biology and behavior of their children and grandchildren. I marveled that my parents' trauma could've caused depression and anxiety in my children and me. How many of us are victims of our parents' trauma? My parents' generation suffered from wars, plagues, and the Depression. I'm sure very few were untouched by the difficulties that arose in their generation. Most of my generation and those that have followed are basically spoiled. Many never give a thought to what their parents or grandparents went through, and with guilty clarity, I knew I was indeed to blame for that very behavior.

I started putting together the pieces of my father's war experience, but I didn't know much about his childhood. Being a quiet man, he never talked about it. I wasn't close to his parents, who had lived across the country in Massachusetts.

Then I thought of my cousin, Trish. She'd grown up near our grandparents and knew them well. I was eager to reach out to her. Trish and I didn't grow up together, but when we were adults, she tried to get to know me. She flew from

New Bedford to California once on business when we were in our thirties. Trish stayed with me, and we created a bond that would last the rest of our lives. She became the sister I never had. I was single with two kids, and Trish was single with three kids. We became each other's rocks. Trish had the best life advice, whether parenting or dating. When I was dating a man I was crazy about, she asked if he would still want me if I lost my legs. I thought about her question, and I knew he wouldn't. When we finally broke up, and I was upset, she told me that being upset was a choice. She said everything was a choice, and I could choose not to be upset. She changed my perspective, and I'll never forget all that life-altering advice she gave me.

Now, that friendship would be invaluable once again. Trish's childhood had been vastly different than mine. She'd grown up hearing all the stories from our grandparents about their journey to the United States from Canada. Plus, Trish's dad, my uncle Rene, told her many stories.

Trish and her new husband had moved to Tucson, Arizona, a few years ago. This project was consuming all my thoughts, and I thought about driving over and visiting her for a few days, but I wanted the information right away, so instead, I called her.

After the usual pleasantries, I brought up the reason for my call, "I don't think I ever really knew my dad, Trish." I shared with her everything I had discovered about my parents' younger selves.

She was shocked when I told her the truth about my

father's letters. It was apparent to us that my father had told no one in the family what he had realized when he reached Italy. We contemplated that and decided he must have been embarrassed after all the razzing his brothers had given him about being foolish to stop dating and save all his money to get this girl he hardly knew. We couldn't imagine what his brothers would have said if they had known the truth. Poor Dad was stuck from the very beginning, but he had no way of knowing how unhappy his decision would make him.

I wandered to the kitchen and poured myself a fresh glass of water. "Trish, I need to understand more about where Dad came from." I settled back onto the couch. "How did our grandparents and great-grandparents decide to come to America?"

"Of course." She sighed as if it were going to be a long story. "I'll share everything I can remember."

"Was their life in Canada hard? Is that why they left?"

She paused for a second, then sighed again. "Yes, Adela, life was hard for them. Both great-grandfathers worked in the logging industry in Quebec. It was back-breaking work, but there was never enough. Both of their families decided to leave around the same time in 1907. Surely, you heard the story about how Mémé put that pine sapling into her bloomers as her family prepared to cross the border into the United States?"

"I do remember that one." I smiled, "She was ten, right?"

Trish laughed and said, "Yes, ten years old. Dear old Mémé."

Even though I hadn't known her well, my father's mother had always impressed me. Each year, she would drive herself and Pepe from Massachusetts to California in her car to visit us. She had saved her money to buy her car and wouldn't let anyone else drive it. From the few stories I had from my mother, Mémé seemed to be a take-charge kind of woman.

My Italian ancestors had some things in common with my French-Canadian ancestors: the dream of a new and better life. But while my father's family found it, my Italian grandmother could only seek it for her daughter.

Newly settled in New Bedford, Massachusetts, my grandparents, Adela Lambert and George Fortin, met at church and bonded over their shared experiences: learning English and adapting to life in a new country. After a short courtship, they were married in 1916.

Trish told me all the stories she could remember. I kept seeing similarities in the lives of my Italian ancestors and French-Canadian ancestors. They both had diseases to worry about—tuberculosis and the Spanish flu. They both had gardens they depended on to nourish their families. It didn't matter that they were oceans apart; their needs and difficulties were the same. The difference was that life would get much better for my French-Canadian family sooner because they made the right choice to come to America. But my Italian grandmother's life would get much worse, and the dream of coming to America had only one chance of being fulfilled by my mother marrying my dad.

My father was born on April 23, 1919, right in the middle of the Spanish flu epidemic. When Trish and I realized this, we were surprised that our grandparents never talked about what that was like. From what I researched, it was much worse than what we went through with the COVID-19 virus. These people were just used to hard times. It made me feel so spoiled researching the lives of my family. Both sides dreamed and worked hard to give their children and their children's children a much better life. It brought tears to my eyes to think about their struggles and hardships, all of which benefited me.

My grandparents had four boys: Armand, then my dad George, Rene, who was Trish's dad, and Leo. My Pepe built the family house in 1921 in New Bedford, Massachusetts. He built it in fits and starts, piece by piece, saving money where he could. The basement was constructed first, with just a kitchen and a small bathroom. This is where the family lived while he finished the rest of the two-story house. When the project was finally completed, the house had three bedrooms and one full bathroom. To my Italian family, one full bathroom all to themselves would have sounded like a total luxury, but to me, one bathroom for six people sounded like a nightmare. As I wrote and learned about my family, I reminded myself of my many blessings.

In 1928, there was a strike in the New Bedford Mills where Pepe was a foreman. Thirty thousand men and women went on strike for six months in protest of a ten percent cut in their wages. My grandparents and their family were already living well below the poverty level. Trish told me that as foreman, our grandfather felt he couldn't participate in the strike. Everyone was fighting everyone because of unethical practices of "undercutting" or firing one man and hiring one or even two women to take their place at even lower wages. When everyone fought each other, the cohesiveness necessary for unification was destroyed. Grandfather wanted to help bring everyone together. Also, since he was making a foreman wage, someone would easily take the job he couldn't afford to lose. Every morning, he was forced to cross the picket line where thousands of people lined up with babies in their arms and children by their sides. They threatened and taunted our grandfather with shouts of "Scab" while he fought back his urge to join them. Day after day, grandfather continued to enter the workplace while hundreds of his coworkers scorned him. He couldn't see how any other choice would be beneficial.

Mémé looked after their children. She tended her garden, cooked constantly, made her family's clothes, and patched them whenever they got frayed. The younger boys wore hand-me-downs, their shoes soled with tire rubber. At times, the soles would flap open, and the boys tied strings around them to bind them together. We take so much for granted today, I realized, as I thought of my large closet full of shoes. My Italian grandfather made shoes out of wood with straps of cloth for his children. Both of my grandmothers had to sew clothes for their families. There would have been only fleeting moments for just relaxing or having fun. How did it change and shape my parents as they witnessed their parents' hardships?

At the end of 1929, life in America took another drastic downward turn. On Black Tuesday, October 29, the stock market crashed. Jobs were scarce, banks were closing, and homeless people jammed the streets, unable to support themselves. My father was ten years old when the Depression hit. He surely remembered how hard it was for his family and those he loved. Many years later, when my mom was 10, she was in the middle of World War II with even more devastating memories.

I'm sure both my parents remember not having enough food to eat when they were young. Both families depended greatly on the gardens that their parents grew. They both had chores like harvesting vegetables, and they both had to conserve water and wear old clothes. My mom left school very young because of the war, but my dad also had to leave school early to go to work. It was common for children to drop out of school during the Depression. My father joined his father and brother Armand and went to work in the mills when he was a young teenager. The pay was minuscule, but the family needed the money. Pepe earned $20 weekly, while his sons made just $15. The mills operated around the clock, and the three of them worked the third shift, from 10 p.m. to 6 a.m. Day after day, they straggled home, exhausted and hungry, to the stew that Mémé kept warm for them. Both of my grandmothers, oceans away from each other, canned their vegetables to ensure that nothing ever went to waste.

Trish told me that despite their difficulties, the family loved to get together and enjoy what they had. The aunts, uncles, and cousins would get together, push the furniture aside in the basement, and dance the Quadrille, a French folk dance. I closed my eyes and imagined them all dancing and having a good time. How grateful they must have been for those special moments. Trish and I agreed that our grandparent's hardships must have made them really appreciate the good times.

In 1939, war broke out in Europe, and the economy shifted with a renewed focus on manufacturing war materials. Beginning in September of 1940, men were drafted to join the military nationwide. My young father, George, was called to join the Army on April 15, 1941, just before his 22nd birthday. Soon afterward, Trish's dad, Rene, joined the Marines, and the youngest, Leo, joined the Navy. Armand stayed behind, excused from the draft because he had flat feet.

Grandfather and Grandmother with sons before they went to war

Trish told me that because their sons were going to war, our grandparents had a family portrait taken that year. Mémé looks almost hopeless, her heart heavy with worry. Trish said Mémé believed her boys would never come back to her. That was one thing my Italian grandmother didn't have to go through as she managed to keep her family close through the crushing war. I can't imagine watching either of my sons go off to war. How devastated my grandmother must have been.

My dad left for Fort Meade in Maryland for training around the same time that Trish's dad left for Quantico, Virginia. Uncle Rene told Trish that the two brothers met in Washington, D.C., after their initial training before they were to be shipped out again. Lonely for family, they slept near each other on park benches the night before leaving. Trish and I wondered if they slept at all, as they must have worried about the war in Europe and the possibility that one or both might not return home. In the soft early morning light, the two brothers said goodbye one last time. Trish and I sighed together as we thought of how our fathers must have felt that day so long ago. After they parted, Uncle Rene went to San Diego for more training, and Dad was dispatched to the Desert Training Center in Indio, California, known as Camp Young.

I thanked Trish for the heartfelt talk about our fathers and grandparents. I was grateful for everything she remembered. She possessed the gift of a storyteller and helped me discover some of what my father's childhood must have been like. Now, I wanted to learn more about Camp Young and what my father experienced there and in the war. But that would have to wait, as my mom was ready to share more of her history.

TEN

Mom looked rested and refreshed when I went to see her the next day. She didn't seem interested in my talk with my cousin but was anxious to tell me more about her story. We sat down, each with a cup of tea, and got started. It was good that I was a fast typist because Mom was in rare form as we jumped back into her childhood.

* * *

Thump. Nina fell out of her chair-bed again with her hands to her ears. The winding scream of sirens blared atop the police station a little over a kilometer away. Somehow, it sounded like it was right next door. Since the Germans arrived, the alarm sounded increasingly more often. Agnese heaved her belly out of bed and went to the crib for Amelia while her husband gathered a few supplies. At that time, Agnese was at least seven months pregnant. The whole family met at the front door, and Agnese and Giovanni counted their three children before sprinting to the forest's edge.

The tiny waxing crescent moon hardly lit their path through the cobblestone streets. Soon, they reached the hillside, just yards from the forest's edge. Giovanni took young Amelia from Agnese, and they made their ascent through smoke and chaos. Germans were firing at the planes passing overhead while bombs dropped all around as families ran for the trees. Agnese fell headfirst into a large hole. Nina screamed, and Joseph sprinted to her side, skidding to a halt on his knees in the weeds. He and Giovanni each grabbed an ankle and hoisted Agnese back onto the hillside above the hole. Before anyone could say anything, another cannon fired from behind the church; the enemy in the sky could drop a bomb anywhere at any moment. They had to keep running. Giovanni and Joseph half carried Agnese while Nina dragged Amelia by the hand. They ran together like that for what felt like forever before they could finally plunge safely under the cover of the trees. Nina looked down at her little sister. Amelia's tear-streaked face was contorted with fear and confusion.

Agnese was also crying silently on a soft patch of weeds nearby. She held her belly and sat still for a moment to see if she could feel the baby moving. Then, after what felt like ages, she let out a long, slow sigh and smiled. "I'm okay. The baby is okay, "she said.

Giovanni dug a shallow ditch and padded it with some rags he'd managed to bring along. Finally, he settled his wife into a comfortable situation. That night was one of many sleepless nights in Passiano for a lot of families.

When they returned home, the Italian and German troops patrolled the streets at curfew every night with extra caution. They went from house to house, confirming no one had any candles lit, but they didn't need to. No one wanted to end up on the list of the dead or missing. Most families ran and hid in the forest during air raids, but some never made it. Others stayed home, but no one was stupid enough to light a candle, even if they could afford one. During the day, people scanned the skies and stayed as silent as possible, listening for the rumble of a bomber. Passiano was like a living ghost town.

Somehow, life went on. Her sister, Carmelina, was born on March 15, 1941. Carmelina was a beautiful baby with a full head of dark hair. She was a calm infant, hardly ever crying, often entertaining herself by pulling on her toes and cooing. This was a blessing for Agnese. Due to the lack of food and the other stresses of the war, she experienced a slow and difficult recovery after the delivery.

On calm days when the bombs weren't falling, Nina continued attending school with Insegnante Papalo. The boys continued to grab her bonnet and steal her pencil and paper.

Today, my mother makes sure she never runs out of anything. She has a basket on her coffee table with paper and pencils. It's interesting to think just how many things in our childhood shape our habits today. Blankets, pillows, food, and so many things are always abundant at my mother's house. It causes her anxiety whenever she is running low on anything.

One day, when Nina was at school, the sirens sounded in the distance. Her teacher announced with suppressed panic, "Pack up and go home." So they all left, headed toward another night, afraid of what might fall from the sky. Nina returned home to find everyone downstairs just as a bomb reverberated through their little village from somewhere in the distance. The fighting was happening somewhere else that day, but it forced everyone into the downstairs area. Nina's family went into the kitchen and huddled up next to a small coal fire to keep warm.

Hours passed in near silence. "I'm hungry, Mama," Nina finally whined.

"I know, Nina. I'm sorry. Eat this orange. Make sure you eat the peel, too. We don't have anything else." I wonder what my grandmother thought as she looked at her children sadly. She must have been thinking about how she would try and fix things in the future if an opportunity presented itself. Maybe she prayed for that opportunity.

Joseph was observing and listening to his mother from the corner. Finally, he spoke up, "Mother, I could go looking for food!"

"Absolutely not," his mother shrieked. "It's past curfew, and there's an air raid near."

"Fine," Joseph said, his voice barely tinged with a respectful tone, but eventually, he dropped into the corner with his arms crossed.

Across the fire from him, Nina was trying to choke down a piece of orange peel. Agnese could do nothing but sit and watch her children suffer.

As a mother myself, I can only imagine how horrible it must feel to watch your children starve and freeze. Agnese barely ate anything herself, so she must have been weak. Everything went to the children. I know my mother, and I would have done the same thing in that situation. Listening to my mother's story, my heart broke for her and my grandmother.

They all awoke cold and shivering. The coals had died sometime in the night, leaving a frosty chill behind. Before Agnese woke up, Joseph tried to slip out the front door. He'd nearly reached it when Nina skittered up from behind to step in and block his path.

"Where are you going?" she whispered.

"We need supplies," he said.

"Can I come?" she asked.

Joseph hesitated, contemplating her usefulness. "It's too dangerous," he finally decided.

"Be careful," she conceded, moving out of his way.

It was early morning, and the soldiers would have just finished breakfast. Joseph shoved his hands in his pockets, trying to look casual as he strolled the outskirts of the German camp. Occasionally, with a few sideways glances in each direction, he'd quickly bend down to pick up discarded tin cans. Most were empty, but occasionally, he found leftover rations lining the inside of the can. At some point, a soldier took notice of him. When Joseph realized he had a tail, he took a sharp left and headed to the road that led into town. Half a step later, he abruptly turned and ran back into the cortile.

"That was fast," Nina said when he entered the flat.

"I almost got caught," he said, unloading his treasure onto the table.

"But it's just their garbage," Nina said.

"Yeah, well, I didn't want to attract attention. The Germans don't like me poking around in their trash."

His pockets empty, he said, "I'm going into town now. We need more food".

"To Cava?" Nina asked.

"As far as I need to go," Joseph shrugged.

Nina poked her head outside and watched her brother run down the cobblestone path. The German had forgotten all about Joseph, so he was free to roam again. On his way down the hill, he was stopped by a peculiar situation at the general store. Hovering just out of sight in a nearby doorway, Joseph watched a few Germans tossing things from inside through a broken window. Some of them pocketed items, and others loaded up bags with supplies. One of the men in a more detailed uniform was standing at the back of a truck surveying what was being loaded. One of the soldiers spotted Joseph. He gestured for him to come closer. Joseph froze with fear before approaching with caution. The soldier smiled, held up a pair of shoes, and pointed to Joseph's bare feet. Joseph shook his head in protest. He liked walking barefoot. The soldier wouldn't take no for an answer through.

He tied the laces together and hung the shoes around Joseph's neck before returning to the transport van. The back door slammed shut, and the German unit loaded themselves into the front cab. When they disappeared around the corner, Joseph finally let out a long sigh of relief. What if they'd had locked him up, too?

He sprinted to the next alley and ducked into it to cross to the next street. He needed to get away from there, fast. A few blocks later, coming around a corner, he saw a local police officer. Before he could turn around, the officer demanded that he stop. Joseph considered running, but he didn't think he would escape.

"Where'd you get those," the police officer asked, pointing at the brand-new shoes.

"Someone gave them to me."

"Don't lie to me," the officer pressed. It was no use arguing. Joseph knew he looked basically homeless, and besides, he was just a kid. The officer continued, "Give me the shoes. Come on, you're going with me". He pulled out handcuffs, clipped them to Joseph's wrists, and hauled Joseph to the jail. Without further conversation, the officer put Joseph in a small jail cell. It had only been a few hours when he finally heard his mother's voice reverberating throughout the building.

"Let my son out!" she yelled. Nina and Amelia hid

behind her legs, terrified. They'd never seen their mother this angry before.

"Signora, he stole these shoes and lied about it," the officer said, holding up the shoes.

Carmelina in her arms, Agnese leaned over the counter and narrowed her eyes.

"My son doesn't steal and doesn't lie. Let him go!" she said, increasing in volume with every syllable. Something in her eyes must have told him she was not a mother to mess with because he relented and let Joseph go.

"Peppino!" she shrieked with her arms open wide. Joseph hugged her, and then they headed silently for the front door. One more final look of complete disdain from Agnese signaled their departure from the police station, and she exited with her children in tow.

Mom sat on the couch with a throw across her lap as I sat in Dad's favorite recliner across from her. Again, my mother was near tears with emotion as she related each of these stories. My grandmother was desperate to keep her children safe. I understood why my mother held her in the highest esteem all these years. I so wish I could have known my grandmother. Through my mother's stories, I was getting to know how powerful this woman was.

No one mentioned Joseph's run-in with the police to Giovanni. He and Joseph sat in near silence at the kitchen table, flattening some of the discarded cans from the Germans into plates. Their last set of tin cups and plates had fallen apart, so these new tins were a windfall. The smaller ones didn't need to be changed at all to use them as cups. Together with their wooden utensils, the family finally had another complete dining set. At last, they kept one of the larger cans to cook and used one of their new plates as a lid.

I now knew why my mom loved new pots and pans. I took her to the store last week, and she just hovered over the cooking display even though she didn't need anything. She has always kept everything in her kitchen looking new. She went through so much, but it makes her appreciate all the material things she now has.

While Joseph and Giovanni had been working with the cans, Agnese lit a coal fire across the room. Nina mixed flour and water with a single egg to make a batter. She glanced at her brother, who had been sullen since his visit to jail. His head was between his hands, and he was glaring at the table like it had personally attacked him. When Nina reached for the newly made pot, his head snapped up, but his eyes were still focused on something else. She put the batter into the pan and handed it to her mother to put on the fire. Agnese piled coals on the lid, and the family sat together around the warmth of its flames until the pancake was done baking.

My tea had grown cold while I listened to my mother tell her story. I'd forgotten it after the second sip. The sun was now high above the house, and my stomach was rumbling for lunch.

"Oh! You're hungry, Adela. Let me make you some food," my mom said as she brushed away a tear and took a deep breath.

"No, no, Mom." Despite my hunger, I could hardly imagine eating after listening to Mom's tales of starvation and scraping leftover food out of cans. "I feel guilty eating after knowing you went through that."

"I did, but that's no reason for you not to eat now. Come let me make you some spaghetti," she insisted. While she puttered around in the kitchen, she continued, "A few weeks later, more German soldiers arrived. They were rowdier and seemed more desperate. Some even seemed hollow. When you looked into their eyes, there was nothing there anymore. There were rumors that they'd just come from somewhere where the fighting was more intense, and I was no longer allowed to wander the streets alone. "

"Oh, Mom," I cried, "I had no idea your childhood had been so extreme. I knew it was hard, but this is different." I had a hard time swallowing my food as I listened.

Agitated, her voice got louder, and her body stiffened as she replied, "This isn't even the worst of it yet. No, the worst was about to come. I still can't believe I'm sitting here talking to you. I should be dead."

She took a little shuddering breath and continued in a quieter voice, "Things really got bad in 1943, around the time they closed my school for good. The air was still, and the roads were calm."

"What do you mean, Mom? How did everything go calm?" I asked.

She paused for a moment, then answered, "It was as if

both sides had decided to take a break from the war, just for a little bit."

It reminded me of the proverbial calm before the storm, and I knew she had another harrowing story to tell.

Nina liked keeping busy and often visited her aunt's house to see if she could help. One day, she took her blind cousin Alfonso out to help him deliver groceries from their store to customers. The stillness broke just as Nina led her cousin back home through the front door of her aunt's house. Her aunt was in the middle of asking how their deliveries went when the sirens rang again. Moments later, the ground shook from an explosion nearby. Smoke rose from behind a building across the street.

"We must go into the shelter, "Aunt Conchita said as the color drained from her face and her eyes widened in fear. Her husband started gathering their children and some supplies.

Nina stood there, rooted to the ground. She started panicking when they tried to pull her out the front door. Between sobs, she said, "I want to go home. I want to be with my mom." Ignoring her pleas, her Aunt Conchita grabbed her hand tighter and led her into the street.

People were running and screaming. Babies were crying. Nina followed her aunt and uncle into the bomb shelter, but the cramped space and musty air suffocated her. Another bomb exploded nearby, vibrating the entire area around them. Dirt fell on Nina's head, and she cried out, "I want to go home!" By then, her cheeks were streaked with tears. She clutched her chest and said, "My chest hurts. I can't breathe. Please let me go home. I want my mother." Her uncle tried to push her deeper into the bunker, but she dug her heels firmly into the ground.

"Fine," he said, giving up. "Be careful."

Nina ran out of the bomb shelter so fast that she didn't even have time to hear if her aunt was protesting. She darted past a few soldiers quicker than they could catch her and sprinted toward home, where no bomb shelter waited to trap her. Nina reached a villa, a place to sit with benches, trees, and flowers, and stopped running to catch her breath. She was afraid to stop too long, so she got up and crossed the yard slowly, still panting. When she reached the middle, she heard, "Piccola ragazza!"

She turned to look back. A policeman ran towards her. "What are you doing?" he asked. "It's not safe out here."

"I'm going home," Nina replied, continuing her pace.

"You need to go back to Cava. There's a bomb shelter there. You can leave when it is safe."

"I need to go see my mom!" she cried.

"You can see her when it becomes safe, trust me!"

Before he could finish, Nina burst out.,"I need to go home!" She repeated over and over.

"Okay, okay, okay," he said in exasperation. Once again, panicking had gotten Nina her way. "Just stay out of the road, walk close to walls and under trees when you can," he warned, "and be careful."

She ran away before he could change his mind. As she sprinted, she glanced up repeatedly to see if the sky was falling. Her heart pounded, and her home seemed so far away. Maybe she should've stayed; maybe it would've been safer. She shook her head as she panted; she needed to be with her family.

Finally, her home was in view. Someone was standing in the doorway. It was her mother waiting. When she spotted Nina, she opened her arms wide. Nina sprinted, sobbing as she ran into her mother's embrace. Her family had been waiting for her. She had done the right thing.

"That's it. We can go now," Agnese said. The family poured out of the house to escape to the forest again.

A few weeks later, on a day that started calmly but left Nina with the trauma she would remember for the rest of her life, she headed to town with Giovanni to find supplies for the family.

The schools had finally closed earlier that year, and while she didn't regret not seeing the bothersome boys, she felt a little lost, having so little to do, and she missed her favorite teacher, Insegnante Papalo.

As she went along next to her father, she counted the number of cobblestones she stepped on. Somewhere around 43, she lost count and looked up. As if she had wished him into being, Insegnante Papalo, young and handsome, if a bit thinner from the war, appeared on the other side of the street.

He smiled, pulled off his hat, revealing his head full of

dark hair, and waved. Nina hoped he would cross the street and talk to them.

Just as Nina and her father waved back, a rumbling started beneath their feet. For a frozen moment, all movement stopped. Then they lifted their heads. A British plane blocked out the sun. A projectile dropped from the plane, glittering in the light, whistling downward. Nina raised her hand and pointed at it.

Without hesitation, her father dove on top of her and covered both their heads. From beneath his arms, she watched as her teacher tried to run from his place beneath the bomb. He was too close.

For just a millisecond, Nina was blinded by the flash. And then she wished she couldn't see. Her beloved teacher was right in the path of the bomb's destruction.

His body exploded. Chunks of Insegnante Papalo rained onto the street, against the building, and over her and her father, embedding in her hair. One of his legs skidded across the road and into a thicket of trees on the edge of the forest, the skin charred and black.

The dust settled around them as they pushed themselves up. Giovanni looked to the sky, watching for another bomb. Nina stared wide-eyed at the wreckage of her teacher. What was left of him was crumpled into a heap centered in a pool of blood.

A sharp pain stabbed her heart, and she thought she must have been hit by a piece of flying glass or shrapnel, but when she looked down, her chest was bloodless. Still, the pain settled in her chest tightened, and she wondered if she might be dying.

Giovanni searched the sky again before scooping his daughter into his arms and running to see if the teacher was still alive. He touched his fingers to the warm corpse and shuddered. There was nothing that could be done.

They ran toward home, darting through the wreckage as fast as they could, hurdling over bodies and debris. The smoke stung their eyes, and the smell of death filled their nostrils no matter which direction they turned. Halfway down the street, a woman stumbled out of a shop holding her stomach. She was covered in blood, hardly standing on her buckling knees.

Before Nina could shield her eyes from more gore, the woman collapsed and let go of her front. Her body was skewered with shrapnel. A few people rushed out of a nearby building with a chair. They heaved her onto it and tried to get her inside, but she was beyond hope. The woman stopped breathing and fell out of the chair halfway back to the door. "Shut your eyes," her father told her. But it was too late; Nina had already seen too much.

They were on the move again when they approached their cortile. The door burst open, and Agnese wailed, "Oh, Thank God!" Her glance darted over them, taking in the splatters of blood and the shrapnel embedded in their clothes, and cried, "Is Nina okay?".

Giovanni looked at his daughter with a wrinkled brow. "Mostly," he said, "she is not hurt."

"But there's blood," she screamed.

"It's not hers," he said, going to the window to peek outside. Agnese rushed to her daughter's side to examine her while they continued to speak.

"What happened?"

"The bombs hit the village. We should stay put for now. I don't think it's safe to run for the woods yet."

Agnese's response sounded terrified, but Nina had stopped listening. She couldn't hear over the buzzing in her ears. Closing her eyes made everything worse. All she could see was Insegnante Papalo lying on the street with his glasses smashed into his face.

ELEVEN

I had to stop writing and gather my thoughts. My mom appeared on the verge of tears after putting these awful memories into words. My heart broke for her. How could she have mentally survived such a traumatic experience as a child of nine?

She tried to convince me she had healed from the memories as we took a short break, but I knew that she'd never completely recovered. She'd carried so much with her all these years. When she related her stories, they were always so vivid, like she was remembering something that happened yesterday. I guess it actually was like yesterday for her.

My father had been a soldier, and as I had researched his war experience, I'd been quick to realize so much of his dysfunctional behavior must have stemmed from Post-Traumatic Stress Disorder. But it suddenly dawned on me: how could my mother not be suffering from PTSD as well? There was no diagnosis or attention to the issue back then, not even for soldiers. It was just life, a bleak and hopeless reality that many mid-1900s Europeans faced daily.

After our brief break, Mom had recovered and was ready to continue her story.

On September 9, 1943, Nina once again ran for the cover of the forest, with its thick protective tree trunks that stood like sentinels over the village.

She hadn't even heard the bomb landing in front of the church early before the sun had risen. She awoke to her mom shaking her and shouting, "Run!"

Nina jumped from the bed, fumbled for her shoes, grabbed Amelia's hand, turned out the door, and started to run, dragging the four-year-old behind her. She looked around for the rest of her family. Where was everyone? Where was Joseph? Behind the church, the Germans climbed into their trucks, one after another, rumbling to a start. A distinct clanging of the large guns being loaded clanged behind her in the darkness.

After what seemed like forever, Nina and Amelia reached the forest's edge. Finally, the sun peeked over the mountain tops in the East, illuminating the hillside below. Nina expected to see her mother, father, and brother running up the hill with someone carrying two-year-old Carmelina. Instead, she was met with only smoke searing her nostrils and a deep sinking feeling in her stomach.

It seemed like days, but the sun had just moved to the spot directly above them when she finally spotted Agnese with Joseph by her side and Carmelina in her arms. It had only been a few hours.

When they reached the cover of trees, Nina called out, "Where is Papa?"

"Look there, Nina," Joseph said, pointing to the bottom of the hill. Giovanni and Uncle Giro pulled a mattress up the slope with Nina's sick grandmother on it.

All their family members had made it somehow. But others hadn't been so lucky. Her family sat in stunned silence while others around them mourned their losses.

There was something different about this battle. Rumors flew under the trees. One man whispered that the Americans had invaded Sicily and were on their way to the mainland.

Her father also had news, "The Americans landed," he told Nina's mother.

"How do you know?" her mother asked.

"One of the German units heading out was talking about it."

"Maybe that means it'll be over soon," Agnese hoped out loud.

Nina hoped so, too, but she hardly knew what that would mean.

The reality was, with the Americans actively landing, there came more brutal fighting and bombs dropping.

The family fell silent as they settled in under a big tree. By evening, the villagers that had waited in their houses were now running for cover. Many never made it in the shower of debris and shrapnel. Some were even killed by angry Germans who'd heard rumors the Italians were siding with the Americans. Flares dropped near them, lighting up the trees and the homes.

The Allies dropped flares so they could see where the buildings were, making the forest one of the safer places to hide. That night, the family stayed cold and hungry but safe under the protection of the trees. Agnese told her children folk stories to keep them distracted and calm. Nina was hardly listening, though. Her mind was on the shores of Salerno. She wondered how the battle was going. Who was winning? What would happen to them now?

TWELVE

I had been sitting with my mom for weeks now and had most of her stories written down. I was anxious to start researching my father's war story.

I called the National Archive and gave them the information on Dad's discharge papers. The voice on the other end hesitated: "Er, I'm sorry, but that record was part of the Archive Fire in 1973."

"What's that mean?" I asked.

"It was lost."

"What?" I was stunned. How could his military records be gone?

"I'm sorry, ma'am. I'd recommend searching for his unit records. Can I help you with anything else?"

"No, thank you," I hung up and sat for a moment, feeling the pain of loss fall over me again. How had I never asked him about his time in the war? Maybe it was because I'd never heard him or my mom discuss it.

Maybe when I was young, I didn't want to hear any

more history. My mother was always, forever repeating her stories about the war, so maybe it felt redundant to hear other stories from that era. But that wasn't fair; I couldn't blame her. Dad wasn't an easy guy to talk to either, but I should've tried. Maybe I didn't want to suffer any more rejection. When I think of everything I should've said or asked, my eyes fill with tears of regret. Now, when it was too late, I wanted to know everything.

I was going to find out what I could. Indeed, Mom remembered a few of Dad's stories. I sat with Mom and wrote down what she remembered, but it wasn't much. I wonder if she ever had much interest in what Dad went through in the war. So, I got to work reading war books and stories online. What I was able to discover about my dad's war history was pieced together from online research of his army battalion and commanding officer documents. I've found enough to paint a vague morbid picture of how he lived, survived, and recovered.

Through my online research, I discovered that in 1942, Dad was dispatched to the Desert Training Center in Indio, California, known as Camp Young. The camp covered 18,000 square miles and was the world's largest Army post, under the command of Major General George Patton. At the time, Patton was the first commanding officer. I was curious if my dad had any personal contact with Patton. It seems strange that he never mentioned being under one of history's most famous commanding officers. Patton was known as "Old Blood and Guts." He believed the best defense was to attack continually. I wonder if Dad was subject to Patton's rousing pre-battle speeches, peppered with plenty of profanity. Did he cheer loudly after hearing the speeches? Did he admire Patton's leadership? Camp Young was huge, and maybe Dad had never encountered him. I will never know.

Patton purchased commercial radio broadcasting equipment with his own money to set up a radio station at the camp. Most of the time, the station played news and music, but occasionally, Patton would take over the programming using the microphone he kept at his desk. I imagined my dad and his buddies listening to these speeches, resting on their bunks while mentally preparing for war. How do you prepare for war? Especially being the gentle person that I know my father was.

Dad was assigned to drive a Sherman tank for the newly formed Company B of the 191st Battalion, which was composed of men from the northeastern seaboard of the United States. He trained in the California desert from April 1942 to February 1943 and then departed to join the Allied forces in North Africa. This campaign was called Torch, with General Dwight Eisenhower in charge of the Allied troops. Rommel, the Desert Fox, led the Germans. Rommel was a seasoned warrior and a brilliant enemy. Eventually, Rommel was pushed out of Africa and then Sicily onto the Italian mainland with most of his divisions intact.

George's battalion was held in reserve during the battles in North Africa until he was shipped out to Salerno, Italy, in

September of 1943. It was George's first fighting experience. This was one of the most ambitious water assaults of a fortified enemy beach in the history of warfare. Code-named Avalanche, it was a monumental screw-up that almost cost the lives of all the allies involved. The Italians had surrendered, and the Allies thought that German opposition on the beachhead might be light or nonexistent. In order to achieve surprise, the landing in Salerno was carried out without previous naval or aerial bombardment. Surprise was not accomplished. The Germans were not fooled; their spies in Sicily had warned them of the date and strength of the pending allied invasion.

Hitler had anticipated that the Allies would try to crack his "European Fortress" at Salerno and had placed his 16th Panzer Division to defend the beachhead. On September 9th, 1943, George and the 191st tank battalion arrived by naval warship at Salerno harbor. He soon had his first taste of bloody war, in a battle much worse than the Allies anticipated. The allied troops were too thinly spread to be able to resist concentrated attacks, resulting in heavy casualties. Nevertheless, George's tank battalion held its ground with the assistance of naval and aerial support despite the German attacks reaching almost to the beaches in places.

I shuddered as I read about this battle, imagining my father in the middle of it, moving forward in his tank.

Despite the Germans' preparedness, the Allied forces were able to capture Salerno. The Allies had learned new aspects of amphibious assaults in North Africa. They were now experienced and established their presence in the Mediterranean.

While Nina's family waited for twilight in the dark early morning of September 9th, under the flimsy cover of a Chestnut tree, George was floating just offshore with Company B of the 191st Battalion to the south, near Paestum. The fireflies danced in nightmarish choreography across the shores while he watched from a distance. His countrymen were dying while he drifted silently with the remaining reserve crew. The whole ship was eerily somber and at the mercy of the psychological warfare the Germans were employing from loudspeakers on shore. Forced to listen to eerie chants floating across the water of "Come in and give up" and the haunting tune of "Deep in the heart of Texas," the soldiers waited uneasily. There was nothing they could do to help without orders to send in more units. The battle ebbed and flowed almost as if it were following the tide of the waves hitting the shore.

Finally, George was told to get ready to move out and prepare his tank for battle. His company hit the shores late on September 10th like an avalanche set in motion. They were met with German ferocity in the din of battle, the air thick with bullets and blood. The Germans possessed weapons the Americans had never imagined. Like something you'd see in a science fiction film, radio-controlled flying drones and mini tank drones came from nowhere and exploded, blasting the American "iron coffins" into fiery infernos. Sherman tanks were fast but had negative qualities, like an under-protected gas tank that could explode with a lucky hit.

The battalion of tanks sported a new waterproofing fabric for transport from the ship to land, which was supposed to release quickly, but on the beach, crews struggled to get it off, making them vulnerable. With bullets whizzing past, they took turns fighting with the tangled tarps and wires, improvising the best they could. Eventually, with their enemy closing in, many cut the fabric off with axes and hopped inside to join the fight. The Germans were entrenched, battle-hardened, and willing to kill. George pushed forward in his tank to support his brothers in arms.

In the middle of one of the many torrents of bullets during those first few confusing days, George's top gunner was hit and fell, landing on top of George. There wasn't room for the unresponsive man in the tank, and George obviously couldn't drive with a dead body on top of him. While he continued to drive, his other buddies hauled the gunner up and off the tank. They had to abandon their brother on the battlefield, unable to carry his body. The only thing they had left of him that day was the blood that stained their uniform and an unspeakable inner wound.

It was a jarring story. The decisions that had to be made in the middle of combat were beyond my comprehension. How could they live with a choice like that? As I wrote down the stories my mom remembered and read more from the few records and accounts from my dad's battalion I found online, I resisted digging into every detail. Did I even want to know it all? What would I find in my search for the truth? But maybe I needed to know. You watch movies about the war. You know it happened. You see it on screen in countless documentaries. But you never really feel it until you picture someone you love in the middle of it all. Knowing my father had been in the war hadn't been enough to open the floodgates of empathy until I read his history and learned how much he suffered. Where he was and what he did was an entirely different view than the distant lens I'd been looking through before. Despite the pain it caused me, I needed to know more.

The 191st Battalion continued to press northward, traveling over narrow, rutted roads, harassed by German air and ground forces. Movement was dangerous and tedious. They were all at risk if a tank got stuck or slid out of position. Since my father's personnel records are gone, it's difficult to say much about what he did, but I was able to find out every place his battalion traveled. His experience in the war wasn't unlike many others, and he was lucky to have made it out alive.

* * *

Upon reading numerous commanding officer reports, I was able to shed light on how horrible it was for my dad. While I read, I put myself in his shoes and wept, as I'm sure he had many times while he was there. I always thought my mom was the one who had it the worst during the war because she often talked about it. It wasn't until later in life that I learned those who suffer the most are often the ones who suffer in silence. My father never said anything when my mother told one of her many stories. She was a child protected by her parents, but she never realized that my father was almost a child himself. He was only in his early twenties. No one was protecting him. He must have been terrified, never knowing if a new day would be his last. That same fear probably plagued my mother, but even on the worst days, she still knew her parents would protect her.

However, while she sat there telling me her story in her living room, she didn't seem to have much empathy for what Dad went through in the war. Maybe it just wasn't real to her. My mom pushed past that brief mention of my father landing when the Allies invaded Italy and onward with her own story. Mentioning the boys who never made it home made her skip well ahead in her story, from when she met my dad to when the war was over. I had to reel her back into our timeline.

"Wait, wait," I said, touching her arm. I didn't realize how frail she'd gotten. Her skin felt thinner than usual under my fingers. Then, her deep brown eyes snapped back into the present and focused on me. I said, "Go back to the forest. Your family was hiding, and Dad arrived on shore. What happened next?"

Without a moment's hesitation, she jumped right back into her narrative.

The Germans had been friendly to young Nina up until then. At that end stage of the war, she thought they were upset that their fellow soldiers were dying, but it was more than that. They thought the Italians were siding with the Americans. In many ways, that was true. She'd heard that the Americans were met with pizzas on the shores of Salerno, which made no sense to her. While the Allies advanced toward the Axis lines, Italian soldiers surrendered, abandoning their Nazi allies. In many places, they dropped their weapons and welcomed their liberators. Nina was baffled. They were enemies for so long, and now they were their allies? Apparently, it made no sense to the Germans because they were furious. Even as my mother and I talked and tried to make sense of the behavior of the Germans and Italians, it was hard to understand what had transpired. Finally, we concluded that the Italians were tired of war, death, and the fear they felt and wanted it to be over. The Germans saw their triumph slipping away and retaliated against the Italians.

First, the Germans struck back by looting shops and factories, throwing things they couldn't use into the streets. Then, as they began to retreat, prison transport trucks came back around to round up as many Italian men and soldiers as possible. They wanted more men for their ammunition factories or anything else they could force the Italians to do to help them win the war.

Giovanni and Joseph stayed out of sight as much as possible. Then, on the day before the Germans left the village, the soldiers went around the neighborhood, going from house to house, assembling as many men as they could find.

As the soldiers drew close to their home, Giovanni

raced to uncover the small space behind the stove, and he and Joseph squeezed themselves in. Little Carmelina wailed as Nina's mother rearranged things around the stove and hissed at the other girls to act normal.

Without a moment to spare, the soldiers were pounding at the door.

Nina's heart raced with fear, wondering if the soldiers would check behind their stove. She tried to look anywhere but the stove as a group of Germans entered their home. They searched under the bed, in the closet, and the garden.

Finally, they moved on to the next home. German boots faded into the distance as they continued their search for other men. Giovanni and Joseph hid for a few more hours in case the Germans returned, but thankfully they did not.

Nina was only nine, but she remembered the battle grew extremely close that day. They could hear the chaos growing in Cava, just a few kilometers below their village of Passiano. Homeless Italians started flooding Cava and Passiano from neighboring towns and villages being bombed.

I stopped my mother and asked her where the homeless came from and why. She didn't have a clear memory, so I did some research later. To the east in Foggia, the Germans had set up an air, rail, and vehicle transportation center to move their troops around southern Italy. At one point, the Allies carpet-bombed the entire city, killing thousands of people. Those who survived ran for cover and safety as they were surrounded by the bodies of those who had been hit by debris or shrapnel. Their homes and everything they owned were destroyed, and they left on foot with nothing, looking for a bit of kindness from surrounding towns and villages. Nearby, Naples was hit the hardest, and to the south, Reggio Calabria was devastated as well. They seemed to come from all over as they arrived in Cava and Passiano with just the clothes on their backs.

The families in Passiano did what they could to help the refugees coming up the hill from neighboring towns and villages, offering what little food and shelter they could spare. Mom counted the people as they staggered into her humble home, practicing what little addition she had been taught in school. In all, fifty people crammed into the downstairs of their humble dwelling. Everyone, including the six families that lived in the cortile, was afraid of the roof falling on them and slept each night on burlap sacks on the broken concrete floor of their cortile.

Meanwhile, Americans and Germans fought for passage through Cava, going north. George was somewhere nearby, part of the American forces, fighting his way through muck and smoke to liberate Nina's country.

One night, packed in the cortile with her neighbors and the refugees, Nina was startled awake by a kick in the face. She sat up, looking at the person on the burlap sack near her with anger. She'd gotten a foot in the mouth for the third time that night. Across the rows of sleeping people, she spotted her brother sitting against a wall. Apparently, he wasn't sleeping well that night, either. In fact, she was sure nearly no one was actually sleeping, except maybe the small children. Finally, weariness flooded her, and she closed her eyes, hoping to find sleep.

A boom violently shook the door, and Nina woke up startled. She couldn't go back to sleep; she never could when she knew people were dying. People around her were waking up and whispering. She strained her ears to hear the closest conversation. It was a young couple she'd taken note of when they had arrived because they looked so beautiful together. Walking hand-in-hand, the woman was tall and blonde, and the man was the most perfect man Nina had ever seen. The woman had been so thankful for a place to stay that she'd hugged Nina in gratefulness.

Now Nina could barely hear their whispered words.

"What do you think will happen to our home?" she whispered to her love.

"I don't know, Dolcezza," he replied. His hand was resting on her head, slowly rising and falling with his chest.

"It will be gone," a sobbing neighbor chimed in.

"You don't know that," the husband replied. "At least we'll be alive.

The group quieted down, but then a young kid about Nina's age got up to go to the bathroom. In the silence of the night, she heard liquid hitting the wall outside in the garden. She would never go to the bathroom at night. No matter how much she had to, everyone would hear. When he was done, the boy returned to his place among the sea of burlap, and Nina waited out the nearby booming sounds. It wasn't until they finally stopped for a few short hours that she was able to sleep.

The following day, Nina was in the chicken coop collecting eggs when a shadow fell from behind her. When she turned, the beautiful blonde woman was standing behind her. "Can I help you bring in the eggs?" she asked Nina. Nina nodded, grateful for an extra hand. Between their family and all the refugees, they would need all the food they had to feed everyone. Nina's aunt had come from Cava the day before with a bag of potatoes, and Joseph had managed to scavenge a few handfuls of spaghetti noodles left behind by one of the last German incidents. They'd be able to make enough food for at least a few days.

Nina walked through the kitchen door with the tall woman in tow. All the other women were already in the kitchen preparing their next meal. While the women cooked and gathered food, the men sat behind the big stone pillars outside and kept watch for more air raids.

Nina skipped out of the kitchen, happy her mom had extra people to help with cooking for once. She wanted to play outside, but her mom called out, "Nina, don't leave the cortile."

She glanced at the main entryway, but her dad was sitting there. She couldn't escape. Instead, she climbed on a ledge and watched the smoke rising in the distance over the scorched mountains. The smell inside the cortile had become nearly unbearable. There wasn't enough water to clean all the bodies that dwelt there, and of course, the lack of soap made it impossible to maintain good hygiene.

I tried to imagine the stench of so many unbathed people so close together. My mother said it was even worse than the stench of death on the air outside, where bodies rotted in the streets.

If you had a good nose, you were in trouble. On that day, Nina wished she had a bad nose and considered how hard it might be to jump from the ledge and run into the forest for a breath of fresh air. Weighing the chances that she might get caught in the battle, she decided against it.

Two days later, they were almost out of food. Then, finally, they received word that the Americans had miraculously won the battle in Salerno. The last of the Germans retreated, and the refugees were free to go home, at least those with homes left standing. But, after taking in a horde of extra mouths to feed, things remained difficult for my grandparents and their children, with minimal food left to eat. Their garden was nearly stripped clean of vegetables and fruit.

Most of the Americans followed the Germans to the north. Life under the Allied occupation wasn't much different from life with Germans, at least not yet. Dead bodies were left in the wake of the battle. Most were German, but there were also a lot of Americans, Italians, and British. Nina and Joseph wandered the streets to Cava shortly after the battle passed. They wanted to see if their grandfather's store was still standing and pick up supplies, if any were left.

Joseph stopped with a jolt, eyes open wide after they rounded the corner to enter the main road. If they'd thought there were a lot of dead soldiers on their path up until now, it didn't compare to what lay before them. Nina clutched her brother's arm as he slowly approached one of the German soldiers. The swastika patch on his arm flapped in the wind where his arm used to hang.

"He's never even shaved," Joseph said, his voice shaking. He turned to look around at the many bodies before him, "They must be eighteen, nineteen. Maybe even younger. They were going to take me. I could have died. I would have died." His eyes widened.

Nina stood silent momentarily before thinking aloud, "I still don't know. Who is the enemy? The Germans pray to the same God. The Americans pray to the same God. We all pray to the same God. So, how are we supposed to be enemies? We don't even know each other, and we're supposed to kill each other?" She looked at her brother, but he had no answer. He didn't know either.

"I'm going to bury him," Joseph said, rolling up his sleeves.

"We're supposed to be getting food for Mama," Nina protested.

"I'll go with you and borrow a shovel from Grandfather. But then I must stay. I need to do this," he replied with a look in his eye that she dared not disobey.

They walked into Salt and Tobacco together and hugged their grandfather, but when they left, they parted. Joseph had the borrowed shovel in one hand and as many crosses as he could make with the supplies available in the other. Nina trudged up the hill toward Passiano, loaded with almost too many potatoes to carry. It was all that was left after the Germans raided Grandfather's store. As she rounded the corner heading for the village, she saw a soldier whose skin was all black. His uniform differed from the Germans, and she didn't know where he came from. She assumed with his black skin; it must be somewhere far away. She had never seen anyone like him, and it frightened her. He tried to hand her an onion, but she started running towards home. He followed and was right behind her when she reached her front door and her mother. The young black soldier handed Agnese the onion, who said thank you with a smile.

In the days that passed, Joseph formed a crew of boys and young men to help him bury the fallen soldiers and civilians caught in the wrong place at the wrong time. Meanwhile, Nina did her best to adapt to a new normal. She fetched water in the mornings, which was even dirtier than ever, so they had to boil it and strain it a few times before using it. The rest of the day, she helped her mother with her sisters, Amelia and Carmelina. In the afternoons, she cooked what little food her mom could scrounge together for dinner. Nina sometimes wondered if she would ever return to school but decided she still preferred this life over daily bullying; besides, it wouldn't be the same without Insegnante Papalo.

* * *

After spending another day with my mother listening and writing, I went home shaken by what I had learned. I frequently found myself in that state after one of our interviews. My mother wasn't doing so well either, as her memories came flooding back as if it was yesterday. Often, a tear escaped her eye, sliding down her cheek as she talked. Glad to be home, I slumped on the couch, drained of energy. I couldn't get the many stories of my family out of my head.

It wasn't just what they went through but the beauty of how they treated one another. I felt the compassion of these people overwhelming. They had nothing and still were willing to share whatever they had. I hope people today would behave similarly if faced with similar circumstances. When my grandmother gave an egg to the German soldier, she was glad to help and didn't even see the uniform. There was so much empathy for their fellow human beings. My quest to find out what went wrong with my life seemed so minor in the light of what my grandparents and parents had been through. Drained and tired, the tears started to flow. My issues seemed so petty; I was ashamed.

I knew as I fell into a fitful sleep that this journey I was on would forever change me.

THIRTEEN

A few months after the Battle of Salerno, Nina met George.

One day in January of 1944, Nina sat outside on a barrel at her grandfather's store, swinging her legs off the edge and watching her blue skirt sway in the wind with each kick. The other children were playing nearby.

The milkman was supposed to arrive soon, and she didn't want to miss him. He was one of her favorite people to see when she was at her grandfather's store. His handsome smile made her happier no matter what was going on in the world.

This time, however, another man caught her eye, George Fortin. The weak January sunshine bounced pleasantly off his blonde head as he slowly approached her on the narrow cobblestone road.

My father was so very handsome, and I smiled as I listened to my mom talk about what an impression he had made.

Next to him, his shorter, fairer friend seemed to walk somehow with more authority. His name was Robert

King, and he was George's best friend during the war. Maybe Robert puffed out his chest more, or perhaps his deep red hair made him seem more intense, like a flame. Whatever it was, it was hard for my mom not to stare at the two soldiers in their neat American army uniforms and polished boots. They were so different from anyone she'd ever seen. She shyly watched the two soldiers as they approached her and the other children.

George reached into his pocket and pulled out a candy bar, which he broke into pieces and offered to all the children. Who was she to say no to any food, much less candy? Nina ran forward with her hands outstretched, but her grandfather, watching from the doorway of his shop, hooked Nina's suspenders with his cane and pulled her back. She'd gotten her piece of chocolate just before she was yanked away but was upset because she wanted to be close to the American soldier to look at him.

That look of disappointment must have captured George's heart because he was back with his friend the next day. This time, he approached Nina's grandfather directly and offered cigarettes. Her grandfather smiled and signaled his thanks. They had a broken, gesture-filled conversation before George turned toward Nina, who was peeking out from behind the doorway.

"Nina, this nice man has some candy for you," her grandfather said. "In fact, he brought some for all your siblings. Why don't you take him to your Mama and Papa up in the village? George made a gesture demonstrating he would follow her. She bravely grabbed him by the hand and walked the two soldiers to her home.

I expect George was missing his own family and longed to be in a family environment. It's hard to say why he wanted to meet Nina's family.

When they reached the cortile, Nina's parents greeted the two American soldiers enthusiastically with kisses and hugs in typical Italian fashion. I think most Italians were feeling incredibly grateful and anxious to show their gratitude for the retreat of the Germans. Likewise, Nina's family was honored to meet these two American soldiers and thrilled to express their thankfulness. Giovanni and Agnese seemed almost smitten, saying things like, "Bella, Si?" Agnese wrapped her arms around her daughter, and her eyes shone brightly at the soldiers standing across from her. I wonder how soon Agnese formed the idea that this man could save her family from poverty.

Through sign language and a few words that they had picked up, the family did their best to show their appreciation and make the soldiers feel at home. Soon after they arrived, Nina was sent off to the store with a bit of money to buy dried figs, walnuts, and half a bottle of wine. The family had very little but did everything possible to make the men more comfortable.

* * *

George visited several more times before leaving the area for the next campaign. On the next occasion, he brought

Nina a strand of coral beads. She hung it around her neck immediately, happy to have a piece of jewelry to call her own. Before Nina could stop beaming about her new style, Agnese said, "Take the soldier to the garden, Nina. Give him a tour," and ushered the two out the door.

Outside, Nina led George by the hand to the garden, her chest puffed out and her chin stiff with pride. Since it was January, there was very little to show, but he appreciated it all the same. While they walked, George must have noticed the bald spots on Nina's head. He would have figured they were from malnutrition.

After the garden tour, they walked to the top of a nearby hill so that he could see the view of the valley below. Nina wanted to ensure he saw everything she loved about her home, but he had to go before she could show him all of it. She pouted until he promised to return. He bent down and looked into her big brown eyes and promised her and God that if he survived, he would be back for her and help her family. At least, that is what my mom thought he was promising.

It wasn't unusual for young soldiers to make promises to God; they were all so scared. Later, he wrote to Nina, "We all have a purpose in this world." I wonder if he felt his purpose was helping my mom and her family.

As he prepared for Anzio, I knew he must have been worried he wouldn't survive this next battle. So many soldiers had already lost their lives. Some had been his friends. What if he was following? He brought more gifts for the Farano family. I couldn't help feeling emotional as I thought of my dad and all he must have felt as he visited the Faranos for what he thought would probably be the last time.

When he arrived at Nina's humble dwelling, he piled more candy, cigarettes, and a bottle of tonic on the table. Amelia danced with joy alongside Nina while they grabbed their candy pieces. George pointed to the tonic and motioned to Nina's head, telling her parents it would help heal her scalp.

"Grazie! Grazie," Agnese nearly sobbed. It had been years since my mom's head disease began, and nothing seemed to help. My grandmother must have known this was God's answer to her prayers. Nothing is coincidental in this life. If it were me, I would have known this was an opportunity God granted me because it was what I asked for.

After relinquishing himself from Agnese's tight hug, George bent down and handed a rosary to Nina. She beamed at it with pride. It was simple, but it was all hers and opened the world to her. She'd never been given something so special. She planned to make a little purse to carry it the first chance she had.

"Will you," George said, pointing at Agnese. He continued pantomiming while he spoke, "Write to," now pointing to himself, "my mother, mia madre, and ask about me?"

Despite their limited English, Giovanni and Agnese understood when he handed them an address with his mother's name. Agnese clutched it to her chest as George said his goodbyes. Perhaps my father was pleading with God as he left to allow him to live so he could keep his promise and return to Italy to ensure this little girl and her family were alright. He'd talked to my brother about this promise, and I'm sure it gave him one more thing to live for. He must have worried about what would become of this kind Italian family. If he lived, helping Nina was the one thing that mattered, something to hang on to.

With one last glance back at the family, he called out, "I will come back! Write to see if I survive."

"When you return, you will marry our Nina," Agnese offered in a way that sounded almost more like a demand. It may have been the language barrier created by the mix of English and Italian, or it could have been her desperation. Maybe it was divine will, but George was compelled to reply,

"Yes, si! I will marry Nina when she is old enough." Nina could only guess what the two said but knew it was essential to both of them.

Agnese clutched his mother's address tight to her heart. She was determined to see that American soldier again and nearly depended on it through the rest of the war and even afterward. She went to the church almost daily to pray to Our Lady of the Rosary for George's protection until the war ended.

* * *

I learned from online reports that George's battalion arrived outside Anzio just before January 22, 1944. The Germans called off the coastal watch that night, convinced of a stalemate. As Adolf Hitler was fast asleep, the Allies quickly landed on the beach to establish a military stronghold. By the time the Germans awoke, it was too late. I am so proud to say my dad and his battalion were instrumental in helping the Allies get their foothold on the beaches of Anzio by dawn.

In the morning light, German reinforcements finally arrived with aircraft leading the way while the allied soldiers dug into the beach, christened "Bitch Head," named for its notoriously difficult undertaking. The men took cover in holes and caves, fortifying themselves with their backs to the ocean and nowhere to go but into enemy territory. George and the rest of his battalion lived miserable, muddy lives, waiting for their next opportunity to advance or a German mistake. As the Germans progressed with superior numbers, some Allied soldiers abandoned their duties and ran. Many of the men who tried to run were slaughtered. When only a few men were left on the front lines, tanks were sent to slow the German advance. George's battalion, among many others, lost countless tanks and artillery over those weeks while neither side seemed to gain or lose ground. It made me proud that my father never abandoned his duties and had the medals to prove it. Again, I wished I had researched this before he died.

George's battalion was ordered back to Naples to regroup. Naples was the largest resting camp for Allied servicemen; unfortunately, it was also known for being governed by corruption. American soldiers saw Naples as a place of crime, prostitution, sexually transmitted diseases, and desperation. Southern Italy was severely devastated by the war, but Naples was hit the hardest. I read that from November 1, 1940, to September 8, 1943, Naples was bombed 76 times. The city was in complete ruin with no running water. I can only imagine the filth and ruination my father witnessed as he walked the streets of Naples. Seeing that kind of destruction had to have affected him greatly. GI rations were bartered for goods and services, which included sexual activities. People were starving and had nothing else to trade with but their bodies.

Many years after they were married, my father told my mother a story of walking through the crumbling streets of Naples and being approached by many prostitutes. My mother was horrified as she had no idea how bad it was in Naples. They would grab at his arm and tease him. One of them pulled him by his shirt to her home, which had been bombed, leaving only half of it standing. The stench of rotting dead people under the rubble was overpowering. George felt very sorry for her but could not have sex with her. He laid some money on the filthy bed and left quickly. He felt ashamed that he even went with her but was glad he could give her something to help.

Upon hearing this story, I thought of my beautiful mother and was grateful she was so young during such a miserable time. My mother's village is only 25 miles from Naples. If she had been older, she could have been taken and raped. She told me about a young woman in her village seized by a truckload of British soldiers. They kept her with them for a couple of months, and once she returned to her family, her life was ruined, she was traumatized, and her reputation was shattered.

Gradually, back at my father's camp, replacement tanks and personnel brought the Allies back to normal strength, but the process was slow and inefficient. George was promoted to Private First Class and soon after to Corporal. He trained new soldiers as quickly as possible, but the expectations were overwhelming. Equipment was pouring in faster than they could supply capable men to use it. What took George a year to learn was the same thing he had to teach the new men in a couple of days.

Another story my mom remembered was about a little dog my dad found one day. George was training his men, and a small dog wandered into the camp. Everyone took to this dog right away, but especially George. He named him Prince; the dog followed him everywhere. Prince became George's constant companion and rode in his tank with him.

Back in Passiano, things were about to take another turn for the worst. The battle may have moved past them, but on March 18, 1944, Mother Nature entered the war in Italy.

Nina was playing in the Spring sunshine, enjoying a day of peace and recovery, when the ground beneath her rumbled and shook, the windows rattled, and the house trembled like it feared the dark, ominous clouds filling the skies. Mount Vesuvius spewed her rage in the worst volcanic eruption in 38 years. Rivers of fire surged through the countryside between Passiano and Naples, shooting flames thousands of feet into the air. Most people in the area evacuated their homes, this time running from hot molten lava instead of bullets and bombs. People scattered in every direction, looking for shelter, using umbrellas to shield themselves from falling debris. Bits of ash the size of coffee grounds blanketed southern Italy, destroying homes and farms as they landed. The family stayed barricaded in their home, hiding from the mounds of volcanic ash. After three days, when things were clear, Giovanni tried to pry open the door and found that it wouldn't budge. They had no water, but the well would be full of ash even if they could get to it. Little Carmelina was crying in the corner, getting increasingly dehydrated by the hour.

"What do we do now?" Agnese asked.

Giovanni started up the stairs and muttered over his shoulder, "Grab the sheets." Agnese gathered a pile of sheets and followed him. Together, they created a makeshift rope long enough to reach the ground from the upstairs window. After he climbed down it, Giovanni dug a path to the front door so his family could be free for the first time in days. Nina stepped onto the walkway her dad had created, and the piles of ash went past her knees. The streets were covered in hills of it.

When they exited their home, screams came from the home next door. Nina's neighbor, Mr. Bruchelli, had climbed up on his roof to sweep away the burning ash before it burned his house to the ground. He fell through, dying instantly. His family was devastated. The eruption was worse than war, unpredictable and utterly indiscriminate in its destruction.

Allied troops helped clear some of the ash with bulldozers in Salerno, but nobody came to help in their little village of Passiano. It was at least a year before all the ash was cleared from the village. Gardens and farms were ruined; the food supply was so devastated that the Allies helped by sending food rations.

Nina poked at the powdery, green pea substance her father brought home with the "food" rations. The directions said to combine it with water and heat, but she couldn't imagine how it could become food. Luckily, she was wrong, and soon, impossibly, an edible substance bubbled in the pot she'd hung over a small fire. Bringing a spoonful slowly to her mouth, Nina touched her tongue to what she thought might be pea soup. She silently thanked God for the food her mother's Aunt Enza and Uncle Alfonso brought from their grocery store in Santa Lucia. At least they weren't limited to only military rations. When the roads were cleared enough to travel again, once a week, someone from Nina's family walked two hours to Santa Lucia to retrieve anything Aunt and Uncle could spare from the store.

On one occasion late that spring, Giovanni still hadn't returned from his trip to Santa Lucia to get supplies, and Agnese was starting to worry seriously. So, she took her children on a walk into Cava that afternoon to see her father. On the way down the hill out of Passiano, a man stopped them and asked, "Excuse me. Are you Agnese Farano? Giovanni's wife?"

"Yes," she said with a polite smile. "Why do you ask?"

"No reason, I'm just surprised. You're beautiful," the man said, "I don't know what he sees in other women." He was gone before Agnese's jaw dropped. She stood in stunned silence and looked down at Nina and Joseph, her face clenched in embarrassment.

It was too late, but Nina pretended she hadn't heard. She didn't ask why when her mom returned to go home, leaving Joseph, Amelia, and Nina to visit their grandfather on their own.

They had a pleasant visit with their grandfather and were returning home when the sound of a pig being slaughtered echoed off the cobblestones and cement walls that lined their path. Nina shot her hands to her ears before realizing it couldn't have been a pig. The butcher had slaughtered his lot just the day before to prepare for the summer markets. Joseph grabbed Amelia by the hand and began walking faster toward their cortile, but Nina took off toward the sound. She'd never dared to watch the pigs die, but this was something else. It had to be. The sound led to another small cortile and up a couple of flights of stairs. Inside one of the flats, the village milk lady was pounding her fists on the ground, howling. She flung her body around like a demon had possessed her, standing and stomping her feet and then falling to the ground and thrashing around on the floor. Nina looked around for one of her sons. Why weren't they there to calm her down? Her daughter sobbed silently in the corner, clearly too distraught to help. Nina knew one of the three boys was a soldier. Maybe he'd been killed in action.

"What's going on?" Nina whispered to one of the woman's neighbors.

"Her sons were killed," she wept with her hand to her mouth, "All three. Poor soul." She crossed her heart with her fingers in the sign of the cross and said a little prayer. A vivid memory of the boys laughing and playing in front of the church flashed across Nina's mind.

"What? How?" Nina was stunned.

"There was an explosion on a train up north."

Everyone stayed until the woman finally wore herself down and passed out in a lump on the floor, a photo of her boys clutched to her chest. Her daughter curled up next to her, wrapping a blanket around her as if it would shield her from the truth.

As she wandered up the cobblestone to her home, Nina wondered what life would have been like if her dad or brother—or worse, both—had been taken away by the Germans or enlisted in the Italian Army. She never would have seen them again. What would have happened to her family if they had? How would they have survived?

Instinctively, Nina reached for her rosary in the little pouch that always hung at her side, but her fingers went straight through a small hole in the bottom of the fabric. No, no, no. The sack was empty. How could she lose it? In her memory, she watched the American soldier walk away again.

* * *

At the beginning of October 1944, George's company was in France, attempting to dislodge the Germans. In the middle of the battle, his tank trundled over a land mine. Mom was a little fuzzy on the details but knew the explosion was catastrophic, leaving a smoking, crumpled wreck. I can only guess what happened. Dad must have smashed his head on the instrument panel and knocked himself out instantly. He woke in agony, choking on the smoke pouring into the tank. A fire crackled around him, bringing him to his senses.

Mom said his feet were utterly crushed. He freed his legs and crawled to the top of the tank, where he found his Sergeant holding onto the top. George shook his leg to get him to move, but the Sergeant slumped lifelessly to the ground. His head was missing. Horrified, George again lost consciousness and fell back into the gunner's seat. Prince, who always stayed near George, barked frantically, alerting another tank nearby. The crew approached the smoking ruins, unsure of whether anyone was alive. They pulled George and his dog out and retreated with them to safety.

The next couple weeks were spent at a nearby field hospital in France until George could safely travel to a hospital in Massachusetts. He left France on October 19, 1944, to spend the next six months recovering in the United States in a wheelchair until he healed. He had what some GIs called "a million-dollar wound," one that got you out of the war and back home in one piece.

My dad was awarded the Good Conduct Medal, The American Defense Medal, The European African Middle Eastern Theater Campaign Ribbon with four service stars, and the Purple Heart. All in all, Dad lost four tanks during those brutal years he fought in the war. This was information I'd never heard as a child.

In retrospect, all the information I gathered revealed that my father was a true American hero. He did what was expected of him and didn't give up. But what had it cost him? What had the war cost both my parents? I remember feeling unloved, like I had no allies in this world, ready to run away. Yet, what was once a feeling of alienation was now replaced with an overwhelming empathy for my parents. My mother had never grown past the war. The trauma she suffered was all she ever talked about. She shared her stories of the war and her Life magazine with anyone and everyone.

On the other hand, as my mom always took center stage, my dad hardly talked. It seemed nothing my dad did ever mattered. In his silence, I think he loved her very much. From reading his letters, it was clear it wasn't the life he had envisioned, but after time, it was the life he must've resigned himself to.

I blinked back tears as I thought of my dad. He never gave up as a soldier; again, I wished he hadn't given up as a dad. He may have done the best he could under the circumstances. Maybe both my parents did.

I continued my research into my parents' lives. I'd heard my mother's stories so many times, but writing them down was eye-opening; all the pieces had to fit. It was amazing how well my mother remembered everything from so long ago. I think she relived those stories over and over again every time she told them.

* * *

After the war, things started calming down for my Italian family. Grandmother had her fifth child, Cristina, on July 9, 1945. She was a bundle of joy, and my grandmother was very busy caring for her growing family. Almost a year after the war ended, my grandmother thought it was time to take my father's address out of the sugar bowl and write to his mother, Adela Fortin. My grandfather's friend Dominico, who knew a little English, helped her write this short note. I do wonder why she waited. Maybe she was afraid he hadn't survived. She had such high hopes for my father. I expect he was in her prayers every day. I'm a big believer in manifesting, and I'm sure she visualized my father's return often. She prayed, believed, and brought an amazing story to reality, even though she had to use deception to accomplish it.

August 26, 1946

Dear Madam,

We are some friends of your son and we would like to know his news and if he is back home yet. We promised him before he went from here that we would contact you. He left to us this address to write to you when the war was over. We cannot forget how good he was to our family. Every day we talk about him, especially my little girl, Nina.

We hope he is back home safely and he and his family are all well. Our thoughts are always with him and how good he was to us. We will never forget him and hope soon to have his good news.

I close these lines sending the best to him and all his family,

Agnese Capuano Farano

She sent the letter off, hoping she would hear back soon. Later that month, Nina rushed home to show her mother the embroidery she'd learned at her aunt's house. She burst into the garden, where her mom clutched a letter to her chest with a huge smile.

"Look, Mama!"

Agnese smiled and patted her head. "The American soldier wrote to us, Nina. He says he is back at home and doing well. He is going to send you a package."

"I hope he sends sweets! He always had sweets to give to me when he was here."

That Christmas, Nina received her first gift from the American soldier. Agnese opened the package eagerly and handed her daughter a little gold locket with George's picture and a box of chocolates. "See, Nina, the American soldier kept his promise and sent you a gift. He's good at keeping his promises."

My mother treasured the locket. It was her nicest piece of jewelry. But what about the picture? It was a picture of a man she hadn't seen or thought of in years. And why would my dad send his picture? They weren't sweethearts! My mother had no answers to my questions.

My mother told me she remembers her mother sitting in the corner of their small living room with a kerosene lamp, writing. I can picture Agnese at the table my grandfather made, thinking and writing, trying to make things interesting and easy for my dad to understand. Paper was precious, and I'm sure she put her thoughts in order before writing. As my mother watched from a distance, it never occurred to her that her mother was pretending to be her, as she wrote. Later, all the letters were written by Dominico, a friend of my grandfather who had spent time in an English prison during the war and learned some English.

Dad would write his letters in English and bring them to an interpreter to have them translated into Italian. He then had the original letter to save for posterity, as he mailed the Italian version. When his interpreter refused to help him any longer, Dad wrote his letters in a beautiful flowing script on full sheets of paper, using a pencil, then typed them, saving the handwritten one and mailing the other to Italy. He wanted to make it as easy as he could for the Italian interpreter to read. Although, as I painstakingly pieced everything together, it became clear that some things got lost in translation on both sides, Dad put a lot of thought and care into every letter, making them very detailed.

My grandparents had more of a struggle writing their letters but obviously tried hard to make them enjoyable for my father to read. Unlike the full sheets of paper my father used, their letters were written in pen, with efficient use of space, on small sheets of stationery, some with a little red border, others on blue paper with ragged edges.

All in all, my father's big manilla envelope contained 81 letters written by him and 74 from my grandparents. I never saw any of the letters received in Italy and have no idea if they were saved or not. Unfortunately, I believe I'm missing a few pieces of correspondence.

All the letters were rich with romance, culture, and history. I loved reading each one over and over again. I've pieced together a narrative, summarizing some of the letters and leaving out repetitious ones. I've also added more of my mother's thoughts and memories, plus my interpretations.

Discovering the story of my young father brought me back to a time when the world was very different. He was very unlike the man I knew, and I was fascinated. I wasn't just enthralled; I was emotional. I fell in love with the young man and the person he struggled to become. He reminded me so much of myself. His decisions weighed heavily on him, and he tried hard to avoid making mistakes. Here was a man I spent most of my life blaming for my unhappiness. A man I never understood. Perhaps what appeared to me as sullenness and anger had actually been a profound disappointment? I just took for granted that the picture my mother painted of him was accurate. But there was so much more to this man who started as a kindhearted soul.

I've talked so much more to my dad now that he's gone than I ever did when he was alive. I hope he can hear and guide me as I write this story.

PART TWO
THE LETTERS

FOURTEEN

1947

My grandmother must have weighed the positives and negatives as she decided to proceed with her deception.

In April, Agnese sent another letter from Nina, gently chiding George for not writing back. The letter contained the line, "I think you have every day good time because you have everything in beautiful America," which perhaps perfectly summarized my grandmother's hopes for her daughter and this American Soldier.

She would have been relieved at the positive letter they received shortly afterward.

April 1947

Dear Nina,

I was so happy to receive your photo. You look very attractive on that photo since the last time I saw you. I like the way you fix your hair. I keep your photo on my table where I do my schoolwork every night. That way I am always thinking of you.

Nina, from the first day I met you I've always thought about you. Because you are a good girl and come from a good family. I will never forget the time you held me by the hand and took me to your house.

If there is any little thing you would like to have let me know and maybe I will be able to send it to you if it doesn't cost too much. Everything in United States today costs a lot of money. It makes me happy to know that you're happy when you hear from me and receive gifts from me.

I am going to see some Italian people and have them write this letter in Italian.

You know Nina, America is a nice place. Italy is a nice place too. But in America everybody Italian, French, German, Polish, Portuguese, all talk English.

Maybe I will be able to send you some books so you will be able to learn English.

Nina go to school as long as you can because an education is the best thing in world. I went to school until I was 16 years old and today I am very sorry I did not go longer. I am going to school now but I am not learning as much as I could of learned if I would have continued my schooling. People may tell you schooling is no good but don't believe them. Someday you will want a good job and make a lot of money and maybe visit America or even live here where everybody is happy and have mostly everything they want.

Well I think I've said enough now Nina, so good luck to you and your family.

Your loving friend,

George

April, 1947

Dear Nina,

I received another letter from you a few days ago. It makes me feel good to receive news from you every once in a while.

You know Nina it's lucky that I gave you my address because the address that you gave me was lost in France when I was wounded. I felt so very sad to lose it because I thought I would never hear from you. I'm glad you're writing to me.

What are you going to plant in your little garden this spring? I remember you took me for a walk in your little garden and showed me all the things that were growing there. I used to like to eat the fruits in Italy. Yes, It must be beautiful in Italy right now with everything turning green. I remember the beautiful views from the top of the hill. I would love to visit Italy again someday in the spring.

Did I tell you that my youngest brother was in

Italy too? Yes, he was at Naples and at Anzio. He tried to come and see me at Anzio when I was there. But he could not because there was an air raid and he could not get off his ship.

I saw an Italian movie the other night, the words were translated into English so we could understand. It was about the Germans when they came to Italy. They treated the Italians terrible. They killed a lot of innocent people. It was horrible, I hate to think about what happened there.

I'm so glad you and your family are doing well. Say hello to everyone.

Your loving friend,

George

I found several letters in Italian that weren't dated. I believe most of the early letters from Italy came by boat, and most of Dad's letters would've been sent by airmail, so it wasn't easy to put them in their proper order. When my mother translated some of them for me, I placed them where they belonged. When Domenico, my grandfather's friend, started translating for the family again in March 1948, he always dated the letters. At that point, I think, they were all being sent by air. It seems there may be some letters missing on both sides. I believe there were also letters that Dad never had translated because he didn't respond to some of the questions asked of him.

May 1947

Dear George

I am writing to you right away after receiving your letter. I was very happy to receive your letter. I sent you two letters and I sent you greeting cards for Easter. You didn't think of me, I received nothing for Easter. I am not happy when I receive nothing from you. I feel bad that I worry about you. Just think that ever since I was a little girl I loved you. Ever since the day I met you I have been thinking about you. I thought about you when you were fighting the war and I prayed for you. I was feeling my destiny and I loved you. I am going to take some pictures and I will send them to you. I hope the pictures turn out good. I will write you another letter soon. Don't make me wait, write to me right away. That is the way I am, I worry about you. Everything you send to me I save and take care of. You always tell me that you are very busy and I believe you. How long does it take for you to write a letter. Would you like to know what I do in my life.

In the morning I go see my Aunt she is teaching me how to sew. When my brother comes back from Salerno he comes to get me and we both go home together. After I eat I go see my tutor and learn how to read and write. He is close to my home and there are a couple of others that are also learning. I can't go to the movies or dancing we have no money for such things.

I think of you being so far away. My parents are keeping me for you and they don't want me to go far from home. When my Mom and Dad go out they take me with them. If you send me some books I promise I will try and read them. I am still waiting for the books you promised me to learn english. Dear George I listen to you, everything you tell me. You promise that when I am a little older you will come and get me. Yes Italy this time of year is beautiful and very green. You wish to be here in the spiring so you should save your money so that you can. If you come we will have a feast. I haven't had time to go in the garden lately there is no fruit there now. I'm sorry that your brother did not come to see me I would have sent you something with him.

If your brother ever comes back to Italy make him promise to come and see us.

Thank you for saying you want to send me so many things. I will make believe that you did send me all those things because you have a good heart. God bless you with good fortune that you can make lots of money. Don't think about anything bad or that anything bad could happen to me. Don't worry about me I don't pay any attention to any other man. I would tell my father if someone was to bother me.

I always pay attention to what you are telling me. My family works very hard but we still don't have much.

All my regards to your family

Regards from your Nina

George's photo he sent Nina

When I asked my mother to translate the letters, she had no problem saying yes, but on the other hand, she didn't know the content we would find. I'm not sure she would have agreed if she had known the steps her mother had taken to bring her plan to fruition.

We carefully handled each thin piece of paper, trying not to rip them. My mom translated them slowly, taking in what her mother was saying. I typed as she spoke. She had to stop and gather her thoughts at times as she couldn't believe what she was reading. It didn't make sense to her that her mother would lie like that. I tried to console her every step of the way, telling her that her mother was doing what she thought was best for her family. But as I listened to her translate, the main thought running through my head was, "Poor Dad."

At one point, I told Mom to take a break and got her a glass of water. Everything she was reading was hard for her to wrap her head around. The letters claimed to be written by her and expressed her love for a man she had barely known. I felt sorry for her as I watched her. I was forcing her to do something she had purposely avoided her whole life. Finally, she was discovering the truth after all these years.

After a few hours, exhaustion overtook her, and she went home, promising to return the next day. I was relieved she was willing to come back and finish. I was worried she wouldn't want everything revealed in the book I was attempting to write.

She arrived the next day as promised. We took our seats on the couch, and she continued translating slowly as I typed. Mom seemed to struggle a little, stopping and thinking before responding. Was the writing or the content causing the difficulty? The pages were old, and some words were smudged. She seemed guarded with the emotion she shared with me. She'd shake her head and breathe heavily but gave very little away. In the end, I know she did the best she could.

It took us three days to finish, and I wish my mother would've shared with me all the thoughts that were swimming in her mind, but she continued to be guarded.

In reality, I was just as upset as she was. Having these additional letters translated revealed more of my grandmother's deceit, how she had lied, manipulated, and bullied my father. I longed to dig into the subject with my mother, but I could tell she was too overwhelmed to do anything of the sort as she prepared to leave the moment she was done translating. Weeks later, when I finally asked her what she thought of her mother's choice, she was in total denial even though she had seen the truth on the written page. She refused to discuss it, saying only that her mother didn't mean to do what she had done.

I walked her to the door on the last day, hugged her, and thanked her. It hadn't been easy for her, and she still didn't know how to process everything she'd learned. But, again, I told her it was alright; her mother was doing what she felt she had to do to save her family.

I printed out what I had typed, numbering the letters according to dates. I fit them in the notebook I had made for my father's letters in order of where I thought they belonged. Now, I had a complete story of how my father fell in love and into my grandmother's trap. I say my grandmother because she was the one who I believe came up with the idea and wrote the majority of the letters until she died. Still, my grandfather was undoubtedly involved, as well as my uncle Joseph and Domenico. They had a secret little group with the common goal of betraying my father for their gain. My mother shared with me how she witnessed them huddled together, whispering in candlelight as she watched from the bedroom doorway.

June 1947

Dear George

I am telling you this is the second letter that I am writing you and you are not responding. Please let me know why. Maybe you don't write to me because you are sick of me. You are making me suffer. You make me so mad. I excuse myself and I am upset by myself. I understand you are suppose to send me some books. You didn't send them and I am still waiting. I understand everything you want me to do and I remember everything. I do everything you ask me to do. When I get older you will take me with you to America. I feel bad when you don't respond to me. Let me know if you really love me like I love you. I want to know if you love someone else. Is she Italian? The day that you met me in front of my Grandfathers store I have always thought of you since then. I always think of you and I want to know if you love me. I don't want to be unhappy in my life. It is terrible to be so far away from you George. Let me know if you sent me the english books. I would like to have some more American dress magazines. I have started to sew dresses in the American style. My Aunt is helping me learn to sew and I am trying to do really good work. She sews for other people and I want to do that to. Do you want me to work in America? I want to earn some money so we can be happy.

There is a lady that came here from America and she met my Mother. She said there are so may beautiful things in America. How lucky you are to be happy in America. I hope everything is good with you.

Regards to your family
Regards from your Nina
Translated by Nina Fortin 2014

From this letter, I see that the guilt trips, manipulation, and a bit of bullying started early on. At that point, my Dad must have mixed feelings about his relationship with my mother. From what I gathered from his interviews in different newspaper articles after returning to America, he hadn't been serious about going to get her. He said he'd just been teasing, but those articles never explained what changed his mind. But now I knew it was my grandmother. He must have also remembered his promise to God before the battle at Anzio. I bet that promise nagged at him as he thought of his comrades dying during the conflict.

July 1947

Dear George

I am letting you know that this is the third letter I am sending you and I have not received your news. Maybe you are tired of me. Let me know why you have not written. I am really worried about you, and I have been crying. You can't imagine how I feel. George I sent you my picture that I found that my mother had taken of me in the garden. I did not look well but now I am feeling better, and I am working at feeling even better. You haven't been writing to me and I am worried. Tell me why you are not answering my letters. I don't deserve this George! I hope you send a letters soon. Remember that I loved you since I met you.

Regards from my family and give regards to your family

With affection from your Nina

Translated by Nina Fortin 2014

I can't imagine what must have gone through my mother's head as she translated that paragraph. "I don't deserve this," and "Remember that I loved you since I met you." These are obvious words of manipulation. There was no doubt that Grandmother Agnese was on a mission and not going to give up.

July 11, 1947

Dear Nina

I'm terribly sorry I didn't write to you sooner. I didn't realize how you felt about me. I took all three of your letters to Mrs. Morelli today so she could translate. After she read them to me I couldn't feel more terrible. Don't worry Nina I don't think I could ever forget you. I enjoy your letters, please keep writing to me.

It makes me happy to know I have a little friend in Italy writing to me. I'm very proud of you Nina for the work you are doing. You don't waste your time like other girls your age do. You must be about thirteen years old now. American girls your age don't help their mothers make dresses and embroider. Girls thirteen years old in this country would rather play or go to the movies. My mother is good at sewing too. She does embroidering and makes dresses and she makes white shirts for us. We never have to buy any shirts.

American children seem so spoiled but not you Nina. I'm very impressed with you. I didn't have much when I was growing up. My parents couldn't afford to buy us toys but that was ok, we understood. Today my brothers and I save our money. We've been taught not to waste money.

I'd like to travel and see Italy again. It takes a lot of money to travel so I'm going to have to start saving now. When Mrs. Morelli reads to me your letters you are always saying that I am going to forget about you. I'm sorry I haven't had much time to write to you Nina but I will never forget you. Please forgive me and I will try to write to you more often.

I'm trying to save my money, Nina. I don't want to spend my money going out and having a good time so I read. I have quite a few books now, I'm starting a little library for myself. They are mostly educational books from school and I also buy other books.

Have you been bathing yet in the Mediterranean Sea or is it too far to go. It can't be very far from where you live. I go almost every day, I take my dog.

She loves to play in the water as we walk along the surf. I'm getting a good tan from my walks on the beach. I get out of school at 12:30 every day now and that way I have the afternoon off.

I bought a little trinket from one of the girls at school who made it. I think you'll like it very much.

Give my love to your family Nina and most of all to you.

Your loving and affectionate friend

George

My Grandmother's manipulation was starting to work. She'd easily convinced my father that this sweet, unspoiled Italian girl would make a much better wife than the choices he had in America.

.July 27, 1947

Dearest George

To respond to your letter I am writing you right away. When I received your letter I was very happy to get your good news. I am glad everything is fine with you and everything is fine with us too. I didn't know what to think I had a bad feeling in my heart because I didn't receive your news.

I love you very, very much and I think I always will. I am always a good girl for you. My father and brother work in the factory making furniture at night. They make furniture for people that don't have a lot of money.

My Grandfather has two stores one is to sell magazines and one is to sell tobacco. When you come we will take a walk to my grandfathers stores and then take a walk to see his farms.

I am very pleased that I am in love with an American. I am very pleased that your mother works and when I come to America I will work to. I like to work. Did you like the picture I sent you. The dress I am wearing in the picture I made myself. I received your picture and you cut your hair. You should let your hair grow. I liked the picture of your family they are beautiful people.

I have some sad news. My father was hiding some black market tobacco. Someone found out and came to take it. They choked and killed my mothers dog and took our chickens. We were all very upset .

You asked me if I ever bathed myself in the Mediterranean Sea. I sometimes go to the beach with my Aunt Mary. We go very seldom because we don't have the money for bus fare. If I go anywhere it is usually with my Aunt Mary or my brother Joseph. I never go anywhere by myself because my mother wants to keep me pure and good. I am so sorry my writing is not good.

Regards to all your family,
Regards from your Nina
Translated by Nina Fortin 2014

I asked my mother about the black market. She said her father hid black-market tobacco in a space between the oven and a pig pen. Sometimes, when he was away, working in another city, the family would run out of food. Her mother then sold some of the tobacco to feed the family. This was very dangerous and illegal; she feared going to jail.

One night, perhaps tipped off by a sale Grandmother made, gangsters came looking for the tobacco. Threatening the family, they grabbed the dog, twisted his neck, and killed him. They lost their dog and chickens that night, but the gangsters didn't discover the tobacco and never returned.

My mother's voice amplified, and her back stiffened as she told me, "I can't believe my father put us in such danger."

As the letter stated, her family did keep a close watch

on her, not wanting her to attract the attention of another man. When her parents became fixated on the American Soldier, she was no longer allowed to have a normal life. My Grandfather and my Uncle Joseph never let my mother out of their sight.

As my mother told a story explaining how Joseph watched her constantly, noticing if boys looked at her, she shook her head in frustration. She told me that one day, her friend Mario dropped by with a magazine all the village children shared and passed from family to family throughout the village. Unknown to my mother, Mario had a crush on her. He'd tucked a love letter in the magazine, hoping she would read it. But my mother was too busy washing clothes and cleaning all day and went to bed early, forgetting the magazine on the table. Joseph found it and the letter in the morning. He dragged her out of bed by her hair, accusing her of leading Mario on. She didn't know what he was talking about and protested in tears.

Joseph knew their parents' plans could be destroyed if she fell for some Italian boy.

She told me, "I didn't even care about boys. I was too busy taking care of everybody. I was just trying to survive." She sighed and said she occasionally wanted a little fun and wished her brother and father would leave her alone.

Another time her father slapped her across the face because he thought she had red lipstick on. He rubbed her face with a cloth, but there was no lipstick. They were obviously earnest about their ruse.

She never mentioned what her mother thought about her hanging out with boys. But then her mother was weak with her pregnancy and sick with disease.

I pushed for more details, but it was clear my mother didn't want to figure this out with me and didn't even want to talk about it. But then my mother never ever said anything negative about her mother.

July 21, 1947

Dear Nina,

In your last letter you said you were crazy about me and you would love me no mater what happens. Is that really true Nina?

I had some similar thoughts Nina but I am so much older then you. Ever since the first day I set eyes on you I said to myself there's a nice girl from a nice family. Right there and then I wanted to give you everything I could to make you happy. And when I'd go back to camp I wanted to rush back to see you the very next day. Do you realize how much older I am then you? Does it make a difference to you? Does your mother know how you feel about me? What would she say if she knew? Does your father and mother read these letters? Maybe if they did they would stop you from writing to me. I would never want that to happen Nina because I am so happy to receive your wonderful letters.

Nina, a lot of girls here put make up or powder and lipstick on their faces. I don't think you need any of that stuff. I think you'll look much better without it. Anyway some girls put too much on and they look terrible.

Nina, how old do you have to be in Italy to get married? I wish you were old enough to get married now. I'd marry you right away. I hope you keep on loving me until the day I go to Italy and get you. How old are you Nina?

What day, month, and year were you born? I think I asked you that before but I never got an answer.

Don't you want to tell me? You don't have to if you don't want to just keep sending me a picture once in a while so I can see you grow up into womanhood.

Nina I understood from one of your letters that you bought a book to learn english. It's going to be hard to learn the english language but I can tell you are a mature, intelligent girl and I know you can do it. It would help if you could find someone that speaks english so you could practice with them.

I told a friend of mine that there was a girl around thirteen years old in Italy that was in love with me. She said I was silly and that I shouldn't bother with you because you were to young and didn't know what you were doing. She said you would meet some nice

Italian boy and forget all about me. Maybe that is what will happen Nina. You know Nina, I am about fifteen years older then you. You are young but when two people love each other I don't think age matters. We will just have to wait and see what happens.

If your mother reads this letter she will probably think I'm the one who is making you fall in love with me. It seems we might be getting serious Nina. Is this really what you want?

Ever since your last letter Nina everything seems brighter. I'm happier in my work. All the music I hear over the radio sounds sweeter. I walk around with my head high and say to myself, "It's a wonderful world we're living in."

Nina, I dreamt that you were here with me and we were walking by my mail box and we saw a letter there from your family. But when we got there it wasn't the letter from Italy it was another one. That was the first dream I ever had of you.

Nina, I believe this letter is getting a little long I better stop now and I'll write you another long letter soon. Give my regards to all. Good luck, Nina, and take good care of yourself. All my love and kisses.

Your beloved friend,

George

Grandmother must have been so pleased with this letter and my dad's evident emotions.

In the letters, my grandmother invented the story that my mom was on a mission to learn English. In reality, she never tried at all, and she never believed she was going to America. It was interesting that my father had guessed my mother's correct age and was okay with it. But then my grandmother lied to him and made her a year older. I think all the questions about age and the miscommunication made them concerned that he had a problem with her age.

July 1947

Dear George,

I am telling you that I talked to my family and I told my Mom I don't care if you are older than me. Tell me if you are happy to marry me.

The year is passing and there are a few more years to wait. Let me know if you are happy because I am happy about going to America. You wanted to know my birthday and it is March 30th.

I love you and think about you all the time. I have loved you since I saw you in Italy and I want your family to know that. How can I ever forget you George. Tell me what you did to me, let me know if you really love me. I started loving you like a brother because I didn't know what love was until now. Please stop worrying that you are 15 years older than me. I am happy and want to be with you in America.

I am so glad you had a dream that I was with you in America.

Regards to your family and regards from your Nina.

Translated by Nina Fortin 2014

My Grandmother poured pressure on my dad to commit to loving Nina. It was obvious to me that she gave a lot of thought to these letters and how she could manipulate my father into making promises.

July 1947

Dear George

This is Nina's mother responding to your letter. I am letting you know that my daughter Nina talked to me and her father. She made us read your letter. We are happy you and my daughter are now happy. My daughter says she doesn't care that you are older then her. You wanted to know how old my daughter is, she is 14 she was 10 when you met her and she turned 14 on May 30th. If you are thinking of marrying her you have to wait. Let me know if you are happy with what I am saying to you. We do not know what Nina is thinking she is very young and innocent. She doesn't know what love is and has never had a man friend. It looks like she does love you and is very sincere. She is sacrificing her life and you really have to think about what you are doing. Tell me what you are thinking? Why would you want her to study? I used to always tell her to study, she needs to study her Italian first.

We don't have the money for her to get a tutor to learn english. I have three children in school and I do not have money for a tutor for any of them. We have no money and have to get rations from the state. Just to get a loaf of bread is difficult and now bread is on the black market.

Give my regards to your family.

Agnese Capuano Farano

Translated by Nina Fortin

It is interesting that my grandmother told my father my mom was 14. My mother turned 13 on March 30, 1947, and she was nine when my father met her. Some of the letters say her birthday was on May 30th, I guess it was translated wrong, but it is obvious my grandmother misled my father about my mother's actual age.

July 31, 1947

Dear Nina

I went for a ride tonight about 10:00 p.m. in my father's car. I was all by myself. I went to a little place where they sell beer and wine, and I had two bottles of beer and listened to some sweet music. I had you on my mind all night. And When I got back home about midnight I decided to write you.

Nina, I'm going to quit school and go to work next month. I will make twice as much money than going to school and I'll be able to save more too. I'm going to be a bookkeeper in a store.

I thought you would probably like to hear more about my life. I will tell you what I can remember. I was brought to the house I live in now when I was two years old. I was always very shy and quite. I was always mother's favorite and she seemed to like keeping me close by. When I was ten years old my mother wouldn't let me go out of the yard alone. When I was sixteen years old I had to be home when it got dark or by seven o'clock at night. I didn't do to well at school, I was too shy. I was never very talkative. I was sixteen years old and still in the eight grade. So when I was seventeen years old I decided to quit school and go to work.

My first pay was nine dollars a week. I was very glad to have that nine dollars so I could help my parents. I gave my parents $8.50 and had 50 cents left over to spend.

I was working in a mill where they made cloth for men's suits. The next highest pay I made was $11. And then I made $13 and then $16. My pay steadily went up until I was making $25 a week when I was twenty-one.

Then one day I was drafted into the army, and I had to be trained to fight. It broke my mother's heart to see me go. I was always so close to my Mom.

When I got in the army I met all kinds of people

from all over the country. I did a lot of dirty work in the army. I washed a lot of dishes and did a lot of guard duty. I was always a good guy. I tried to never fight or argue with anyone. You know Nina I always tried to be honest, dependable, and reliable. One day in a restaurant I asked a waitress for change for a dollar, and she gave me change for a ten. Of course I made it right and gave her the money back. She was so happy and now every time she sees me she remembers what an honest guy I am. You know Nina it pays to be honest. People respect you and remember you. A lot of the guys I know keep the wrong company and do wrong things and get into trouble. My mother raised me right.

Nina, be good to your mother. I'm sure everything she tells you is right and she wants the best for you. You only have one father and mother, don't ever forget that. Give your parents all the respect they deserve.

Nina I bought you a box of paper, envelopes and a pen. I will send it out to you soon. It's nice paper and I hope it improves your writing. Are you working on your english? You should work on it a little every day. And if you can see someone who talks English there in Cava say some of the words to him in English and see if you pronounce them right. I would really love it if you could speak English next time I see you. I am going to start working August

18. I'll have your pictures on my desk where I work. I'll be proud of you when people come over to my desk and admire your picture. They'll ask me who the pretty girl is. I'll tell them that you're my sweetheart far away in Italy. I'm having a nice colored picture made of myself. And when I receive it I will send it to you as soon as I can.

All my love and kisses, Nina. Give my regards to all.

Your beloved American Friend,

George

Did this honest letter give my grandmother any sense of guilt? My dad was so genuine and sincere, and she outright deceived him. I want to think it wasn't easy for my grandmother to do what she did.

I really felt connected to my father when I read his letters. As a timid introvert, this long-distance relationship fit my dad perfectly. Writing a letter, I'm sure, was so much easier than going out and trying to create relationships. He could experience a connection with another person by sitting down and writing a letter. The distance made it easier for him to dream and fantasize about her, and loneliness made it even more appealing.

August 24, 1947

Dear George

We have received everything you sent us. You

don't know how happy I was to get your beautiful gifts. Thank you so much for thinking of us and sending paper and envelopes. My sisters were so happy to receive the candy and they are blowing you kisses. The picture I received is now my favorite picture. I am so happy what you do for me. We received the package, but we didn't receive any mail. You didn't respond to my mothers letter. She told you all about me and how old I am.

I know you want more pictures of me and my family. My mom is pregnant again and has nothing to wear for a picture. I wish to have a baby brother. My brother was supposed to go and be a soldier but he didn't go because he didn't pass the medical exam.

Let me know if you are doing well in your work. I asked you before and you didn't respond about your work. You didn't let me know if you are happy with what my mother had to tell you. You make me worried. My mother still wants to know if you are going to wait for me. She wants to know what year you will come for me. She also wants to know if you want me to come there by myself. She said I can not come by myself you must come when I am 17 and then I will come with you. She will not let me come by myself, I have never been anywhere by myself.

We sent you a little card from Amelia's first communion. The pictures from Amelia's first communion did not come out good and that is why we are not sending them to you. We can not get good pictures taken because we don't have money we used my Aunt's little camera which is not very good.

Because of the war a lot of the young people are sick today. The sickness Typhoid was a sickness that if it was malignant they die. We thank God that we today are all OK. I am very scared of this sickness Typhoid. We feel so bad for all the poor people that have this disease. My little sisters were so happy to eat the chocolate you sent.

Regards to your family and kiss your Mom.

Hurry and write to me right now.

Regards from your Nina

Translated by Nina Fortin 2014

In 1943, during World War II, typhoid was prevalent in Italy's central and southern regions, which air raids and bombings had ravaged. After the war, famine and hardship continued, with flooded fields, polluted water, and low food supplies in numerous areas. Additionally, more than 50,000 cases of typhoid and paratyphoid fever were reported between 1943 and 1949. Typhoid cases continued to escalate in Italy in 1950 and 1951, mainly in rural areas like where my grandparents lived, where the hygiene standards remained low due to poverty and neglect.

Italy had more typhoid-reported cases during that time than all other European countries. My grandmother had many things to be afraid of; typhoid was just added to the list.

September 7, 1947

Dear Nina,

I received your nice letter a few days ago and I appreciate the nice little medal you sent me. I shined it up and put it with your picture. I also had your mothers letter read to me. It looks like your parents are ok with our relationship. Did your mother write that letter? The handwriting looks just like yours or maybe you wrote it for her. From what I understand Nina, you are 14 years old and will be 15 years old on May 30th. Is that right Nina?

Nina, I have a cousin who just got married last week. She is only 17 years old. When she realized she was married and was leaving her family she started to cry. Will that happen to you, Nina? You have about 2 years to think it over. You don't know where you are going to live here or how you're going to live. This is a beautiful country to live in. Love is blind and a gamble they say. If two people are in love they will do everything in there power to make each other happy. You'll understand more about love as you get older. When a boy meets a girl and they want to be together all the time and give each other everything to make each other happy the best thing for them to do is get married.

I'm letting my hair grow now for the winter and when its full grown I'll have another picture taken and send it to you. I hope you liked my large photograph I sent you. I'm sending you a small photograph of myself that I had taken when I first went in the service when I was 21 years old I hope you like it.

I had my teeth cleaned at the dentist yesterday. The dentist said I had one of the best set of teeth he ever saw. I hope I can keep them that way forever. You also have nice teeth, Nina, so take good care of them. Brush them at least twice a day. You won't be sorry. Italians usually have good teeth anyway. In America lots of people have bad teeth. There are people here with false teeth at the age of 18. Thats because they don't eat the right food and eat too much candy.

I pray to God that someday I will have a nice little wife to live with and make happy for the rest of my life. I hope it will be you.

Think everything over Nina. Make sure you know what you want. I also want to know that you are learning your English.

Your beloved and affectionate friend,
George

My father continued bringing up their age difference. My grandmother continued reassuring him.

My mom mentioned she'd found out Dad had a girlfriend for a while who had false teeth. In those days, it was not uncommon for a young person to have false teeth. I read that in the 1940s and 1950s, before fluoride, flossing, and dental implants, dental disease was widespread. When people could no longer live with the symptoms caused by severe dental health issues, they'd visit the dentist and replace their teeth with dentures. Others just wanted new white teeth and had their teeth switched with false ones for purely cosmetic reasons. Dad, obviously, didn't want a woman with false teeth.

September 1947

Dear George

I am responding to your dear letter. I received two of your letters after so long. Why are you taking so long to write to me. You make me worry about you. I am glad you received the medal I sent you. You are thinking that I am still little but I am older now. Don't worry I write my letters with my own hands. I don't go anywhere to have my letters written.

I am very glad your cousin got married and you went to your cousins wedding. You said your cousin was never away from her mother. Someday that will happen to me, I have never been away from my Mom. I hope someday you will be able to bring my father over to America. When I come to America I want you to have my Mom and sisters come to America also. What George do you think of that?

Don't worry about my teeth, I take care of my teeth. My teeth are always very clean. I went to the dentist and he told me I would eventually have to get a wisdom tooth pulled. He told me I have beautiful teeth.

You keep telling me that I have to learn english. I am unable to learn english. When you keep asking me my Mom knew someone who could teach me and she asked him to teach me english. He tried to teach me english but he fell in love with me and wanted my parents to save me for him. My parents won't allow me to go to him anymore.

My mother told him that it was impossible that they save me for him because I love an American man. My father and my brother talked to him also. He left very upset and then came again in 15 days with the excuse that he wanted my father to make him a piece of furniture. He asked my brother again if he could save me for him. My brother told him that he doesn't tell me what to do, my father does. It was better when I was little and didn't have these problems. When I come to America you can teach me english. Now my brother doesn't let me go anywhere by myself and I have to be careful when I go anywhere. I can't even look at a man because they will make something out of it.

I received your picture and you are so handsome in that picture. We put your picture on the coffee table where we can see it everyday. My Mom was so happy to hear that you are Catholic. I am so happy that you are thinking about me and my sisters. They loved the candy that you sent.

Regards to your family George

Regards to you from your Nina
Translated by Nina Fortin 2014

Since the whole correspondence was a lie, my grandmother seemed to feel the freedom to lie about little details as well. For example, this letter states that Nina had gone to the dentist, but she never visited a dentist until she lived in America.

While the English teacher fiasco served as an acceptable reason why Nina wasn't learning English, I think grandmother was also trying to make Dad a little jealous. In the letter, my grandmother also attempted to get a feel for my dad's reaction to bringing the whole family to America. He never responded to the question; perhaps it was lost in translation. But I think my grandmother always intended to bring the entire family to America.

November 1947

Dear George

George it is months that my daughter did not receive your news. I want to know why you have not been writing to my daughter. I do not understand why you are not writing. She has been waiting for the arrival of your letter, I hope it comes soon. Because you are not writing to her I am going to get another picture to send to you. One of my neighbors boyfriends who is in medical school told me to get Nina iron shots because she is so tired and depressed. She does not feel well and is very worried that you are not writing to her. You know how much she loves you please write to her right away.

You saw her as a little girl you have to see her now she is growing into a beautiful woman. You would not recognize her today. One of my friends married an American woman named Elena. We went to meet her in town and she told Nina to learn how to cook very well because American's like to eat. We gave her your address and she took a picture of Nina. When she arrives back in America she will write to you and send you Nina's picture. Please let me know if you hear from her.

How is your health, we are worried about you. Maybe something happened to you. Or maybe you are trying to get distant from Nina.

You are far from her eyes and never far from her heart. Nina is sacrificing her life always home by herself waiting for news from you.

You should write her if you love her. We are all worried about you over here. You are not paying attention to Nina or thinking of her and I do not want her upset.

We love you and wish you good things.

Write soon, I know nothing else to say.

Agnese Capuanno Farano

Translated by Nina Fortin 2014

A friend attending medical school had my mother's blood tested. Nina was tired all the time, and they discovered she had thalassemia. Thalassemia is a blood disorder passed down through families, where the body makes an abnormal form of hemoglobin, the protein in red blood cells that carries oxygen. The condition results in excessive red blood cell destruction, leading to anemia. Anemia is a disorder in which your body doesn't have enough normal, healthy red blood cells, resulting in exhaustion. They thought that she had thalassemia major at the time, which meant she would have needed blood transfusions and would probably die by the time she reached her 18th birthday. My grandmother was devastated by this news and swore that this would not happen to her daughter. Her daughter was not going to die.

She started feeding my mother raw egg yolks daily to build up her blood. I'm sure this made my grandmother even more determined to get my mother to America. Luckily, when my mother got tested in America for thalassemia, they found it was thalassemia minor, which only causes slight anemia. My grandmother conveniently blamed my father for my mother's depression and laid another guilt trip on him. At the time, my mother didn't know what her mother was up to and didn't think about my father, much less suffer depression about him.

November 1947

Dear Nina,

I received your mother's beautiful letter. Was it your mother who wrote it? It was written very nicely. I'm sorry to hear that you were sick. I promised that I would answer all your letters and I didn't. I know I was unfair. You should of punished me a little by not writing for a long while. But I know you can't. Because you've got too much of a big heart to do a thing like that to me. I love you more than ever now since I received your last letter. I never knew what love was like before. But now I know. And it took 24 years to find out and it had to be with you when you were ten years old. But your growing into womanhood now. Nina, I was always a bashful boy. I didn't go out too much before I went in the Army. I was always my mothers favorite boy.

I always minded my mother more than my brothers. There was lots of girls who liked me and I liked them but I never got the courage to approach them and talk to them. In a way I'm glad I wasn't a wild boy like some. Because I'd have been married by now if I was and probably unhappy too. Don't worry about me anymore Nina, because I'm going to answer all your letters now as soon as I receive them. And this time I really mean it. I don't want you to get sick and worried over me anymore. Nina, you should't stay home all the time on account of me. Go out and enjoy yourself. Have fun with the others. But be careful of the fresh boys of course. They have ideas sometimes with pretty girls. Be careful where you go alone. Try to have your brother go with you if you go far. Go out with girl friends to the movies. I hope I hear from that lady you told me about. I'll let you know if I hear from her. Well, Nina, I wish you all the luck in the world and don't get sick anymore. Give my regards to all.

All my love and kisses,
George

As my dad wondered why my mother's handwriting looked the same as her mother's, you would think his intuition would've kicked in, but he believed what he wanted to believe.

I'm sure my dad felt a little guilty about my mother's sickness. He believed she was alone, waiting and missing him. He probably thought she ran to check on the mail every day. But, of course, she was oblivious, and my grandmother was the one anticipating his letters. Grandmother had very little in her life to look forward to, and his letters would've filled that hole.

November 1947

Dear George,

I am writing to you to let you know that my mother had a baby. She has blue eyes and blonde hair like you. My mother looks at your picture all the time, she loves that picture and wanted a baby to look like you. If the baby had been a boy my parents would have named him George but since she is a girl they named her Angelina after my Aunt in Paris. I am happy having a baby sister but I am sorry of my mother who got sick from the delivery.

I now have to be the mother of the house because I am the oldest. The post office has done a lot of favors for my Mom to deliver your packages and letters so they asked us for cigarettes from you. Please send a pack of cigarettes for the postman. Please write to me right away so I don't worry about you. I will like to hear your good news. When I go to the post office and there is no news from you I get very upset and worried for you. I hope the next two years will go by fast so that we can get married because I am not happy right now.

Regards from me and my family to you and your family.

I am always thinking about you George.

Always Nina

Translated by Nina Fortin 2014

My grandmother's health never returned to normal after having Angelina, her sixth baby. She may have known deep down that she would not live to see her children grow up.

George never responded to the news of the new baby, and several letters were sent over the next couple of months, repeating the information and questioning why he wasn't responding. It must have worried my grandmother greatly when she didn't hear from my father. I'm sure she laid awake at night thinking of things she could tell him that would convince him he should marry her daughter.

My mother said my grandmother spent a lot of time looking at my father's picture and commenting that her new baby daughter looked just like him. It sounded to me like she was falling in love with him herself. I'm sure she had all her hopes and dreams for the future wrapped up in him. The thought that he might find another woman in America must have been a great worry. In addition, her health was not improving, causing more concern.

I believe my father must have dated from time to time, forgetting about my mother. That would explain why he didn't write for months at a time. But my grandmother was never going to let him forget her little Nina.

FIFTEEN

1948

By 1948, my father had been writing to Italy for over a year. Nina would soon turn 14, and Dad would be turning 29. My grandmother never regained her strength and was becoming increasingly weaker. I wonder if she had felt better, perhaps, she would've told my mother more about my father and maybe shared some of the letters. Instead, she most likely mainly focused on her health, fearful she would die.

January 10, 1948

My Dearest Nina,

Today I'm going to write you a long letter and try and make up for all the letters I haven't written. I'm so sorry I didn't send you a card or a present for Christmas. I promise I won't forget you on your Birthday. I don't want to make you any promises Nina because I would hate to disappoint you. I have four letters on my desk from you right now. I have never seen a girl have so much patience as you do. Another girl would have given up writing to me long ago if I didn't answer all her letters. That's one of the things I like about you, you just don't give up. I know I have a lot of explaining to do about not writing. Well it's like this I was tired of my job and I quit. Now I'm going to school again and I just bought a car and I had to borrow money to buy it and and I won't get any money from the government for a while yet. Now I owe a lot of money. And I've got to go to work after school so I can make more money to pay my bills. I go to school from eight in the morning to one in the afternoon. And if I can get a job from two in the afternoon to ten at night I'll make enough money to get by. And this summer I would like to get a new car. But if I go to school and work too I won't have much time to myself. Well I'll save money.

I know Nina that you think that I have forgotten about you. I had an idea you'd say something like that. I don't blame you for saying that. I'd feel the same way if I was writing to you and you didn't answer my letters. But don't worry every day I have you on my mind. How can I forget you with your pictures all around my desk. You see I have a lot on mind.

I've also been having trouble getting together with Mrs. Morelli so that she can read me your letters. I called Mrs. Morelli about five or six times and every time I called her she was busy or she was out.

She was really busy over the holidays like everyone else so I waited until the holidays were over to see her. She's a swell lady, Nina, and from your letters she says you seem to be a very intelligent girl. I'm not going to go out very much now because I want to save the little money I've got. Nina, I'm looking at the picture of your family all together. I think you all look very good in it your father looks young. How old is he?

The Farano Family

You have four little sisters now. I'll bet the baby is cute if she looks anything like you. But I doubt she looks anything like me. I like children myself. They're so much fun.

Nina, in your last letter you asked me if I was engaged to someone here. No Nina, I'm not. I could have gotten married many times. But how can a guy get married if he isn't in love. I'm sending you a picture of a girl who wanted to marry me. She's very pretty and she's nineteen years old. She asked me to marry her. But I couldn't because I didn't love her. A lot of people get married today when they don't really love each other.

Sometimes they get married because they want to see what it's like then later it leads to separation and divorce. They destroy their lives and are unhappy. I've seen a lot of people do that. I'm leading a very happy life here with my folks and my brother. Maybe I would be married if it hadn't been for the war.

Nina I don't want to make you any promises about marriage. I just don't want to disappoint you. But you say you want to know right now if I will marry you. Couldn't we just continue to write to each other like we always have? Anything can happen in two years, I could get killed or go blind. I don't want you to count on anything Nina. You might have read about the Italian girl that came to America and the man she was going to marry got killed in a plane crash.

Let's just continue to write to each other Nina. If our feelings continue to grow and we love each other when you turn 17, I will come and get you. Is that alright with you Nina?

If I bring you to America I will get you some nice clothes like they wear here. I will also make arrangements for you to go to school and learn english. You'll be surprised how fast you can learn. A german girl I know learned how to speak english in 6 months.

Who knows Nina maybe we could have a wonderful marriage in spite of our age difference. I'd like to take you to see New York, Hollywood and an Italian Opera. I saw an Opera two months ago. Most of the Operas are in Italian. We'd get a nice little place to live here in New Bedford where I've lived all my life. It's not very far from the coast or Cape Cod which is very nice.

Nina it would be so hard to leave your family and come here. I would be the only one you know here in a strange place. You would meet a lot of nice people here. Hopefully it wouldn't be lonely for you. You say you sent me a bundle. I hope it gets here soon. I'm anxious to know what it is. I'm glad to hear that you are brushing your teeth. Because that's very important and they are nice teeth too. So a boy was getting fond of you at school while you was learning English. I don't blame him because you are an attractive girl. The boys that are fond of you must hate me when you tell them about me. If a boy in Italy can take you away from me good luck to him. I will send some cigarettes for your father and the man in the post office.

Mrs. Morelli is having some trouble reading your letters. Is there anyone there Nina that could write your letters for you in English. I know you are very private about your letters and don't want anyone to know what you write to me. I understand I feel the same way. But we have to find a better way to get together and understand each other.

Nina, my hair is full grown now just the way you like it. I'll have my picture taken again soon and send it to you. I hope you'll like it. What kind of work would you like me to do, Nina, when you come to America? I can learn something for four years and the government pays for it. You know, Nina, there's a lot of things I'd like to buy you. I walk down the busy street and look in the store windows and see a a lot of pretty things. But they cost a lot of money today. You know prices are going up here all the time too.

Please don't ever stop writing to me Nina because if you did I'd lose the best little friend I ever had.

Your loving American friend,

George

I think my dad was conflicted. He didn't want my mother to count on anything. Maybe it was a little pushback to my grandmother's pressure on him. But, on the other hand, the idea of a sweet, unspoiled young girl waiting for him had to be appealing.

At this point, Domenico started doing all the translation, starting with a letter from Nina's father, making it clear to me that he was in on the deception.

January 23, 1948

Dear Mr. Fortin.

We are all very thoughtful about you here. It is a long time we never had your news. We will hope you and all family will be OK. So I and all family we are OK. Nina she is always thinking about you and she like to know what happened because it is long time you did not get your news. We think maybe your friend who writes Italian is away if you can not get someone who write for you we don't mind if you write in english. Will you please let us have soon your good news and let me know if you got my Christmas post card.

We hope you had a good time in the holiday time. We had good time! Nina she talk always about you she never forget your goodness to her. She wants to learn to write english. Well will close this few lines hoping to have soon your good news sending to you all best wishes and regards from all the family and to your family.

Giovanni Faranno

and a kiss from Nina

Translated by Domenico

February 1, 1948

My Dearest George

After months I have received a letter. You don't know how happy I was to receive your letter. I went and read it by myself and I got a real bad feeling from you and in that moment I was crying. I hadn't receive news from you in so long it had been upsetting. I had gotten myself sick when I didn't hear from you.

Tell me why you don't want to love me anymore. Let me know everything because I am always crying and I deserve to know. You don't know how much I love you. I didn't expect you to hurt me like this. You aren't keeping your promise to me. You are telling me all this about another women and making me hurt. My mom was also very upset. She was convinced I was to leave to come to America and be with you and leave my family. Over here we love you. I have been hurting and wanting my Mama but she is sick.

I am sorry you had problems with your money and paying for your car. In the beginning I was thinking about you like a brother and now that I am a young woman I love you like a woman would. I thought you loved me like I love you. You made me all those promises for when I grow up you would bring me to America. Now you don't know if you want me. I didn't know what love was and you showed me how to love through your letters. How can I forget my first love? My family sends their regards and regards from an affectionate Nina who thinks about you all the time.

Translated by Nina Fortin 2014

Remember, my father had sent a picture of a girl he'd been dating who wanted to marry him. I don't think Domenico understood when he translated and thought my father was in love with another woman. I can only imagine how upset my grandmother must have been, thinking her plans were going up in smoke.

February 1948

Dearest George,

I am writing you a few lines to let you know I went to see my Grandfather. I hadn't seen him in ten days. I didn't go to see him because I didn't feel well. My grandfather said I looked very pale. My grandfather wanted to know why I didn't look well. I didn't want to tell my grandfather what has been going on between us. My grandfather wanted to cheer me up but I told him I didn't want to hear it. I told him I didn't want to talk to him about you. My grandfather told me not to make myself sick over you he said I shouldn't be worried about these things at my age. My grandfather didn't want my mother to marry my father and wouldn't look at him for the longest time.

I am glad you talked to the American lady Elena. She saw that we are a good family, and my father works hard for his family. When her husband comes back here I will give him a picture to take to you.

I am always thinking of you George. Someday George we will be happy together.

Regards from your Nina

Translated by Nina Fortin 2014

The visit between my mother and her grandfather never took place. And, of course, I also knew that my mother was never sick or depressed over my father. So my grandmother must've written this letter from her own experience with her father. Maybe she visited him and felt depressed over my father's lack of attention.

February 1948

Dearest George

After so long we finally got your news. In the beginning you send us your news and now we finally receive your news again. You have reassured us that you are well. We are glad your family is well also. We are left feeling very bad that we didn't think anything like that would happen that you don't want to come that you want to love an American woman.

My daughter cried a lot, you have broken her heart. You are not a man that keeps his promise. My daughter since she was a little girl has kept her promise to you and has been making a sacrifice. She has been sacrificing her youth for you.

You should understand what it means to make a sacrifice. My daughter is now in bed crying. She has been thinking in the past when she was your woman and you were passionate in your letters and wanted to marry her. I don't know what to do she is upset and doesn't want to eat. She has gotten very skinny and frail and not well. What should I do with my suffering daughter, she has been suffering for you. After so long you now decide you want an American after she now loves you. She will always love you. You have been for her, her first love. I never thought that you would do that to my daughter. My husband is speechless to your behavior. My cousin loved a man so much and he left her and she died of a broken heart. I'm worried that my daughter will do the same thing. You better think hard about what you are doing.

My family and I give you our regards. I hope I will someday be your mother in law. think well what you are doing and don't make my daughter suffer.

Agnese
Translated by Nina Fortin 2014

They were still upset, thinking my dad wanted to marry the girl in the picture. I don't think my dad ever knew how much worry that picture caused. He was having trouble at that time getting the Italian letters translated.

March 17, 1948

Dear Nina,

I'm writing to you in English this time. I didn't read your last letters yet. I called Mrs. Morelli on the telephone the other night and asked her when she would have time to read me your letter. She asked me when I would give up writing to you. She thinks it's foolish for us to write to each other. I'm not comfortable with going to see her anymore. You will have to find someone to read you my letters and write for you in English.

I hope you understand Nina that a fellow my age has to go out once in a while for a little fun. I go out with a girl about once or twice a week. I hope that doesn't change things between us. I hope you don't mind.

I wish I could spend spring in Italy. I know how it is there in spring. I wish I could see your little garden and the view from the top of the hill.

Maybe the Americans will have to go to Europe

again the way it looks between America and Russia. It sure looks like another war. They're talking a lot about communism in Italy. If Italy turns communist, America will not help her anymore. So we'll have to pray to stop communism in Italy.

Nina my automobile really runs nice, I wish I could take you for a ride in it. I keep a picture of you in my car. My friends are always asking me questions about you and what my intentions are. My friends all think it will never work out between you and I because of our age difference. I don't care what anyone else thinks, everyone has their own opinion. Life is what you make it. If we decide to be together and it doesn't work out we have no one to blame but ourselves. You know Nina twenty years from now I'll be 49 and you will be 35. I'll be settled down in an old rocking chair and probably won't want to go out anymore. You will still be a young lady and might want to go out to parties and dances with people your own age. Or maybe we will have a bunch of kids. Who knows what the future will bring. It may bring happiness or sorrow but we won't worry about that right now. We could even have a war soon that will end all possible life on earth. Scientists say the earth could go up in a ball of fire and end all life.

Nina, I'm going to send you a little package soon. I have been wanting to do that for a long time. Since I got this automobile, money is really tight for me.

Nina, I wish you all the luck in the world. Give my regards to the family.

Your loving American friend,

George

Dad continued bringing up the age difference. Little did he know Nina was young for her years, not old for her age. He mentioned he was dating someone, but at that time, the interpreter must have missed his meaning. It was so difficult for them to communicate. It's incredible that they actually got together. From then on, they will have even more difficulty communicating because Mrs. Morelli would no longer help my father. He wrote all his letters in longhand and then typed them to make it easier for Domenico to translate. He saved all of his long-hand letters and most of the Italian letters, creating a future treasure trove I could dig into.

March 29, 1948

My Dear George

I'm writing you this letter to give you my news on March 29, 1948. I am happy that I received your letter. I received a letter from Elena and I thought it was a letter from you until I saw it was from Venice. I am happy about the way Elena talks to me. She said she talked on the telephone to you. She said you love me and I hope it is that way. When I met you I felt you were a nice, good person, that's why I felt affection for you. I have always remembered you and am happy to hear your news. I always try and remember what you write to me.

I know my mother will give us a nice wedding. Just because I am very young we can still be very happy. The age difference does not make a difference. As long as we love each other the age doesn't matter. You have so many things to think about and all the things we have to do.

My family, we all love God and we are all Catholic. We don't even think that the communism will come to Italy. We love America because the Americans have been good to us. I never want to lose all the good that the Americans have done for us.

Let me know your beautiful news. Please talk to Mrs. Morelli on the telephone and be nice and make up. I send your mother a kiss.

Regards from the family
I think of you all the time
Your Nina
Translated by Nina Fortin 2014

Domenico wasn't the best translator, so it's possible he missed the fact that George was dating, or it's possible he didn't tell Agnese to spare her getting upset. She wasn't feeling well at that time.

March 31, 1948

Dear George,

I am responding to your letter that I received. I am glad to hear you received my mothers letter. I am a little bit happier with your last letter and I am glad you are now answering my letters. Now I am happy to write to you because I know you will answer me back. I always worry that you will stop writing to me. I remember the necklace, tank key chain and rosary you gave me when you were here. I was happy when I received your letters last July it's been a long time since you wrote me those beautiful letters. I really wanted to love you after receiving those letters. I saw Elena the American lady again, she has a very pretty face. She told me a lot of nice things about America. She was telling me how I must present myself when I come to America. She said I have to be sophisticated and respectful. She said I shouldn't try and have fun because the world is difficult. She talks to me as if she is my mother. She said I can have fun in America if I don't over do it. She said there is good fun and bad fun. She said when two people love each other just taking a walk is very nice. When I go anywhere I go with my brother and never alone. Do you have the address of Elena so she can tell you about me? If you see or hear from Elena please let me know what she says about me. I was with Elena until she left to go back to America she says she loves me and I love her. My grandfather is feeling a lot better from his bladder sickness. I warn you don't let me wait , write to me don't worry me.

Happy Easter to you and your family from me and my family. I love my little sister so much I wish you could see her with her blue eyes.

Kisses from your Nina.

Translated by Nina Fortin 2014

I imagine my grandmother asked her friend Elena all kinds of questions about America. What she learned probably fueled her mission even more. My grandmother encouraged her daughter's friendship with Elena in hopes of getting her excited about going to America. Nina was oblivious to what her mother was really doing. By this point, she didn't want to hear.

Another letter, signed "from your loving Italian girlfriend. Nina," assured George they were against communism and questioned where the package he had promised might have gone.

In a letter they received a few days later, he explained that he hadn't sent it yet because he had been strapped for money since buying his car. But he promised that he would soon send pictures of himself with his dog, Cigarettes for her Dad and the post office, perfume, candy, earrings, toothpaste, and tooth brush, dress patterns, writing paper, and a few other things that he'd been saving for her.

My father finally sent that package. My mother told me the whole family used that one toothbrush.

April 30, 1948

Dear Mr. Fortin,

I am the man who writes to you. I am a friend of Mr. Farano so you will believe on me your friend to. I wish to thank you for the nice mind you have for me, you will send me some cigarettes and a dictionary. That will be very useful for me and for Nina. I hope you will not take note of all the mistakes that are in my letters because I never been to school to learn english. I was a prisoner in England for three years where I learned these few words. I am happy to have soon your news you will believe on me your friend.

Best regards and wishes.

Domenico Salsano

Now, Domenico was their only way of communicating, and he did the best he could. Somehow, my grandmother convinced him this deception was best for Nina and the family.

May 5, 1948

Dear George

Just a few lines to let you know my news. We are very sad we have a very great loss last week. My grandfather is dead. I think you will know him, he had the tobacco shop in the middle of the village. I have been very sad for the great loss to my mother he was her father.

He was very good with my family. He was only seventy years old. But we can do nothing about death. We know very well every one will go to leave this world one day. Well George I do not wish to make you sad.

George a while back you said you will be having nice good time with a nice girl with your beautiful car in this lovely spring time. George you have made me very sad because you said to me in your letter that you go out with one girl. I do not like that because I am very jealous. It is better you don't tell me those things. I like you very much and I will always be faithful to you. I do not go out if not with my mother. I don't mind if I can not get any good time now because I hope I will be happy with you one day. I love you George, you are very nice boy. I have trust on you and you have on me.

It is nice over here we have started to go in the seaside. I hope you come in Italy this summer so we can go in seaside.

Well George it is long time I never had your news. Why you don't write to me very often. Let me know your news and what good you do in America.

Love and Kisses from your Italian girlfriend.

Nina

Translated by Domenico

It was interesting that it took this long to mention my father dating. Maybe they went back and reread that letter from March when my father had written he was dating someone several times a week. However, that relationship must have ended soon after it started. In the following letter, he states he only has my mother on his mind. I think Dad had a hard time with dating because he was shy and introverted, or maybe because of his PTSD.

May 26, 1948

Dear Nina,

I just received your letter and I am answering it right away. I am sorry to hear about the death of your grandfather. I know your mother must be very sad about it. I don't know what it's like to lose someone in the family. I've been pretty lucky so far.

Nina you think I'm going to have a good time this summer with a girl. Do not think like that. I haven't been out with a girl in a couple of months. That's a long time is it not? I do not care to go out with girls when I have you on my mind. I am working and going to school during the week. On Saturday and Sundays I help my father and mother around the house. I plowed the garden and cut the grass and planted more grass this weekend.

The weather is beautiful right now.

My mother is listening to a program on the radio. It's about people all over the world. They talk on the radio and say how much they love Americans.

Well I have to go to work in a couple of hours so I better rush if I want to get this letter in the mail.

Love and Kisses,

George

June 12, 1948

Dear Nina,

I mailed a package to you today. I sent you a lot of books to learn English. Try and learn a little bit everyday and I'm sure you'll be speaking english in no time. You can give some of these books to the man who writes for you he might want to improve his english. Also give him some cigarettes and some gum. I only sent you a few packs of cigarettes but in the future I will send much more.

I'm going to see a friend of mine on Saturday. He is getting married to a french girl, he is Portuguese. He doesn't live far from New Bedford only twenty miles. He was in my outfit in the army. He saw my tank get blown up. He was in the tank behind mine when I drove over a land mine. He thought I was dead when he helped pull me out of the tank. He told me one night when he dreamed of me he dreamed that I was killed and he cried in his sleep.

Nina when you are able to write and speak English you can write to me all by yourself. And do they have telephones there? They must have! Maybe someday I could call you up in Italy from the United States. But it may cost too much money. And you could talk to me in English. I know you will talk good English some day.

Well I've got to sign off now, Nina, give my regards to everyone and I want to tell you I'm still thinking of you as much ever.

Love and Kisses,

George

June 20, 1948

Dear George,

I am writing to answer your nice letter. Thank you for the books you sent. I have started go to school and I like to learn soon how to write to you myself. George I am always thinking about you and how good you are to me and my family. We are pleased to know you sent more books for me and the man who writes for me. I am very pleased you went to your friends wedding. I am to go to my friends wedding next week. She is getting married to an American boy. He is still in the army and is just back from Germany last week.

After three months he will be back to America with his wife.

Well George this is a very lucky girl and I hope I will be to when you come to Italy to take me back to America with you. You will be surprised when you hear me talk to you in English.

Love from your Nina

Translated by Domenico

While my father's hopes were still high, no English learning was going on. With their poverty and her mother being sick, Nina didn't have time to receive instruction in Italian, let alone English. The imaginary girl in the letters might have had the motivation to learn English, but my mother wasn't that girl.

July 10, 1948

Dear Nina,

I am at the beach today for the first time this summer. And it is going to be very hot. I am here with my dog. I came here about nine o'clock in the morning. It is Friday the 9th. For the past two weeks I have been thinking more and more about you. Everywhere I go when I see a young girl with dark hair and dark eyes it reminds me of you.

This past week has been my vacation week. And I am enjoying it. I wish you were here with me. I have been traveling quite a bit too. I have been taking my folks riding everywhere. We have been going to the races quite a bit too. My oldest brother, Armand, is a mechanic on a midget car. My dog just went in the water all by herself. I never force a dog to go in the water. It scares them. And they never like the water after that. My dog loves the water. And she plays a lot too. She likes all the children on the beach. I didn't go in the water yet. I am just sitting here in the sun writing to you. I was the second person on the beach and now there is many people with their children.

Well you should have received the big package by now with all the books in it. Those books should make it so easy for you to learn English that you ought to be able to write a letter to me by Christmas time. Even though you can not write a whole letter you can try to write a few words to show me how you are improving. Because when you come to America you want to talk good English because everybody talks English.

The other night I saw the heavyweight championship fight of the world between Joe Louis and Joe Wolcott on Television. You must know what that is. It is just like the moving pictures but it is on the radio in your own home instead of at the theater. They are getting all kinds of things in America now. I don't know what it is going to be like 10 years from now.

Nina, don't forget to send me another nice picture of yourself. I haven't had a picture from you in six months. Make this picture a nice one because I want to put it in my car with the others.

I want it to look better than all of them put together.

Nina, I still love you as much as ever. But people tell me I'm foolish to bother with you because you are so young. But I don't care what they say. We are the judges of that aren't we, Nina?

Well I am going to bed now, Nina, and God Bless you. Give my regards to everyone.

Love and Kisses,

George

Everyone was against my father and his Nina. I bet he thought he would show them what a sweet, unspoiled wonderful wife he would have. But meanwhile, mom was only fourteen at this point, and grandmother had her threatening my father that she'd stop learning English if he didn't write more often. I'm surprised Dad didn't realize something was wrong with this picture.

September 20, 1948

Dear Nina,

I am ashamed to be writing to you this late. I don't blame you for sometimes threatening to stop learning english. I've been very busy lately. I've had a lot of work to do on my car. I painted it and it looks like a new car. Everyone tells me how beautiful it is.

I knew you would be disappointed in me for not writing. But I always make up for it; don't I Nina? I always have you on my mind Nina. I don't want you to stop learning english Nina. I will try and write more often. Learning english is the most important thing for you right now. Because when you come to America you want to speak good English and you will receive your citizen papers that much sooner. And you will be an American like the rest of us.

My younger brother Rene and his wife had a baby a few weeks ago. It is a little girl. They came to to our house tonight with the baby. The baby is so cute. It is the first time that my dog, Dixie, has seen a baby so small and she was all excited about it.

My mother works with me now in the same mill where I work. She travels back and forth with me to work.

My youngest brother Leo has a new girlfriend again. He has more girlfriends then I can count. She is a french girl from Fall River which is 13 miles from here. I let him borrow my car to go out with her. They want me to get a girl and go out with them. I knew you would be jealous if I told you I went out with a girl. I haven't been back out with a girl since you told me how jealous you were last time. Don't worry Nina as long as you love me I won't do anything to hurt your little heart. A lot of people keep asking me when I am going to get married. And I tell them that I am getting married in two years. If I wrote to you once a week would you answer all of my letters, Nina? But they would be short letters because there won't be much to say.

Well, Nina, there isn't much more to say at present so I will close saying good luck to your father and mother and brother and sisters and don't worry about me I will write oftener. I love you as much as ever. I am going to start preparing a Christmas package for you soon. I don't want to forget you like I did last Christmas. And don't forget me either. A beautiful big photograph of you will make a nice Christmas present for me.

Love and Kisses,
George

September 27, 1948

Dear Nina,

I am keeping my promise. I said I would write to you once a week and that is what I am doing. I hope I can keep it up. You said that you wanted to know my news here so the only way I can do that is to write to you more often otherwise I forget everything that happens around here.

Yesterday my brother went to the races with his midget racer and it got all smashed up. It got tangled up with another midget and it turned over. My brother, who is the mechanic, rushed over to the driver to see if he was alright. He was alright. He didn't have a scratch on him. He was lucky. Everybody thought he was killed or hurt very badly. Two ambulances rushed over to where he turned over and they didn't have to take him to the hospital. I'll send you a picture of the drive and his midget in my next package. I went to see the midget auto this afternoon at my brother's garage and it was a total wreck. But my brother says he can fix it but it will cost a lot of money.

I took my dog to the doctor today to have her treated for distemper. That is because if the dog bites anybody when she has distemper they will catch a poison from her.

My brother, who is the mechanic on the midget, and his wife were here at our house tonight to see us. My brother's wife always asks me when I am going to get married. And I keep telling her that I am going to marry in two years. But she and my folks say that I need to get married. That I am going to be an old bachelor. That is what they think. They don't know what they are talking about do they, Nina?

Well, Nina, keep looking pretty and grow up to be the prettiest Italian girl Italy ever had. And you don't have to answer all of my letters if you don't want to. Just write to me when you are able to. Good luck and I hope your English is improving very rapidly.

Give my regards to everyone.

Love and kisses from the bottom of my heart.

George A. Fortin

Midget racing was quite popular in the 1940s, but the cars were virtual death traps. Many of my Uncle Armand's cars had accidents. The cars looked like cannons on wheels. There were no roll bars; fire suits and seat belts were not mandatory. The helmets were made of leather and offered little protection. Auto racing was curtailed in 1942 because of rationing that was taking place for the war effort. The ban was not lifted until late 1945. In the years that followed, there was money to be made in auto racing. Unfortunately, I don't think my Uncle ever made very much money.

October 12, 1948

Dear Nina,

This is Columbus day. It is a holiday but mother and I are working in the mill just the same. This is a famous day for America. If it hadn't been for Columbus coming here from Italy America may not have been discovered. Every since that day of discovery America has grown and grown into a wonderful country.

Nina, my dog, Dixie, is dead. I had her put to

sleep by gas because she was getting to be to vicious a dog. She almost bit two or three people already and I didn't want her to bite anyone.

I had her put to sleep because I loved her very much. Remember I said I wouldn't sell her for all the money in the world? Well I meant it. I miss her very much.. When a person gets attached to a dog like Dixie It is pretty hard to get rid of her. To me she was the most beautiful dog I have ever seen. I used to take her for many rides in my car. I could of sold her for a lot of money but I didn't want to have her mistreated by anyone. She is dead now and I know she is alright. My little niece, who is about four years old, was at my house a few days later and asked me where my dog was. I told her my dog was running around somewhere and it was not true. I had tears in my eyes when I told her that. I hope I will get over it in a few weeks.

Nina, did you receive the Readers Digest Magazine that I sent you yet?

I am getting worried about you, Nina, please write to me soon. Don't break my heart. I go to the mail box every day to get your letter but there is none. And then I wait until the next day. Good luck to your folks, sisters, and brother,

Nina, and all my love and kisses to you.

George

That story about Dad's dog made me so sad. Dad was a compassionate man. We did have a dog once, but one day I came home from school, and the dog was gone. My mother never liked animals and wanted her home perfect without dog hair and messes. I'm sure she had my dad give the dog away. I think we had it only a short time.

In a letter dated October 20, 1948, Dad stated that he had mortgaged his car for $500 to help his brothers start an electrical business. He also had a bit to say about California, where he would move our family in 1955.

> California is on the west coast where Hollywood is. I think California is the nicest place to live in the United States. The sun is always warm there. A lot of people are moving to California but there isn't enough housing there. In some places eight people are living in one room.
>
> That gives you an idea what a housing shortage we are having. To have enough houses for the people in the United States it would take another five years to build them. And it still wouldn't be enough because people are coming here from all over the world.

Further on in the letter, he shared his thoughts about how he hoped to live and raise his children:

The only trouble with this country is when people make a little money they spend it right away on cars and foolish things. And then prices go up all the time. Many people think of having their good times while they are living because they say they will be dead for a long time. They say life is short and make the most of it. They have televisions in most of the pleasure places now like restaurants. You go and eat and drink and watch television. You can buy anything you want. If a person wants to make a dress she can buy any kind of cloth any color and any design.

Today women work just like men. When both men and women work and have children the children are taken care of by someone else or are left to wander off and get into trouble. Many parents have children and they don't take care of them. They don't care what happens to them. When we get married and have children we want to bring them up to be real Americans. I don't do much for pleasure lately. I work all week and Saturday and Sunday I go to a movie or stay home when my married brothers come over with their wives and babies to see us. I could go out with some girls but you don't want me to. So I don't go anywhere. There won't be many places to go to this winter. I am going to try to do a little more work to make a little more money so you can come to the United States.

I found reading what my father had to say about parenting fascinating. What happened to him? He obviously had every intention of being a good father. So why did I always feel ignored?

October 30, 1948

Dear Nina,

I am sorry but I meant to write to you a few days sooner. But if I miss a week or so I know you will understand. I am well occupied these days.

My father and I are helping with the carpentry work at my brother's electrical store. They are going to have a beautiful store. They are going to sell a lot of electrical fixtures for houses. They want it ready for Christmas because that is a good time to sell.

Nina, remember the blond soldier who was with me when I first met you? Well I never knew where he lived and I wrote to Washington, D.C. to help me to locate him. I received a postal card today telling me where he lives. His home is in Ohio about 1000 miles from here. I wanted to get in touch with him for a long time because he was a very good friend of mine in the army. He was very good and kind to the Italians. He gave them bread, candy, cigarettes, and many other things. I am going to write to him tonight and tell him I tried to locate him. Do you mind if I tell him about us. And let me know if you want his address. I am going to see him next summer on my vacation. I wonder if he still remembers you. I will never forget what a nice fellow he is.

Nina, you are going to be 16 years old May 30 is that right? These last two years are going to be the longest years of my life waiting for you to be 17 hers old. But I don't mind waiting that long because I know you will be mine to live with and love for the rest of my life.

President Truman, who was vice-president with the late President Roosevelt came to Fall River a few days ago. He was supposed to come here to our city but he couldn't make it because he had some long speeches to make in Boston and New York.

I wish President Roosevelt was still living because he was the best president the United States ever had. They are voting for a new president November 2nd. I hope President Truman is elected. Being a President today is a very had job because we have control of three-fourths of the world. If the wrong man is elected it could be a catastrophe for the whole world. We had a depression in 1929 and I hope we never see that again.

Today you can go anywhere you want and buy anything you please. They sell little radios now that are the size of a pack of cigarettes.

Everyone is working and happy. It is hard for me to explain to you about America and what it has to offer. You will just have to see when you get here.

Nina, did you receive the first little magazine yet? Because you are supposed to receive it in October.

I will close now and I am hoping to hear from you very soon. Good luck to your folks, brother and sisters and everybody.

Love and kisses,

George

The soldier my father mentioned was Robert King, who accompanied him the first time he saw my mom. Dad never received a response. The 191-tank battalion records list that Lieutenant King was transferred to Company A from Company B. He was wounded the month before my dad received his wounds. I wonder if he died from his injuries. I can't imagine he wouldn't write back to my father unless something was very wrong or maybe he never received the letter.

All my father's talk about the glories of America must have been music to my grandmother's ears. But I wonder if she understood how hard my father had to work.

November 7, 1948

Dear Nina,

This is Sunday night and it is a very beautiful moonlight night outside. My brother Leo is gone out with his girlfriend. My father is sleeping and my mother is reading the paper.

Nina, it is getting pretty monotonous working

day after day week after week and not going anywhere with friends.

I could join a men's club. In a men's club they gamble and drink liquor and that costs money. When they drink they go out with bad women. I could do all that but I don't want to. Many of these men do get married and then carry on with there bad habits. I see all these things Nina and I promise you I will never be like that. As long as you are true to me, I will be true to you.

Nina if you should change you mind about marrying me it would be hard to forgive you. I might even get drunk and spend all my money because something like that would hurt very much. When two people write to each other for many years and make promises to each other and something goes wrong it's very hard to forget.

President Truman was elected President again for four more years.

Nina, a German girl nineteen years old came to America by plane to marry an American 33 years old. When she arrived here she was greeted by her boy friend and young brother. The young brother greeted her with a kiss on the cheek. Now she is going to marry the young brother instead of her boy friend. Let's not have that happen to us.

There isn't much more to write about at present.

Give my regards to your father, mother, brother, and sisters and all your friends.

Love and kisses,

George

November 25, 1948

Dear Nina,

I finally received your letter a few days ago. That is why I am a little late writing to you. I was waiting for that letter for so long.

Today is Thanksgiving and it is very quiet here today.

Next month is December and I am hoping you can write me a letter all by yourself. Even if it is only a few words. I don't mind having Domenico translate letters for you but he must be getting tired of writing for you. I feel grateful to have someone like him to translate letters for you. I appreciate it very much. Tell him I will send him some cigarettes soon. Domenico said in your last letter that he was embarrassed because of all the mistakes he makes when he writes. In America all people that come here to live from Europe are ambitious. They have many more opportunities than they had in Europe. A great many Europeans had a difficult life in Europe. As soon as they come to America they find a great difference.

They are more thrifty than the average people. Most of the European people that come here to live make the best Americans because they appreciate being an American. So, Domenico, don't feel bad when you make a few mistakes in your letters.

My grandmother came to America from Canada 47 years ago and does not read, write or speak English so you speak and write English better than a great many Americans. A great many Italians have big businesses. They have furniture stores, barber shops, fruit stores, taverns, and spaghetti restaurants. They make good money and they appreciate being here. There are a lot of Opera plays here too and they are all Italians in the play.

I forgot to tell you Nina that in America you can see a moving picture from your car now. The picture screen is out in the open air and you go there with your car and watch the picture. They put a microphone in your car and you hear everything. I had Rome on the radio tonight and an Italian girl sang the song Amapola. The Italian announcer talked very fast and I only understood a few words. When we listen to Europe on the radio sometimes it is not too clear. I am getting a package ready for you. I have it on my desk. I have some chocolates and candy. I have a pair of little shoes made of wood that came from the Philippine Islands. They were a souvenir to my mother from my brother Leo. They want you to have them. They are not to walk on but keep as souvenir. I will try and send you as many things as I can. I will send you another picture of me when I get one from you first. So send me a nice one soon and I will send one right after. If I don't send you everything I plan to send you I will send you another package a little later. Well let me know what you think.

Well there isn't much more to say at present. I wish you all the luck in the world.

Love and kisses

George

The appreciation immigrants had for America obviously impressed my father. After what he saw in the war, I'm sure he admired his country so much more. Having a girl from Italy who would appreciate what America had to offer obviously appealed to him.

In a letter from early December 1948, my dad pushed again for a picture of Nina, "I'm very glad I'm going to receive a picture of you because I'm very anxious to see how my girl is growing into womanhood. I show your picture to everyone and all my friends want to meet you."

In the same letter, he mentioned their time frame. "Well Nina we only have seventeen more months to write to each other and then our dreams will come true. If nothing serious comes up to spoil everything. We have a lot of patience to write to each other like this. We did it for 2 years now and we can do it for 17 months more. We will show these people that we have patience and understanding. A lot of people would not bother to do all these things like we are doing."

Even though this information was off by a whole year, my grandmother did not acknowledge it in her following letter.

December 12, 1948

Dear George,

I am answering soon at your nice letter I had a few days ago.

I am pleased to hear your good news and to know you are all quite well so we are to now is December here it is cold. I don't go anymore to my Aunt I get job in house and is very good for me because every night I am having some English lesson. I hope you don't think I will send you for Christmas a big letter because I am not able to write but I will send you a few words that I know and I will send my photo.

Well George you didn't let me know anything more about your friend Robert if you write to him let him know about us and ask if he still remembers my house. George I am very enjoyed for the parcel you are sending to me you are very good with me. But I like to send you something from here but we can not send anything now. All my family they are very glad to for that nice present. Well George I must close these lines sending to everyone my best always.

Love and Kisses from Nina

SIXTEEN

1949

Nina at age 12

Nina at age 14

Nina at age 15

The beginning of 1949 marked over two years since my Dad started writing to my Mom. Mom was getting older, and her mother was getting sicker, which meant Nina was very busy taking care of the family and didn't have much time to think about anything else.

January 3, 1949

Dear Nina,

I am sorry I am a little late to answer your letter. We were busy during the holidays. Please excuse me. I received your photo which is very nice. It shows me that you are getting taller and prettier. But your hair is not right. It looks better when your hair is longer. You should let it drop down past your shoulders. I like a girl with long dark wavy hair. But I don't care because you are still my little Nina no matter how you fix your hair. In America girls fix their hair many different ways.

We had a very quiet Christmas and New Year Holiday. I stayed home with my folks and my married brothers came to see us with their children. We had a Christmas tree but not to many presents. Now it is January, 1949 and I can not believe it. Time goes by so fast. But when I think of you it seems to go by slow. Next year will be the big moment of our lives, Nina. You will be sailing to America to live. You will leave your family in Italy. That will be sad for you because I know you love your family. When I went to

Europe to fight I was sad also to leave my family. We will see each other for the first time in 6 years instead of looking at each others pictures all the time.

I read a story in the paper tonight about a young Italian girl 17 years old. Her name is Nina too. A boy in America 24 years old is marrying her. She came from Naples. She is in America now and will be married next month. I am sending the story to you. There will be a story in the paper about us someday too.

You know, Nina, I was thinking of building myself a house for us to live in. But I don't know if I should start to build it now or wait for you to get here first. What do you think I should do? I think it will be better if I wait till you get here than we can make plans together about our little house.

I hope you received the package in time for Christmas. Well there isn't much more to say at present so I will close saying good luck to all your family and friends.

Love and kisses,

George

In a letter dated February 1, 1949, she thanked him for all the gifts he had sent, continuing the conspiracy with words of thanks.

A month later, my dad explored possibilities for their wedding and explained some of his financial information:

I try to spend as little money as possible. Because it is going to take a lot of money to have you come over here to America and get married. I don't have to go to Italy to get you. I can make arrangements here to have you brought over on the ship. And you will be very well taken care of. But of course if I have to go to Italy for you then I will go. I would like to see Italy again. But it would cost money for me to take that trip. We want to have a little money saved up to get us started on our way to the future. Wouldn't you rather see me save money for a little home for us or spend it on a trip to Italy? Most of my bills are paid up now and I don't have to spend anymore money on my car. So I am on my way to save a few dollars. I work eight hours a day now but I am going to work 15 hours a day. that will mean more money to save. But It will be tiresome for me. But I will try to do it for 6 months at least.

It didn't surprise me that my dad planned to work 15 hours a day. Dad was the kind of man who never turned down overtime. He worked hard his whole life.

In the 1900s, the textile industry in New Bedford exploded but faded just as fast. When the machinery was running, the conditions were loud, hot, and dusty, with bits of cotton flying everywhere. Three shifts ran continually, 24/7. During New Bedford's textile heyday, the mills employed more than 41,000 workers. Ten-hour days were the norm, so no one would have thought too much of my Dad working 15-hour days. The work was monotonous and grinding. But the millworkers showed up day after day because many others were eager to take their jobs.

My dad always worried about their age difference. In a letter dated January 15, 1949, he wrote the following:

Nina, they say an age difference between a married couple is not a barrier. They can adjust their life to suit themselves. That is what we will have to do and I know it can be done. The way we love each other it won't be hard.

He also wrote:

> I got another job in another place. It's the same kind of job I had before but a much better place. The people that work there are all nice. The boss there likes me because I am an honest and good worker. He wants to promote me to a better job. Right now I am his helper. He will teach me to fix looms which is something I have always wanted to do. My father has done that job for 30 years and I believe I can do it as good as he did. It is not the best job in the world but when a person is happy at his work that is all that counts. You are on my mind when I work so it helps me to get ahead. Before I met you there was nothing to look forward to in the future. But now I know that you will be my future.

It seemed my dad needed something to believe in to keep him going and that was his relationship with his little Nina.

January 20, 1949

Dear George,

With great joy I have received two of your nice letters in this week. I am pleased to have your good news and to know you are all quite well. I am very glad about my brother because he is back from the Army. I like it if he doesn't go away anymore because my father doesn't like to let me go out alone.

Last night I went to see an nice American picture The Miracle of Bells and today is my Aunt's birthday and I am going to dance in her house with my family.

No more driving car for good time with girls. I am very happy about it because you will have your money for to build a very nice house and to keep more money to make a good wedding. Well George you don't have to sell your car because you have plenty of time to save your money because I am only fifteen years old. We are very glad about your good intentions only you never said to me for our wedding if you come here to take me to America. I have asked many times and you did not answer me about because my father he don't like to let me leave my house alone that is what he likes to know and about and what is your opinion. It is with my great joy to have soon your good news. I will close this lines sending to everyone my best always.

Kisses and love to you,
from Nina
Translated by Domenico

Domenico's translations were tough to read, but I was able to read that Nina was only 15 years old. Somehow, my father missed that fact.

My father wanted my mother to come to America so he could marry her there, but my grandfather didn't like the idea of Nina traveling to the United States alone. It would be much more expensive for Dad to go to Italy and then both return to the States, but that is what he would have to do.

In response to "Nina's" query, he replied. "Yes, Nina, I am going to Italy to get you; when you become seventeen, I will take you back here to America and we will have a wonderful wedding." He also explained, "Nina, If I expect to go to Italy I can't go out and spend my money; I have to save it. It also wouldn't be fair to you if I went out with girls and you didn't go out with boys."

The reality of Dad's situation made me furious. He changed his lifestyle, gave up things he loved to do, and worked extreme hours for a girl who never would have gotten on a ship or plane to come to America for a man she didn't know or love, whose letters she never read.

February 5, 1949

Dear Nina,

This is Sunday morning about 3:30 I went to bed about 7 o'clock last night and got up this morning at 3 o'clock. It's hard for me to sleep now because I work at night from 10 o'clock to 6 o'clock in the morning. I have to sleep in the day time. I worked on this same shift before the war. later on I expect to go on the first shift from 6 o'clock to 2 o'clock in the afternoon. That will be much better for me because I will be able to sleep at night.

I am still waiting for my large photo and the pictures I had taken. As soon as they are ready I will send them to you in a package with the radio. I will send you some cloth also from the factory where I work.

I had my teeth cleaned and repaired again and they are just like new again. Take good care of your teeth too, Nina, visit the dentist every 6 months to see if there is any decay. Everyone has decay in their teeth now and then even if they have beautiful looking teeth.

I wrote a letter to the Post Office in Robert's home town. I told them I wanted to locate Robert. I hope to hear from them soon.

Well Nina I am counting the days now until you will be seventeen years old. There is about 478 more days left.

As soon as you turn seventeen years old I will make arrangements to go to Italy and get you. And when you arrive here I will find a place for you to live until we get married. You could live with Mrs. Morelli. She has a big house but her married children are living with her. And I don't know if there will be room. Or you could live here in our house in a separate room. We do have an empty room now that my two brothers got married. And when we get married we can have our own room here until we move into a house of our own or rent a little place. My younger married brother is living with his wife's folks. But he says he wants a little place of his own soon. And my older married brother is living in a 6 tenement house and it is not a very healthy place. The doctor told them to move from there as soon as they can find a better place.

Tell me if you are improving with your English. I am anxious to know.

Oh I forgot to tell you I drink wine now to make me sleep after work. I am drinking some now because I am going to sleep soon. It is Sherry wine. I will have to get used to it anyway because when you come to America I will have to drink some with you because you are used to wine there. Do you always drink wine with your meals? Don't you drink coffee, tea or milk?

Well, Nina, I must close this letter now good luck and God bless you.

Give my regards to everyone and love and kisses to you.

George

My dad still hadn't responded to the comment, "don't worry I'm only 15; you have plenty of time to save your money." Some of the Italian letters took more work to make out the words. Perhaps he missed it. Poor dad actually had 783 more days before he could make the dream he was chasing come true.

He may have been disappointed when he found out that my mother doesn't like wine. She's never touched a drop her whole life. She says she has a virgin stomach.

February 14, 1949

Dear Nina,

This is Monday night and it is a very beautiful night. It was a very beautiful day too, it was just like a spring day. I hope we get a lot more days like that. I was sick last week, I had to stay home from work two days. I had a pain in my right side in my kidneys. I've had that problem a couple times before, it only lasts a few days. It's nothing to worry about. I have been lucky, I hardly ever get sick. I just get a cold now and then.

I am getting a package ready to send to you. In the package I am sending you some cloth that I got from the mill where I work. I hope you can make something with it. And a can of tobacco, my large photo and a few other little things. You may not find much difference in how I look. You see at my age we stop growing and we change very little as we grow older. But at your age you change very much because you are growing all the time. That is why I like to have a picture from you every six months or so.

Nina, what do you expect of me when we get married and we come here to live? You probably have a lot on your mind about how and where you will make your home here. Don't be afraid to ask me about little things like that. And besides a married couple has to enjoy the same things. You like to dance very much don't you? I like to dance too. And go to shows, don't worry we will get along and enjoy ourselves like other married couples. I am an easy person to get along with. I hope you are the same. I think you are. We didn't have any arguments yet in our letters.

Are you improving at all in your English? I hope so because the time is drawing near and you only have about 15 months more to learn it. Because when I go to Italy you will have to be my interpreter. I won't be able to talk to your family in Italian. I will talk to you in English and you will repeat it to your family in Italian. But if I stay in Italy long enough I will learn Italian in a short time. I don't know how long I will be permitted to stay there. Because a trip like that must be arranged with the steamship company. Well we will talk more about that later on.

I think about you more and more all the time. I love you as much as ever. So keep looking pretty until that happy day I get to Italy.

Give my regards to everyone.

Love and Kisses

George

February 14, 1949

Dear George,

With my great joy I am answering your letter. I am very glad to know you work in the same factory where you worked before the war only it is not much good for your work on the night. I will wish you to get new shift later on to be able to sleep at night.

My mother she is making me a good dress maker. I am very happy to learn dress making.

Thank you for the package you send me. All I can send to you is all my love and a big kiss.

I am pleased to know you have been to repair your teeth but you don't need to worry for my teeth because they are all good .

I hope you will get news soon from your friend Robert.

Well George only you are wrong to count the years I will only be fifteen in March. You will have to wait two years more.

I don't care where we live when I come to America I will just be happy to be with you.

So I must close this lines sending to everyone my best always and best regard from all my family and my love and kisses.

From Nina

Interpreted by Domenico

My grandmother first wrote the lie about my mother's age in July of 1947. They repeated the lie in April 1948. I could've believed it was a mistake if it had happened only once, but the 1947 letter was written in my grandmother's own hand and not a translation from Domenico. My grandmother must have realized she would have to correct my dad's misunderstanding as he was beginning to make plans. As would be expected, this was a significant blow to my father.

disappointment when I read that I would
have to wait for you another two years,
Nina, didn't you realize what that
would do to me? Have you ever been
disappointed before in your life? If you
haven't then you don't know what it is like
But if you have been disappointed before
in your life you must know how I feel.
In your letter, 14/11/48, you said that you
would be sixteen years old in May. Accord
ing to your latest letter that is a [illegible]
lie. Your latest letter says you will be only
fifteen in March. I hope this is a mistake. I am sending you back
that letter of 14/11/48, to show you where
you told me you would be sixteen in May.
You have some explaining to do about this
And you better make me understand

February 20, 1949

Dear Nina,

I was very glad to see your letter on my desk today but when I opened it I was terribly disappointed.

How could I have to wait for you another two years? Nina didn't you realize what that would do to me? Have you ever been disappointed before in your life? If you haven't then you don't know what it is like. But if you have been disappointed before in your life you must know how I feel.

In your letter April 11, 1948 you said you would be sixteen in May. According to your latest letter that was a deliberate lie. Your recent letter said you will only be fifteen in March. I hope this is a mistake. I am sending you back that letter from April 11, 1948 to show you what you said. You have some explaining to do about this. Please make me understand what this is all about or I will stop writing to you. It hurts me deeply to have to say this to you Nina, but you said to me in one of your letters to have trust in you. How can I have trust in you now? Here I am in the most wonderful country in the world sacrificing mostly everything I have to wait for you and you do this to me. I hope it is a mistake that you will only be fifteen years old in March. You don't know if your birthday is May or March?? You better find out what your true age is from your mother.

All the plans I've been making to find out I will

have to wait a year more. I write to you every week and that's what I get for being a good man. Well I am going to start writing to you every month now instead of every week to punish you. Let me know if it was just a mistake and not a lie. And I will forgive you. You know, Nina, this changes everything between us. Tell me the truth and everything will be alright just like before.

Well I will say good luck and give my regards to everyone. I will not write to you until I get a letter from you explaining about your age.

Love and kisses,

George

This was my father's chance to end the whole thing, cut his losses, and find an American wife. But, I think he still wanted to chase the dream of the perfect little princess who would appreciate him and be the ideal mother for his children. He was probably also worried about what people would think after so many had told him he was being foolish. I wonder what his gut was telling him. Did he just ignore his intuition?

February 27, 1949

Dear Mr. Fortin,

Will you excuse me if I write to you these few lines. I am very sorry about the mistake I made in the letter April 11, 1948 about the age of Nina. I didn't understand when Nina's mother told me to write to you her age. I was all wrong, the fault is all mine. Everyone is very disappointed about the news. You will be glad to know about your young girl and her family because they are all very good people and they are very trusting with you.

Please believe on me.

Your friend,

Domenico

It's very interesting that Domenico was so noble and took the fall. I doubt my grandparents were paying him anything as they had nothing. Maybe he was in love with my grandmother.

February 27, 1949,

Dear George,

I received your letter just this morning. It was not very good news. I am very sorry for you because you are very disappointed about the mistake that Domenico did. Domenico was very wrong. You thought that we said a lie and this made my Mom very sad. I was born March thirtieth, 1934 and I am only fifteen years old. George I never told you lie because this is all Domenico's fault. He did the mistake, you know very well I can not write english.

We are all very disappointed with Domenico to and you will not be disappointed any more because what I have told you is all true. You have offended me and my family, we do not lie. You said you will not write to me and have lost all trust on me. We have always been very truthful with you. Is it so bad if I am one year younger then what you think.

I am sorry the sacrifice for you to wait one more year. I am all ready to wait if you still love me and will have again trust on me. George I have to let you know that I have cried all morning. When Domenico read to me your letter.

Well George I hope that you will believe on me again and write soon and be good with me again. I hope you write again every week and you will not think about the mistake any more because I have not fault. I hope I have your news soon.

Sending to everyone my best always and kisses and love to you.

From Nina

Translated by Domenico

I could hardly believe the misplaced guilt they were laying on my dad with the line, "You have offended me and my family, we do not lie."

My grandmother, grandfather, and Domenico must've had a big pow-wow about this and how to handle it. Domenico had to take the blame to convince Dad he hadn't been lied to and that it was all a mistake. What would've happened if my grandmother hadn't lied at the beginning? Would my father have thought my mother was too young then and that it was too long to wait? The timing of grandmother's lies seemed to work in her favor.

In a letter I have no record of, my father must have written to Domenico and asked him to ask my grandparents to explain sexual intercourse to my mom. That must also be the letter where he forgave them for lying about her age. However, they never did explain to my mother about sex. When my parents married, they didn't consummate the marriage for a couple of months because my mother was scared.

March 19, 1949

Dear Mr. Fortin,

Many thanks for the nice mind you have for me and the compliments that you have confidence in me. Well Mr. Fortin I have explained all to Nina and her father everything about your age, the married life and the sexual intercourse. They have understand everything and Mr. Farano has made his daughter understand. She says she is ready to make every sacrifice for you because she loves you.

I wish you don't think about the age because now all the men they marry very young girls the only thing we look is if the girl is good and comes from an honest family.

To you my best wishes George and I hope you understand my letter.

Your faithful friend,

Domenico

March 19, 1949

Dear George,

With great joy I have received your letter. I am please to hear your good news and to know everything is the same again and I will not have to cry anymore. You make me very happy that you still love me and have trust in me.

My dear George my father and my mother they have told me everything what you have write in your letter about married life. George I have understand very will and I am very glad to tell you I love you and I am all ready to do every sacrifice. The Italian women, they know very well when they get married they go live with the husband and he is the chief of the house. The wife should respect the husband and trust for that. We learn in the Catholic church that we can not divorce. We live with our husband for good because if not we offend the church.

Dear George you are a nice and very great man because you are very honest man for that I love you. I promise to you that I will make every sacrifice to make you a beautiful wife.

Well George I must go and have my English lesson.

My best regards to everyone and all my love and kisses to you.

From Nina

Translated by Domenico

March 25, 1949

Dear Nina,

I received your wonderful long letter yesterday. It explained everything I wanted to know and now we understand each other.

Married life is what you make it and I believe we can make a happy one.

My married brother Rene who is younger than me had an argument yesterday with his wife. He lives with his wife's folks. He got up yesterday morning and didn't feel good. They started a little argument over some little thing and he came here to our house and he slept in my bed. Next morning his wife came over crying to mother and told her about the argument. My mother and I told her to settle the argument with her husband and be careful how she treats him. We told my brother the same thing and today they are together again.

Nina I am not a married man but I am old enough to know what goes on between a married couple. Each should have respect for the other. When they get into an argument with each other they should settle it before it goes too far. I know about children too. My mother is taking care of two of them now. I am getting a lot of experience. I have read about problems of young married couples in the paper and magazines. Religion is very important, it is always best for the man and wife to have the same religion like us.

Nina I just read your letter again and I think you have a great understanding about things. It makes me very proud of you, especially at your age. There are a great many young girls here in America who get married and they don't have that understanding and then it is too late. And then unhappiness follows. I know now that that will never happen to us. When you come to America with me I want to give you everything to make you happy. I want to buy you clothes and little house for us to live in and many other things to make us happy.

This last letter I received from you makes me want you sooner than two years. It convinced me that I could only be happy with you. I wish you could come to America next year instead of two years. All the Italian people I ever met in America are very respectable people. They are kind and generous and very religious to. That is why I want you for me.

Love and kisses,

George

The previous letter and others make it clear how much thought my father was putting in to make his future marriage work. In a letter dated April 2, 1949, my dad said he'd purchased some books on "Love and Marriage." He commented, "You would be surprised how much I am learning from these books at my age. They tell you everything about marriage."

I'd never guess my dad would read such books. He was so earnest to make his marriage a success. My heart hurt, realizing the disappointment he would experience in that future marriage.

In the same letter, he mentioned an article he had read in the January issue of Reader's Digest about travel to Europe by plane. He said, "In the future it will be very much cheaper to travel to Europe by air. And it will take only a few hours to travel there." He had always mentioned traveling to Italy by boat, but times were changing.

April 3, 1949

Dear George,

With my great Joy I have two of your letters. Well George I am very pleased to receive your good news and to know all is right and you have understand my letter very well and am very glad to know your good news and from your family My mother has been sick in bed two weeks. She is a little better now and we are very pleased.

Well George I am very sorry because I didn't had the parcel yet. I will have your nice present for Easter. Here it is nice weather and I will have a nice walk with all my family. I hope you will have a nice good time in Easter.

George in your letter you told me about your brother and his wife get into argument. I think when there is love and trust between each other every argument is soon ok. We will never get into divorce because our love is the same for each other. We have love and trust and for that we will realize our dreams come true.

Well George I am happy to always have your good news. I will close these lines sending to you my best always and best regards to everyone. From me and my family

Kisses and love to you.

From Nina

Translated by Domenico

Nina was not thinking at all about love, trust, and marriage. I was repeatedly shocked my grandmother didn't share some of my father's letters with her daughter. Maybe Nina was too young to want to listen. A part of me thinks my grandmother didn't want to share my Dad because she was falling in love with him herself. But maybe Agnese figured she would share all this with Nina when she was a little older and closer to the wedding. Perhaps she was just too unwell and weak to worry about it. I will always have so many questions.

April 9, 1949

Dear Nina,

This is Saturday night again. Everyone is sleeping except me. Leo has my car and he is out with his girl.

I received your letter yesterday. It was short but it was a nice letter. You don't have to write to me as often as I write to you. I realize Domenico can't spend too much time writing. Just write longer letters and tell me what I want to know. I know if you wrote the letters yourself they would be longer and you would tell me more how you feel about me. When I write to you it is quiet in my room and I take my time. I try to tell you all I can the best way I can. I am not an expert at writing but I try my best.

It was a beautiful day. I hope it keeps up from now on. I have your pictures in front of me on my desk. I admire your pictures very much but all I can do is look at them. I can't take you in my arms and squeeze you like I would want to. You are five thousand miles away and I am doing my best to be patient. It feels like the time I was in the Army in Europe waiting for the war to end. But it is not quite as dangerous as the war. All we have to do is be patient and wait that's all. Every letter we write to each other brings us closer and closer together. If I had enough money to take a trip to Italy I would go this summer. But it is impossible at this time. We couldn't talk to each other anyway.

My youngest brother is having trouble with his girl lately. Last Sunday he went out with her and she kept him out late and made him miss his bus to Boston. She wanted him to miss his bus. She is a spoiled girl. I loan my brother my car as often as I can for their dates but her behavior makes me not want to. I let him have my car Saturdays and Sundays but now I am letting him have it only one day a week to punish her.

My oldest brother Armand's wife is still sick so we are still taking care of my niece Barbara. His wife Mary is going to have to go to the sanatorium because she has tuberculosis. That can be a very dangerous disease. Armand is very sad and today he cried a little and made me have tears. He loves his wife very much. He asked me to take her to the sanatorium for him because he is so upset and doesn't want her to see him that way. We should all pray that she will get better soon.

We all have sad moments in life. We never know what will happen to us in the future but we must be prepared to face it. We are planning to see each other in the future. We are making sacrifices for each other, but we may never see each other when the time comes. We should never think those sad things but it happens to people everywhere and everyday. Let the next ten or twenty years be the happiest ones in our lives.

I am so sorry to hear that your mother is sick. I hope she feels better soon.

There are a lot of people out of work here in New Bedford and it's getting worse. They say we are going into another depression like we had after the first world war in 1927. Everybody made money during the war while we poor boys were fighting. After the war everybody had a lot of money to spend, that was inflation. Now things are slowing up and people are losing their jobs and don't have much money to spend. I hope another depression doesn't come. There should be enough work for everyone because we were all put here on this earth for a purpose.

Nina, keep trying to learn your English the best way you can. Try to read my English letters yourself with the help of the dictionary. I am going to see someone soon about an easier way for you to learn your English. They have easier ways and that is what you need.

Give my regards to everyone and good luck to you.

Love and kisses from your loved one.

George

Two of my father's brothers were having trouble with the women they loved, and I wonder if that filled my dad with caution or made him more eager to get his bride.

It is possible the short letters were because my grandmother was still sick from the birth of her last child. Unfortunately, she would never recover.

April 20, 1949

Dear George,

I am little late to answer your nice letter because I was waiting for to tell you about the parcel. I am very glad to tell you I had the parcel on Easter Saturday that was the Easter present for me and for everyone because we had the sweets. All my little sisters they were so happy and my father for the tobacco. I am very in joy for your nice photograph you are always very fine on every photo you have send me. Everyone that have seen it say you are very nice. I will let you know next time. Well George I can't get the words for thank you about nice mind you have for me and for everyone. George I am very pleased to say my family and I we had a nice and good Easter holiday and I had a nice good time too. The best day it was Easter Sunday because we went all out to have a nice holiday on the Amalfi Coast with my Uncles car. We had all a very nice day. I hope you had a good time to. Well George I am very glad to know you have your little niece with you. That is good for you because you will start to know what is like to be father. So am I learning to because my little sisters they call me mother.

Well George you like to know about Domenico. He can tell you everything you like to know. So I will close these lines sending you the best always. Kisses and love to you and kiss your little niece.

Nina

My mother told me her family was never in a car and never went to the Amalfi coast. Apparently, my grandmother had fantasies she enjoyed passing on as truth, likely to make her letters more interesting.

My father had asked to know more about Domenico in a previous letter. Maybe his intuition was telling him something was off about the situation, so he wanted to learn more about who translated the letters. I can't even imagine what was going through his head with some of the things thrown at him. But, I guess he decided to think positively and believe he was being told the truth. After all, he was kind, truthful, and honest. How could anyone want to deceive him?

Dear Mr. Fortin,

I am very pleased to let you know about me. My name is Domenico Salsano. I am 27 years old and I am not married yet because well you know I have been in the Army for two years. We are not very well in Italy because there is not much work. My job is carpenter. I am very sorry because I have not ready a photo to send to you but will send one soon. All the happiness to see you in Italy soon.

Believe in me, your faithful friend

Domenico Salsano

April 27, 1949

Dear Nina,

I received your nice letter a few days ago. We are all feeling fine and I hope you all feel the same. I am glad to hear that you all enjoyed Easter Sunday. I wish I could send you more little things to make you happy. But it is so much trouble to send packages by mail. There is so much to be done to send a little package by mail. But don't worry I will send you something once in a while.

I don't have a lot to tell you because I live a very quiet life because I don't want to spend my money. I will need every penny to go and get you and start our life together. All my friends are married or have girlfriends, so it is hard for me to go anywhere with them.

I haven't been out with a girl in over a year now. Now when I am introduced to a girl or see one here or there and they make big eyes at me and smile it makes my heart beat a little fast and I turn my eyes away from them to avoid getting too friendly with them. So you can imagine what agony I have to go through to be true to you. That is why I don't have much to tell you because I don't go out to much.

But I can tell you about the races. I think I told you my brother has a midget racer so we go to the races a lot.

Once on our way home we stopped at a restaurant to eat. We sat at the counter. One of the waitresses sat next to me at the counter and tried to get my attention. I tried to not get into a conversation with her so I kept looking away. When she saw I wasn't going to talk to her she got up and got behind the counter and asked who owned the midget racer and where we raced and had all kinds of questions. She got very friendly and wanted to go to the races with us. One of the guys with us said he would take her to the races. He is married with three children. So you see Nina even married men with children meet many girls and go out with them. That waitress is only seventeen years old and this married man is thirty two. So she cant be a very nice girl. But she is pretty and some married men want a change from their wives and go out with these young girls. That is not being true to their wives.

The only pleasure I have now is going to the theatre and the races. I want a woman now more than anything in the world. You are a little young to realize that yet. When I see these men with their wives or girlfriends it makes me want a girl or a wife too. Well I guess I can be patient a little longer and wait for you.

I went with my brother to see his wife at the sanatorium and she looks good. But she is lonely for her little girl and her husband. She has to stay in the sanatorium for one year because of her tuberculosis. Take care of your health Nina.

There are so many things that we hear about and see around us here in America. People get sick, get killed, get married and divorced. But I am not worried about us, Nina because I feel that we are going to be alright together if we keep doing what we are doing writing to each other. We need to have trust and faith in each other and most of all love for each other, that is the most important thing between two people.

I only saw your family a few times but I know that they are one of the nicest families in Italy. I want to take them for a ride in a car if I can rent one there in Italy.

So you say your little sisters call you Mama. I am glad to hear that, because I believe you will make a fine mother for our children someday.

I am glad to hear about Domenico. But I thought he was married and had children. Now It makes me jealous when you go to see him to help you write your letters for you. Now Nina don't fall in love with him. Be careful because you belong to me. I am only teasing, Nina I know you are faithful to me. Well Domenico good luck and many thanks for what you are doing for Nina and me. I don't know how to repay but when I go to Italy I will see you and repay you some way

Give my regards to everyone and love and kisses to you Nina.

George

In a letter written in April, my grandmother made my mother sound very sweet, promising again that she was learning English and with the hopeful line "One day we will not be sorry about all our sacrifices we have done and we will be a wonderful couple." I'm sure my dad felt like a very lucky man, not realizing he was being hoodwinked and deceived. Every time I read about my mother's fabricated English lessons, I had to curb my frustration.

May 8, 1949

Dear Nina,

Nina, why did we have to fall in love, it doesn't seem right for me to do this to you. When I am so much older then you. You don't realize what marriage is all about. And if we did get married things wouldn't be the same as a young married couple. Oh I don't know what to do. Sometimes it seems only a dream when I write to a wonderful little girl like you. And you are so far away! If I had enough money now and you were old enough I would go for you right away by plane and marry you there in Italy. I wouldn't care what anyone would say to me to keep me away from you. I want you now more than anything in the world.

Love is a funny thing isn't it Nina? We want each other to be together and still we can't be for a long time yet. I didn't know that this would happen to me but it happened when you started to write to me three years ago. When two people write to each other for three years it means they love each other. But I thought we would be together by now and I didn't know we would have to wait so long. Anyone else my age would not do what I am doing to a girl your age.

All I can say is that we should pray to God and ask him if we are doing the right thing. If there is anyone who can help us he can. I think I will ask a Catholic priest if we are doing the right thing.

Well, Nina, I love you as much as ever and I will keep writing to you and give my regards to all.

And Domenico, all my luck to you.

Love and kisses to you Nina,

George

Again, Dad was concerned about doing the right thing. I expect he worried about that all the time. My grandmother reassured him in her response, but in reality, Nina was young for her years, and he was right to worry.

George I do not like when in your letters you tell me always you are older. I wish you didn't tell me anymore because I know well your heart is most young like I am. We say in Italy when we want each other there is no obstacles about the age when there is the right love.

Just what the Catholic priest told to me many times. I have pray to God to help me for doing every thing right and to make me a good girl now and a good wife when we get married.

This response distressed me. If Dad only knew the truth instead of thinking he had a beautiful love story.

My grandmother always complained that my father didn't write often enough; maybe his letters were the only thing she had to look forward to. In a way, it has the pieces of a love story, just not the kind my father expected.

May 31,1949

Dear Nina,

It is a beautiful night and I wish you were here with me so we could enjoy it together. It is getting so I don't know what to do with myself. I haven't been working now for about two months. And it looks like I will be out of work another two months because all the mills are closing. I think we will have another depression like we had in the year 1929. I am going to see my cousin get married on Monday. That is two days from now on Memorial Day. It will make me think of the day when we get married. I have your pictures on my desk. I keep looking at them all the

> time but no matter how long I look at them they won't come to life. If you were here in person it would be so much better.

The second page of this last letter must have gotten lost. From what I can gather from the following letter from Italy, he asked Nina not to make eyes at anyone else because she promised she wouldn't. Also, he must have gone to get his feet examined by a doctor because she responded, "I am very pleased about the examination of your feet because you had good report and you are better with it. We are all very glad about it." His feet were severely wounded in the war. The doctor told him his feet were fine, but he suffered with his feet his whole life. Interestingly, she didn't comment on the fact that he hadn't worked for two months.

At the end of June 1949, George sent an update.

> My sister-in-law at the sanatorium is gaining weight and feeling much better. She will be home sooner than we expect. Her little girl who is staying with us at our house is going to school soon because she will be five years old next month. Nina, I am going back to work in two weeks. I am going to work in the day time. It will be much better than working at night. I was anxious to tell you about it. Now I can save some money again.

In Dad's letter dated July 17, 1949, he shared some of his frustrations. He was sacrificing his health to make as much money as possible to get his little Nina. This broke my heart! He also had to put up with others calling him foolish as an ongoing problem. I'd been trying hard to understand my grandparents' deception, but, in all honesty, I could never betray someone, and their choice perplexed me. My feelings went back and forth, all of it something I'll never truly understand.

Dear Nina,

I have been at my new job a week now. It is nice to be working in the day time. I don't know how long I will have the day shift I may have to switch to nights soon. I am hoping I won't have to work in the mills for long because it isn't healthy. I will work in the mill long enough to save money to come and get you. Hopefully when I come back from Italy with you I will find a job that is better for my health.

I just came back from the hospital where my sister-in-law is staying. She isn't feeling so good today. She said she showed my picture to a nice looking nurse. The nurse wants to meet me. I told my sister-in-law I did not care to get friendly with this nurse. My sister-in-law asked me if maybe I didn't like girls. I told her I do like one girl in Italy. She said I was very foolish and shouldn't bother with you. I am not going to talk about you with her anymore. I am a good, honest respectable man why do people try and do me wrong?

I let my younger brother borrow my car and he broke something on it. It cost me a lot of money to get it fixed.

Then he let his girlfriend drive it. I am very good to him and he should be good to me and take good care of my car. It doesn't pay to be good to everyone because sometimes they take advantage of you.

I think Dad grew disappointed in people in general and thought Nina and her family were different. This was so unfair and brought tears to my eyes. Tears were not unusual when I read Dad's letters. Over the subsequent few letters, his brother Leo would continue to meet Dad's bitter expectation.

July 27, 1949

Dear Nina,

I thought a lot about you today. My youngest brother Leo is getting married on Labor Day. That is about six weeks from now. He always said he would never get married but this girl made him change his mind. He is getting married and he has no money. That is no way to get married and I would never do that. He owes money to my father, mother and me and he wants to get a car besides. He borrows my car two and three times a week now.

His old car does not run anymore. He will need to borrow money to get married but he just wants a small wedding. When we get married we will have enough money for my trip to Italy and for both of us to come to America and for a honeymoon. I just hope I won't have to sell my car because here in America a car is a necessity.

Well I am the only one left now in my family who is not married. A lot of people think I will stay single or I will be a bachelor the rest of my life. But we will surprise them won't we Nina? My oldest brother whose wife is in the Sanatorium sold his cottage and his car. He did not make any money with his racer. I am expecting a letter from you soon. I hope it is in the mailbox tomorrow with a picture of you.

Nina, they announced on the radio that we can go to Europe in six hours by airplane. Isn't it wonderful? We are getting everything today. Cars go faster and planes go faster. I only hope that we keep peace with all the world and don't have war among nations.

All my love,

George

August 14, 1949

Nina, remember what I said about being too good to everyone? Well I have been very good to my brother Leo and let him use my car to see his girl. I

> always keep my car in very good condition. Well I am very sorry to tell you my brother was in an accident with my car. He got it all smashed up on one side. He hurt his knee and his girlfriend hit her head on the windshield and broke it. She is ok but her head does hurt a little. Well it wasn't my brothers fault but my car will be smashed up for a while until I can get the insurance money and fix it. I was so proud of my car before the accident but now I feel disgusted with it. But I will fix it and it will look like it did before. When someone borrows something from you they should take care of it like it was their own. My brother passed in front of this other car at night, the other car was going too fast. That's how the accident happened. He should have been more careful and waited for the other car to pass first. Leo is getting married in three weeks. I hope I can fix my car by then so we can use it for the wedding.

My father's level of tolerance exceeded normal expectations. Here his brother was careless with my dad's car, yet my dad still planned to repair it for Leo's wedding.

In later years, when my dad was retired, and his house was paid for, Leo was still trying to take advantage of him, asking Dad to take a loan out on his home so Leo could expand his business. My mother was the one that said, "no way, we aren't doing that."

Perhaps that giving nature allowed my dad to go

through with the wedding to my mother, even after he found out he'd been duped.

August 27, 1949

Dear Nina,

I am sorry to have neglected you. I hope everyone is alright. I have so much on my mind lately and so much to do. I settled with the insurance company for the money I wanted. Now I can have my car fixed by the mechanic. It will cost me only about half of what I collected and I can save the rest.

My car should be ready for my brothers wedding. My poor brother lost his license to drive and it wasn't even his fault. My oldest brother Armand is coming to live with us so he can be close to his daughter. Leo and his new wife will live where Armand was living and use his furniture. Leo and his wife can live there until Armand's wife comes back from the sanatorium.

I have so much to do I don't know where to start. I want to do some of the work on my car myself so I won't have to pay the mechanic so much. I am also studying in school to be a mechanic. I wish I was finished with school so that I could fix my car myself. Don't worry if I don't write as often, I am just so busy, but I love you as much as ever. I know you understand and have confidence in me. At this time I need all the help and encouragement you can give me. I have much on my mind. I have to save enough money for our wedding. I have to make arrangements for your trip to America. I have to find a place for us to live if we can't live with my parents. I am thinking of these things all the time. And I am always thinking and wondering if our marriage will be a success. Maybe I worry about things to much. Maybe I should only write to you every week about things that happen now and only think about our marriage when the time comes. Yes I believe I should not worry too much about the future and forget a little about the past and only think of the present. I hope you understand my letters and if there is something that you don't quite understand please tell me and I will try to make them more clear.

I have two of your letters on my desk. I will try to answer your questions and give you the information you want. I am working on the first shift now. It is just the job I wanted. They like my work at the mill. That is why they gave me that shift. I am happy now. Well I will go to bed now.

Good luck Domenico.

Love and Kisses Nina,

George

A week later Leo and his new wife were on their honeymoon with my dad's car. In the same letter my dad shared some of his medical struggles and other worries.

Well I have to go to the hospital soon for an examination of my feet. Every month I get money from the government for the injury I got in the war. They may start giving me less money if my feet are better. So far they are not better and I get tired when I stand for long periods of time. Do you really want to marry a man with bad feet that is fifteen years older then you?

I met a man tonight that I worked with in the mill before the war about ten years ago. He has a daughter almost seventeen years old. I told him about us. Right away he told me I was foolish to marry you. He said you just wanted to come to America to be a citizen and the only way you can do that is to marry an American. He said when you get here you will probably leave me for a younger man.

I don't care what they say about us. If after we are married and you come to America you want to marry a younger man you can do it Nina. But I don't think you will do these things that people say. Nothing will stand in the way of our love Nina. I am waiting for us to be together someday.

I don't think Dad told many people about his plans to go and get my mom. When he did, they always told him he was foolish. He must have heard some positive comments as well, but he hardly mentions them. I think he was very sensitive about these negative comments because they would have matched some of his fears about his plans.

September 18, 1949

Dear George

We are all very pleased to hear your good news and to know you are all quite well. So are we here only my mother she is not better yet. Just for that I am very preoccupied and I am always very busy. You know well I am the oldest daughter in the family. I must do everything in the house. This is one month I did not go to help my aunt. Well George I am glad to say I had the English book that we think is most easy and is better to learn the English language. We are all very happy about your car because it is all right again and for your brothers wedding because everything has been good. Well George we hope you have been for the examination of your feet at the hospital and everything has been good for you.

Well George I am always thinking about you and I still waiting and we don't care what many people say about us because we have trust together to be happy forever one day. Well I must close these lines sending all the best to everyone and all my love to you and a big kiss from your Nina.

Best wishes and regards from all my family and from Domenico

I loved the historical commentary my father unwittingly shared that added a layer of value to his letters. In another one from September, he mentions, "Last week my folks, and a few of my relatives and me went to a house and there was some moving pictures shown. I was in a few of them. It is funny to see yourself in a moving picture. These pictures make the best souvenirs a person can have. Ten years from now they can look at these pictures again."

Moving pictures fascinated my father. Little did he know that in a year and a half, his wedding would be filmed, and the news would broadcast ~~it~~ in countries worldwide. I've seen the film clip in both Italian and English.

At the beginning of October, a letter from Nina proclaimed, "I have saved all your letters, and I will read them all myself one day, when I am learning good the English language." If only that were true. Even though my mother didn't make that promise, I still don't understand why she never read them. Even when she translated her mother's letters, my mom expressed no interest in reading the ones from her husband.

I get emotional whenever I read my dad's letters, and I imagine I always will. In one letter, he asks Nina's opinion,

> Nina tell me do you want me to send you another radio or save the money for us. And do you really want the Reader's Digest again this year? It cost twice the price of last year. I have a big heart, I could buy

> you many things. Money means nothing to me, but it will mean much to us in the future. So tell me to save it now so we will have it in the future when we need it. I am not going to spend any more money on my car unless I really have to. I pay less to my mother at home now. She is anxious to see me save my money.

And then he expressed happiness that she had received the English book he had sent and encouraged her:

> Just try and read it for one hour a day and concentrate on that. But don't skip a day try and learn a little every single day. Try and form a habit and that is the best way for you to learn.

His dedication to "Nina," who was only a figment of another woman's ambition, was nothing short of heartbreaking. My mom never even looked at any of the English books Dad had gone through such effort and cost to send. Why didn't her mother at least have her study the English books, like she said she was doing? Why didn't she try to add some truth to the lie? When he closed his letters, "Nina, I love you very much," how could I not judge my grandmother? To this day, I go back and forth with that judgment, trying to understand.

At this point, my grandmother was very sick and rarely had the energy to write. Earlier in the correspondence, my

Italian family had often waited anxiously for letters from my father, then the tables turned, and he became the one waiting, anticipating every letter. So many things could go wrong with Nina, her parents, or even Domenico, which could derail the whole interaction. Of course, my father had no idea how precarious the situation was, but still, he worried.

Meanwhile, Leo continued to provide family drama, coming so close to graduating and then dropping out at the last moment to help their brother Rene with the electrical shop. My father shared that he had $250 saved for his travel but needed much more. I then had to shake my head when I read that Leo wanted to borrow a hundred dollars to buy a car. But, at least this time, he acknowledged, Leo still owed him $200, and lending him more would be foolish.

Leo's request for money probably prompted the disapproval Dad expressed toward Leo's wife in the following excerpt:

> Now that he is married things are different. His wife wants to drive the car herself to work in Fall River out of town. She is not working right now but when she does work she spends all her money on herself on worthless things like clothes and jewelry. She is very selfish and does not appreciate what others do for her. One day she slapped Leo's face because he took a drink of whiskey. Last Sunday we played cards and we wanted to show her how to play. We showed her how to play but then she got mad

when she couldn't win. When she went home with Leo she was crying and didn't even say goodnight. We really don't care to see her anymore until she apologizes to us for acting foolish. I'm not sure they loved each other when they got married.

I hope we can continue to have trust, faith, respect, love and patience for each other. Our long years of writing to each other proves that we can make a good life together. I am getting much experience watching these other married people and reading about them. People say "Life is what we make it". Some people go out together for only a couple of months and then get married and a little while later they get a divorce because they never really loved each other. There should be a law against people getting married like that. Well we won't worry about them as long as we will be happy together.

In each letter, it was evident how much thought Dad gave to marriage and what it took to make a good marriage. Each letter like this, where he expressed his confidence in their love, brings me new pain, knowing he had no idea that the love of his life wasn't the recipient of his letters. Maybe my grandmother thought of Nina the way she portrayed her in her letters, but the Nina my father knew was only a literary creation.

December 3, 1949

Dear Nina,

I just sent you a new radio, I hope this one doesn't break. I hope you get it in time for Christmas. I sent you two packages, one with the radio and one with cigarettes and candy. Two cartons of cigarettes for Domenico, on box of cigars and one carton of cigarettes for you father, candy for your little sisters, a carton of cigarettes for your brother and chocolates for your mother.

Nina, in my last letter I told you about my brother's wife. Well, I didn't mean everything I said about her. She was upset and irritated about everything because she is going to have a baby. We all are her good friends again. She is much nicer about everything with us now. She was upset because they owe money to everyone and it will take a long time to pay people back. It also cost a lot of money to have babies.

Nina, when you send me your picture please ask Domenico if I could have a picture of him. I would like to see what he looks like. He has been writing your letters for you all this time and I don't know what he looks like. Nina, I asked the mailman if I could send you some cigarettes and he said I could not. But I sent you some just the same. So be careful. Tell Domenico, your father and your brother not to sell them or tell anybody about getting cigarettes from America. Because it may get me in trouble and I won't be able to send you any more.

Well Nina, be a good girl and take good care of yourself. Give my regards to everyone and I wish you all a Merry Christmas and a Happy New Year.

All my love and kisses,

George

At this point, my grandmother had become very, very sick. That was possibly when Domenico and my grandfather took over writing the letters, if not a few letters prior. I read the letters repeatedly, searching for where the spark my grandmother brought to each correspondence disappeared with her.

December 11, 1949

Dear George,

We are all very sad here and worried because my mother is very sick. She went in the hospital last week. I am the oldest woman in the house and I am always very busy taking care of my younger sisters. They cry everyday because they miss their mother. My father is very sad and is paying a lot of money for medicine for my mother.

Please do not worry when I do not write. I am very proud of you because you love me and I have all my trust on you. I do not care what other people think because I know how great our love is.

I will try and send you a photo of me soon.

I am hoping and praying that we will have my mother home for Christmas. I send you much happiness for a Merry Christmas and A Happy New Year.

Best regards from everyone and all my love and a big kiss from your Nina

Translated by Domenico

December 29, 1949

Dear Nina,

I am very sorry that your mother is sick. I realize all of you must miss her so much when she is in the hospital. I hope her sickness is not to serious. Sometimes it is better to see a doctor right away when a person is sick. Because when it is delayed it may get serious and then it is more difficult to cure. We are all fine here. I will pray to God for your mothers quick recovery. Because we all need our mothers when we are young.

We had a wonderful Christmas here. The weather was fine. Our celebration was quiet. We exchanged Christmas gifts among us but you had the best of them all. You should have the package now. New Year's Day will be here in a few days. We will all celebrate together. Nina, I think of you every day. Take good care of your little sisters Nina while your mother is away. I know you will.

Nina if I tried to forget you I know I could never do it. When I think of all the sacrifices that I am doing for you and me, these things are hard to forget. Your trust in me gives me the power to make these sacrifices. I am trying to do all the right and honest things so that I can make you a good husband and I know you are doing the same for me. Something might happen to keep us apart let us hope that does not happen.

I love you very much. God bless all of you and give my regards to everyone.

Love and Kisses,

George

SEVENTEEN

1950

It was 1950, and my dad had been writing to who he thought was my mother for over three years. My grandmother was close to death. Nina felt exhausted and burdened by all her chores and worried sick about her mother. Her sisters constantly cried because they missed their mother. I'm sure life seemed hopeless.

Letters from Italy became shorter and shorter, and my grandfather and Domenico didn't care for George as my grandmother did. I'm sure my father noticed the difference, although it took a long time for him to voice his doubts.

January 8, 1950

Dear George,

With great joy I am answering your nice letter and we are all very pleased to hear your good news and to know you had a very Merry Christmas with all your family. Se we had good one to because we had our mother at home for Christmas. Now she is better and soon she will go to have nice big cure. I think you didn't understand in the last letter about the medicine I talked to you it was in America. I will put in this letter the medical prescription you will see if this is better and the latest medicine of that so to make a rapid cure for my mother.

I am always very busy in the house. This is two months that I did not go out.

George if I did not write soon sometime you know well because I have much to do and I will let you know about the packages we never had nothing yet. I am very glad because you are sending to me your nieces picture. George my trust is always on you and I pray God to give my mother soon good health and to help me do everything right and to keep me always good and to be a good wife to you. We will hope to be happy soon together one day. All the happiness to have soon your good news. I must close these lines sending to everyone my best always and all my love and kisses to you from Nina

Also best regards from Domenico and all my family

My grandmother was home from the hospital for just a short time. Then, she had trouble breathing and had to be rushed back to the lung hospital in Naples. It was an hour by car from their home. In the following days, grandmother sent a message to her daughter through Don Afonso, a family friend, saying she had to talk to her. It was urgent.

Don Afonso shared the message with Nina and her father, stating that he would gladly take her, but Giovanni said his daughter was not going anywhere.

Did my grandmother have a change of heart? Had she decided to tell her daughter the truth?

"What did she want to tell you? What was so urgent?" I asked my mom.

"I never found out," She answered.

My mind was whirling at this information. Maybe Grandmother was going to tell my mom the truth? She was dying, and her other daughters were too young to be left alone, which would have changed everything. But Grandfather wanted to go to America, and perhaps knowing his wife's desire, he didn't want his plan foiled.

"But you talked to her again before she died." I said, "Did she tell you something then?

"A few days later, Joseph visited her in the hospital." As always happened when my mom spoke about her mother's death, tears sprang to her eyes. "While he was there, the doctor told him she didn't have long to live."

It was January 22, 1950. When Agnese overheard the doctor, she started to cry and begged her son to take her home. She wanted to die with her children around her. Joseph was at a loss as to how to accomplish her request. She was too weak to go on the train, and there were very few cars in Cava. Joseph left the hospital and took the train to get home, promising he would be back.

Once home, he and his father went to Giovanni's nephew, who owned a car. The nephew agreed to get Agnese, and they all left for the hospital. Once they situated Agnese in the vehicle, Joseph held a white handkerchief out the car window as a warning as they sped home to his sisters. At home, they settled her into bed. Between visiting neighbors, Agnese beckoned for Nina. Nina came close. Agnese grabbed her blouse and pulled her closer, "Nina, you can't go to America. You have to stay in Italy and take care of your sisters,"

Nina replied, "Yes, Mama, of course."

She never wondered about her mother's request because she didn't know the details of the letters or what her parents had planned. Twenty minutes later, Agnese took her last breath in Nina's arms. Nina sobbed uncontrollably. The person she loved most in the world was gone.

I wonder if, on her deathbed, my grandmother regretted everything she had done. Her original goal had been to find a way for the whole family to immigrate to America after Nina married the American soldier. Still, as she lay dying, everything was out of her control. Her children were so young it must have worried her greatly to leave them only in their father's care. Amelia was only 11, not old enough to take care of her sisters, Carmelina was 8, and Cristina and Angelina were only 4 and 2, just babies. I can't imagine the fear of not knowing what would happen to them if her eldest daughter went to America. Unfortunately, she'd run out of time to fix it, and explaining it would have taken too long, so she just had to give that simple plea. I'm glad my mother soothed her and told her not to worry, letting her die in peace.

The following day, they took Agnese to the mortuary in a horse-drawn wagon, where the mortician prepared her for burial. On the day of the funeral, rain poured. After they lowered Agnes's casket to the ground, they asked Nina to throw dirt on it. She knelt beside the grave, motionless, staring at her mother's casket, and finally threw a handful of dirt. She needed encouragement from her aunt to rise and leave the gravesite. On the long walk home from the cemetery, the soaked family found it hard to continue. Finally, they stopped at a farmer's house. The farmer and his wife kindly offered warm milk as the family dried their coats by the fire. They waited until the rain stopped and then continued their walk home.

As she finished the story, my mother stared off into the distance. It was apparent she'd never recovered from her mother's death. They'd experienced so much together, watching neighbors ripped apart by bombs, seeing dead bodies in the streets, and fearing disease. They'd run for their lives side by side, then slept in the dirt under trees as their stomachs grumbled with hunger. They would lean on each other, watching bombs drop on the village, lighting up the sky, as they wondered who might have died. They were scared all the time, and they comforted each other.

Often, they would only have half a loaf of bread, and my mother would watch as her mother gave each of them a slice, saving none for herself, even as she wasted away with sickness. Other times, weakness would overcome her mother, but she'd brace herself on the wall to stand up straight and cook for her children. Those memories of a mother's love are still so vivid in my mother's mind; even the revelations she would discover when translating the letters for me over 65 years later wouldn't be able to dislodge them.

But my mother didn't have much time to grieve or worry after her mother died. Grandmother's death made everything more difficult for her. She had to take care of the family without the hope that her mother would be coming home. Despite her grief, she had no choice but to continue cooking, cleaning, and looking after her sisters. Lying in bed and crying for days wasn't an option. The responsibility must have given her a reason to keep going.

Even as my heart ached for her, her loss shed some light on our own relationship. We'd never shared the same intense, life-altering experiences she had in common with her mother. Maybe that was why she never seemed to see me or pay attention to what was happening in my life. Her mother was her biggest ally, and it wounded her very core when she lost her. Perhaps she couldn't be that close to someone again. Maybe she tried, but I don't think she was ever able to move on from Grandmother's death.

Throughout my life, my mother frequently mentioned how her mother didn't have this or didn't have that, usually getting teary-eyed. Mom had always performed the physical responsibilities of being a mother with skill; it was the nurturing of my soul that I rarely received. I guess she just didn't have it to give. Perhaps because she could give me the material things her mother couldn't give her, she thought she was doing well, and I should be fine.

Not knowing the tragedy Nina's family had just suffered, my father sent a couple of chatty letters. He casually mentioned the medicine my grandfather must've requested in the following fragment:

> Nina, I found the kind of medicine that your mother wants, I am sending you a little story in newspaper about it. Streptomycin is a German medicine, it is a new medicine that has been discovered. Maybe that is why it is difficult to get in Italy. If this is the medicine you want let me know how much and I will try and get it for you.

Streptomycin was the first antibiotic that could be used to cure tuberculosis and other infectious diseases. But Agnese was already gone, and my dad's inquiry was too late. There was no certainty that tuberculosis was what she even had.

February 5, 1950

> Dear George,
>
> I am sorry to be so late to answer your letter and to give you bad news. We are all very sad about the

loss of my mother. She died last week, she had a very difficult operation. It was the first time the doctors saw an illness like my mothers. She had a very bad illness of the stomach. We brought her home just in time for her to die. Now we have lost what is most dear to our life. We had a very great mother. We will pray now to God to keep our father always in good health. We will pray for our God to make everyone good and to give me the strength to be a good girl and to do everything to keep our house the same. When my mother was alive I promise her to be a good girl and to take care of my little sisters.

Well George I must close this lines sending all the best to everyone .

Love and Kisses to you from Nina

Translated by Domenico

February 13, 1950

Dear Nina,

I was very heart broken to hear about your mother. I still can't believe it is true. All of you will miss her very much. Now your mother is not suffering anymore because she went up to heaven. From heaven she will always guide you when you are taking care of your home and sisters. Nina I wish I could be there to help you in anyway that I could. You have a really big job now but I know you can do it. You were brought up right and you have ideas of a grown up girl of twenty. I am glad your Aunt and your neighbors will help you. I know you will take good care of your little sisters. I am here in America praising you and praying for you as best I can.

We have our television now in our house. I don't go out anymore to the theater. We have the theater in our house. We get everything on the television. It is very entertaining for the children too. Some day you will have it in Italy if you don't already have television there. Tonight we had a picture made in Italy. I will tell you more about television later on. I am sorry to hear you did not get the parcels yet. It take time sometimes.

We are all fine here, Nina. Give my regards to all.

Love and Kisses,

George

March 3, 1950

Dear George,

With great joy I am answering your nice letter and it has been a very great comfort to me, many thanks for your kind words and the good mind you have for me. Well George I am always busy you know, well I am the oldest woman in the house.

My sister-in-law Anna she has been in our house many days to help me to do everything and she is very good with everyone. She comes to help me everyday. In this world there are the good people and she is very good because she takes care of everyone. Well George we are all very pleased to say we have received the parcel and everything was good. We all thank you for the nice mind and the nice mind you have for our mother. She died before she had your box of sweets which made us very sad.

I am very glad for the nice and beautiful radio you have sent me, it is very nice. Well George I am very glad that you have the television set in your house that is the best and wonderful thing in the world.

You have everything in you house. I will hope to see that nice thing when I will be in your house. Will you tell me everything next time about the television. Well George I must close these lines and I will promise you to take care always of my little sisters and everything in my house. I still love you always with all my great trust on you.

I hope to have soon your good news. I am sending everyone my best.

Love and kisses to you
from Nina

On March 30, 1950, the day of Nina's 16th birthday, George sent the following sentiments:

This day is a special day for us. You are sixteen now. One year from today you will be seventeen and that will be an even better day for us. But that day will be a very sad day for your family because you will be leaving them to go to America with me. Let us hope we are all happy on that day.

April 2, 1950

Dear George,

I am very pleased to hear your good news. I turned sixteen years old last week but the life I am living it is like I am twenty. I am always very busy in the house. I start in the morning at six o'clock and I finish at eight o'clock at night. We have changed the house we are living in. We are now close to our grandmother which is very good for me because my aunt comes to help me. In the morning I have to get everything ready for my father and my brother to go to work in Salerno. Then I make breakfast for my sisters and send them to school. I try to get everything done in the house before they come back in the afternoon. Well George that is my life for now. I hope for a better one next year when my sister finishes school and she will be fourteen then she can help me.

Well George I have always my great trust on you and I hope to see you soon one day in Italy to take me back with you in America.

I will now start my english lesson.

Well I must close this few lines. Sending to

everyone my best always and all my love to you with kisses

from your Nina.

Translated by Domenico

I guess Domenico had been writing the letters for so long that he just continued. I do wonder how my grandfather got him to continue with the lies. Maybe Grandfather thought my mother could still become sick with Thalassemia major and die at 18. When my father arrived in Italy and met Domenico, perhaps he told my father that to persuade him to go through with the marriage. But they may have kept that a secret, thinking he wouldn't want a sick girl. There are so many things we'll never know.

April 11, 1950

Dear Nina,

I received your nice letter today and your beautiful Easter card.

You are so thoughtful, it is those little things that make me so happy and make me love you so much.

We are all happy here except for my sister-in-law Mary. She went to the hospital and was operated on for tuberculosis. They took out three ribs in her chest because her ribs are collapsing against her lungs. Later they will take out two more ribs.

My oldest brother Armand and youngest brother Leo both gave a pint of blood for her. She is really suffering and looks so bad. I really feel awful for her and my brother and I pray for them.

Now I will talk about a happy subject which is us. I am so excited that you are sending me a new color picture of you. You must be taller and prettier now. I am sorry I have been always asking for your photo when you were busy and could not go out. Now I am grateful to you because I will see you again on your photo after looking at these old photos on my desk.

We saw a picture on Television. It was about an airplane trip to Portugal, Spain and Italy. It cost $750 round trip. It showed the Vatican City in Rome and Venice. Venice is beautiful and artistic. We will go to Venice and Rome together. Next week on Television it will be about another plane trip to Paris, France. I wish you could be here with me to enjoy the television.

Nina, I can't believe that you work from six o'clock in the morning until eight o'clock at night. I admire you doing this for your family. I am sure God is with you and helping you and he will repay you by helping you in the future. We must help others if we expect others to help us. I help my father and mother too but I have to work at least eight hours in the mill. I want to do as much for them now because next year we will be married. After we are married we will have the satisfaction of being able to say how much we have helped our families.

Nina, I am listening to some sweet music from Brazil. When I listen to sweet music my thoughts are always of you.

My youngest brother Leo and his wife do not seem happy together. They do not come and see us very often. Before they were married she was working and made money, but she would spend it all on foolish things. When she got married, she quit her job, and now they owe so much money. Now she is having a baby and they have no place to live. She buys things at the store that she does not need. She bought an expensive dress and will not be able to pay for it for a long time. I am glad I did not lend them any money because I would never get it back. Leo owed money before he got married, and she said it was his worry to pay it back. Leo is a good man like me but he married the wrong girl. I hate to say things like that about others but it happens all the time everywhere. I like my younger brother very much but I don't know how to help him. If you want my opinion I don't think she loved him when she married him. She just wanted to get away from her home and have someone to support her.

For us we know there is much love because our letters to each other explains that. We are true to each other and have faith in one another so we know we will be happy together.

I will close now. Give my regards to everyone. I will be waiting patiently for your nice picture.

Love and Kisses,

George

May 1, 1950

Dear Nina,

It was my birthday a week ago, I am thirty one now. I wish I could stay this age until you become thirty one and we would be the same age together. But we can not stop age. I will continue to grow older and you will always be young. I will have gray hair soon and you will be a young girl. Everyone will think that you are my daughter.

A friend of mine is getting married soon and I am invited to go to his wedding. I don't feel like going because everyone will be there with their wives or girlfriends and I will be alone. But I will have you on my mind and I will be careful not to make eyes at the pretty girls. But I can't help it if I make eyes at the pretty girls because it is only nature.

An old friend of mine said he saw my ex girlfriend many times. But I do not care about her anymore, I only care about you. I am true to you Nina and I always will be.

Give my regards to everyone. When I feel like writing a longer letter I will write you one soon.

Love and Kisses,

George

May 14, 1950

Dear George

It is with great joy I am answering your nice letter. I have been very sad because you have been so late in writing to me.

I hope you had a good time on the day of your birthday. It you are thirty one I don't mind because I know how great your love for me is.

I have always all my trust on you and I know well our hearts are together in love the same age It doesn't make any difference if you have grey hair before me. You have said this to me many times and I am not worried. I know well that you will be for me a good husband because you love me. I love you and I am certain we will be happy together.

George I am very glad that you work around the house for your father and mother. For me everyday it is the same. I am always very busy.

I am like an older mother now, my youngest sister calls me mother.

Well George I am very pleased because you are going to the wedding of your friend. I don't mind if you go with a girl that is a friend and have a nice good time. That don't make me worried if you have a nice day with a nice friend because I know you very well and I have all trust on you.

I must close this letter sending all my best wishes to you and my regards to everyone.

All my love and kisses
from your Nina

After years of writing letters to my dad for my grandmother, Domenico probably knew exactly what my grandmother would want him to say. Now, with Grandfather pulling the strings, the letters make Nina seem older than her years. I doubt Agnese would have agreed to George hanging out with "a girl that is a friend," but apparently, my grandfather was okay with it.

May 19, 1950

Dear Nina,

I was so happy to hear from you today. I'm glad to hear everyone there is fine. We are all fine here. I am thinking about you and our future. Our future is always on my mind. I wish I had a lot of money. I know you will be happy only to be with me but there is so much that we could have if I had enough money. I will have enough money to go to Italy to get you and marry you, for our honeymoon and a few clothes. After that we will probably need to live with my parents for awhile. I will have to go back to work in the mill. I don't want to work in the mill all my life.

I want our own little house for just you and me but it costs so much money. I went to see a man about buying some land to build a small house and a little shop but he wants so much money. I could borrow money from the government but I don't like to borrow money and it takes so long to pay it back. We will have to be satisfied with what we have until we can work something out together. Some people get married and they owe so much money. Then they have babies right away, we don't want babies right away. When you come to America we will need to be thrifty and cautious about our money. I will sell my car next year after we take a nice trip around America.

I bought a jacket and a pair of pants today. It is the first time I have bought clothes for a long time. I will need more clothes when I go to Italy. Because my old clothes are wearing out.

Good luck and best regards to the family and Domenico.

Love and Kisses, Nina

George

"Nina" responded that she would be very happy to live with George's parents, but that she hoped he wouldn't sell his car, because she was looking forward to many rides with him.

My father had still not received the promised photo, and he decided to resort to a threat:

> Every time I get a letter from you I have been expecting to see a nice picture of you in it. Nina do I have to beg you for a picture? I should not have to ask you all the time. Am I asking for to much? What is wrong? Why can't you send me a recent picture? Are we losing our love for each other? I don't want you to send me another letter if it doesn't have a picture of you in it. Am I being to sever with you? I am sorry if I am. I will not be writing to you again until I have received a picture of you.

A month later my father apologized:

> I am sorry I did that. I can't stop writing to you now. You are all I have in the world. Maybe I will receive your picture in a few days. I don't want to hurt you and I know you don't want to hurt me. We have been writing to each other for four years. I have all your letters in my draw in my desk. All these letters form a love story between a pretty Italian girl and a former American soldier. We don't want to stop that love story now. I want to write to you until the last day I take that boat to Italy. You don't have to send me your picture if you don't want to. I have many pictures of you on my desk. In another 8 or 9 months

you won't change to much. I think you will be as pretty then as you are now.

In the same letter, my father mentions that America had joined the Korean War and hoped that would not hinder his travel to Italy.

Over two months would go by before new correspondence arrived from Italy, and my father sent several worried letters. He was sure that Domenico must be out of town. Perhaps he was, but it was also likely that my grandfather wasn't as dedicated to this "relationship" as his wife had been.

In one of his letters, my dad explained that he expected to have $2500 saved by March, which is more than he had expected. He was obviously excited to make plans, but he also questioned whether they would ever be together.

Once "Nina" finally responded, she used the easy explanation that Domenico had been out of town. Still, to me, the letter lacked the affection of the previous letters crafted by my grandmother.

August 27, 1950

Dear George

It is with great joy that I am answering your nice letter. I am very sorry I haven't written to you. Domenico has not been here for over a month. Well George be not afraid if I am late to write to you because it is not my fault. But I am very sorry when Domenico is not here. You know George I am always thinking about you and I am very happy because you love me.

I am very glad for your new job and I hope you will save much money. I have great trust in you George but I am afraid about the war

The war is very bad for everybody and I hope it will do nothing to us.

I am very happy to know you will love me always. Please know that

I am so sorry George when I can not write to you. I must close this line sending all the best to everyone and all my love and a big kiss to you

From your Nina.

September 9, 1950

Dear Nina,

I received your wonderful and nice letter. I waited for that letter every day for two month, but I didn't give up. I knew I would receive it and I am a man with much patience. The same way with your photo, I am still waiting to receive it soon. I know you will send me your nice photo when you can. Maybe I should send you a camera and some colored film. I would like it very much to have your photo and Domenico photos in color and all the family. Also a photo of your house and a view of your village. I will think it over and see if I can send a camera to Italy by mail. I hope everyone there is fine. We are all fine here.

Nina, I've been planning to take three months off from my work next year for us. I don't know if they will give me three months vacation. I don't care if they don't, I will quit my job if they don't. I will take about three months for everything that we expect to do. We will go to Venice, Pompeii, Rome, Milan, and a few other places in Italy after we are married. It should take about a month for that and by the time we leave Italy I will be talking good Italian. I will learn my Italian in books with your help. And when we come to America I want to take you all around America and show you many things. There is so much to see here and our roads are wonderful to travel on.

Everyone is sleeping now, but I will stay up a little later because President Truman will speak to us on television about the situation in Korea.

All my regards to you, Domenico. I am sorry, Nina, that this letter is not very long. But it is short and sweet.

Love and Kisses,
George

In response, "Nina" blamed the lack of a photo on her father not being well but held out that there would be one the next week. She also said, "I don't mind if you will send to me a camera for the photo because that is a wonderful thing." That line really sounded like my grandfather!

A confusing statement was offered in the same letter: "If you would like to have a nice good time here it is better to come in the last months. I think in August or September because they are the best months to have a nice holiday because the weather is fine."

George, probably very confused by the statement, responded: "Nina, you want me to go to Italy in March don't you? You said the best time of year to have a vacation is in August and September. I am going to spend only one month in Italy. That should be long enough for us to get married and visit a few places. I want to spend two months showing you around America."

Then, in the letter that finally included the promised photo, "Nina" explained about her father's health: "George, my father is not sick but he is not happy because my mother is gone. It is very bad for a man when he has children and his wife is dead. He never has good times now because of his great loss."

And then the request for a later wedding date was continued: "Yes George I would like you to come to Italy now but to vacation it is better in August or September. If you come in March the weather is not fine. I like you come soon, when you come we will be happy together."

I expect my grandfather was trying to delay the loss of his housekeeper, laundress, cook, and babysitter by giving himself just a few more months. However, months must have seemed like an eternity to my dad after already having a whole year tagged on the endeavor.

October 23, 1950

Dear Nina,

I received your letter and your nice photo. I couldn't believe my eyes when I saw your photo. You are a young lady now. Your photo is a little cloudy and foggy but it does show me how much you have grown. Please send me some more photos that are more clear. Please have some more photos taken soon. It isn't asking too much of you is it, Nina.

All Italians coming to America are questioned in New York when they come in off the boat. They are getting strict now about Europeans coming to America because we must be careful not to let in any one against the United States Government. Because we have all worked together to make America the finest country in the world. Nina, you won't have any trouble to enter America. We have much faith in Italy's future and we are helping Italy all we can. I know everything is going to be alright.

Nina, young children get attached to a person very much when you show them attention. Your little baby sister calls you mama. How do you think she is going to feel when you leave her to come to America?

It will break her little heart and your heart too. That is one thing I will be sorry for. It will make them sad and you sad to leave them. I just hope everything turns out alright.

The war is getting worse now. I don't know how it will be six months from now. We are doing good in Korea but the war is getting worse.

I don't have much more to say now.

Love and Kisses,

George

My father had waited so long for that photo and must have been more than disappointed when it was of such poor quality. After they went back and forth about the date of the trip, it was very interesting that no more mention was made of the timing of his journey until the Korean war leaped into the picture.

November 7, 1950

Dear Nina,

I don't know how to start this letter. But I will start by saying that we are all fine here and I hope everyone there is fine. The weather here is wonderful. I think about you all the time. Time is drawing closer now and I am getting worried about us. In four or five months I hope to go to Italy for you. I have made many plans for us. But sometimes plans don't always come out the way we expect them to. The war may change some of our plans. It looks very much like it is going to be the worst war we ever had. I made this great promise to you about three years ago. So far I have kept my promise to marry you no matter what happens. Now if something should happen to keep us apart we must have courage to stand up and face it and look to God for encouragement because God is the one person who can help good Catholics like us in time of need.

You are young and have many years ahead of you. We don't know what will happen in the future, but it does not look good. Soon they may start this great war and stop ships from going to Europe and America. I may have to go to war again even though I was wounded because there are many things I can do to help fight in a war. War planes can come to America now from Russia and bomb our cities. President Truman was almost shot at. We have never had a war on American soil like Italy has.

So let us hope and pray that this great love story and friendship we have had throughout our four years of writing does not end with sorrow. We will keep looking and waiting for our future happiness.

There is a program on the television which shows moving pictures of the last war. Once a week they show a part of it on television. So Far they showed us the war in Africa. Tonight we may see the invasion of Sicily and the invasion of Salerno. All these moving pictures we see were taken in the last war in Africa, Sicily, Italy, France and Germany by our great General who was commander of our forces in Europe. Tonight I may see your little village of Cava it is very interesting to watch because I went all through that area. I hope to see Anzio because that is a place I will never forget. We never thought that we would come out of Anzio alive. Well, Nina, I hope to get a photo of Domenico soon. Give my regards to everyone.

All my love and kisses,
George

November 28, 1950

Dear Nina,

I am sorry to be a little late to write to you. I hope everyone there is OK. Everyone here is OK. We had a terrible wind storm last night. All our lights in the house went out. Our television set was out too so we could not have any programs. Some places had much damage. This morning it is much better. We had a nice turkey dinner on Thanksgiving day. I hope all of you also celebrated Thanksgiving day.

I am working now in another mill on the third shift. I will work on this shift until it is time for me to go and get you. I work from 10 pm at night to 6am in the morning. I will feel tired for the first week and then I will get used to it. We saw Salerno and Naples on television from the invasion in the last war.

Well Nina, I just received your letter with your photo. That photo does not look like you at all. There must be something wrong with that camera. It must be to small to take good pictures. Were these last two pictures taken with that small camera? They don't look like my little Nina that I have been writing to all these years. You need to have a photo taken at a studio by a good photographer. I have been proud of all your photos and showed them to everybody. But these last two photos I don't like them and I don't want anyone to see them. I am being frank with you Nina. I am having some photos taken in a few days for you. I always go to a good photographer who has a good camera. I want you to do the same thing. I always choose the best photos to send to you. Now Nina, I am sorry if I am disappointed and not satisfied with your last two photos. I guess I am all mixed up. I am working hard at the mill and I will probably be in this war soon. I have many worries now. So have good photos of you taken and make me happy. I have a photo here that I am very proud of, it is the color one of you wearing a necklace.

Give my regards to everyone and good luck to Domenico.

Love and Kisses,

George

With my grandmother gone I'm sure it was not a priority of my grandfather to get Nina's picture taken. They didn't have decent cameras, and a professional picture would be very expensive.

December 6, 1950

Dear Nina,

I received you nice letter a few days ago and also your photo.

Do not be sure about coming to America. Don't not tell everyone that you are sure you are coming to America. We should never be sure about these things. Anybody from America can write to anybody in Europe and Italy but when it comes to traveling to Italy and America that is a different thing. There is so may things to be arranged. There are so many things that can stop us from traveling to Italy and America. The war can stop us. I might change my mind or you might change your mind. So we must be prepared for these disappointments that may come. This is something that is hard to forget. We have been writing to each other for more than four years. We seem to be losing our love for each other. There is something wrong between us. You don't want to send me good photos of you and I don't send you any more packages. Maybe it is better for me to find a good girl here and have some good times again. Later maybe I'll get married to a good girl here. I am getting older all the time and we may not live through this great war that is coming.

Well Nina we will keep writing just the same and maybe we will find our love again. Keep up your spirits and we might be married next year. We will either be married or forget each other.

I am sending you my photo. I had two of them made. One for you and one for Domenico. I will send the other one in my next letter.

Love and Kisses, Nina

George

My father seemed to finally be acknowledging the change of tone the letters had taken since Grandmother passed away, and he was having some very justified doubts, which he had voiced with strong words. "We seem to be losing our love for each other. There is something wrong between us." Without my grandmother directing the writing, the letters lost the spark that pleased my father and convinced him he was in love.

December 19, 1950

Dear Nina,

I just woke up from my morning sleep. I go to bed at about 6:30 am in the morning after work and I can only sleep three or four hours. Then I sleep a few hours at night before I go to work at 10 pm.

They are drafting many more young men now for the war. They are drafting about as many men now as they did when I went to war. We are losing the war in Korea now. Many of our soldiers are being killed. The Chinese communists out number our soldiers there by 5 to 1. In other words we do not have enough soldiers there to hold them back. They are pushing our soldiers out of Korea into the sea. So our President has made a speech last week which has changed everything and put everything on a war basis. We were having a good time with our cars and televisions and other luxuries while Russia has been producing tools of war. Now we face a crisis. But don't worry Nina, I still love you. We must keep writing to each other. Now men of draft age who are subject to be called into the army must stay near home. They can not travel far from home for a long period of time. If total war does come soon I may not be able to go to Italy for another five years. So our dreams and our plans will be disrupted. That is life! We all have disappointments. We must hope and pray for the best. I am sending you another photo like the last one for Domenico and I hope he sends me one of him.

Give my regards to everyone and Good luck to Domenico.

Love and Kisses, Nina

George

December 30, 1950

Dear Nina,

I received your very nice letter a few days ago. I am glad to hear everyone is fine there. We are all fine here. I am sorry I was not satisfied with your last photo. I hope I didn't hurt your feelings. I am very glad that I will get a nice photo this time. I'm glad that we have more of an understanding between each other about the future. Marriage is a serious thing. Either we will be very happy in our marriage together or we will be unhappy. I know you are trying to do all you can in your home to take care of your sisters and keep the house clean. It is a big job I know because my mother works very hard in our house to keep it clean for us.

My sister-in-law was here last week and my Mother told her that you are coming to America and live with us. She told her she was going to teach you many fine things about taking care of a home. That made me very happy because I don't talk about you very much to anybody.

January 1951 is in a few days it will be the beginning of a great year for us and everyone or it may be the most disastrous year of our lives. The year 1951 is a hard year to predict. This war in Korea will decide the new year. Let us hope and pray that I get you in America safe as soon as possible before the government makes new laws and restrictions about transportation from Europe to America. The more I think about these things the more I worry about us.

That is why I want to get you here before I am unable to. I will soon get in touch with a travel agency and arrange the date for me to go to Europe for you. Now Nina, tell me what month do you want me to come to America? If you want me to come in March I will arrange for passage on a ship some day that month. If you want me to come sooner let me know when. If we wait to long it may be too late for us and they will probably stop all ship transportation of civilians and use the ships for war. They did that in the last war and they can do it in this war. As soon as we decide when to take you to America I will make the arrangements and I will probably need your help. So if the Travel Agency wants to know some things about you I want you to give me the right information. We want to be sure of everything. We must be careful and not make any mistakes about our passports, and documents. You will have to prepare your documents to enter the United States. All I do here is give them your name and address. You must make sure your documents are correct or it will delay us in Italy.

Well Nina, that is all for now. So don't forget to let me know what month you decide to leave Italy. This is a serious thing now, Nina. So think about it and if you want to change your mind you still can.

Give my regards to everyone. Happy New Year to all your family, relatives and friends and Domenico.

A very Happy New Year to you Nina.

Love and Kisses,

George

EIGHTEEN

1951

The year 1951 arrived. My dad had been writing to my mother for over four years. Finally, the time was drawing near for him to go to Italy and get her. So many hopes and doubts must have been entwined together in his mind. As I read his letters, my heart ached, knowing what he would soon learn, that the love of his life had no idea who he was.

January 6, 1951

Dear George

With my great joy I had just this morning your nice letter. I am glad to hear everyone is fine. I am very glad because you are not bad about my photo any longer. With this letter you will be getting a good photo. George we did not have a very good Christmas this year because we did not have our mother. But you are making me have a nice and happy new year. I was happy to hear what your mother said. She will be my mother to now and she will never be sorry to have me in her house. I will help you and your mother on every thing.

George my father and my family are very glad about your decision to come. Whenever you decide to come I am ready to come with you. When you go to the agency and you let me know the right information and all the documents you want I will send them to you. Well George I am always ready because I know I will be happy with you and I know you love me so I go with you and I will never change my mind. I have always my great trust on you and I am very glad to get a new mother in America.

I will send all my best regards to every one and all my love and kisses to you

from your Nina

January 16, 1951

Dear Nina,

I went to the Travel Agency and the Immigration and Naturalization office today and they informed me that before I can prepare to have you enter America you have to be my wife. I have to go to Italy to marry you and return to America alone. Then I have to prepare the necessary documents for your entry into America. I am preparing to take the airplane sometime in February. I am sorry it has to be this way

Nina, but there is nothing we can do about it. Now you have to bear with me and help me all you can because it is going to take money and many headaches for me. About six months ago I could marry you in Italy and take you back with me right away. But the government has new regulations now. You have to be my wife before I can prepare documents for your entry in America. I have to prepare them here in America. When everything is ready for you to enter America you will take an airplane alone to America and I will meet you when you get here.

I will stay one month in Italy. Nina, do you agree with everything I have said in this letter? Now you must answer this letter as soon as possible so I know everything is alright. Tomorrow I am preparing my passport and will get an inoculation from a doctor for marriage.

Good luck, Nina, and give my regards to everyone.

Love and kisses,

George

Little did my father know that none of his plans would go according to the details of this letter. My grandfather would refuse to let George leave without Nina, requiring them to both stay in Italy for eight months until her documents had been processed. That was an inconceivable amount of time for George to be without income.

January 21, 1951

Dear Nina,

Most of my documents are ready. I am ready to leave for Italy by plane in two weeks. I will probably be in Italy February 8th. My plane will go to Rome. I will take a train to Naples. We will make arrangements for our marriage as soon as I arrive in Cava. Can you get a wedding gown there? We just want a small wedding. Domenico will be my best man at our wedding. I am taking my camera with me and we will take many colored pictures of us and your relatives and friends and the places we visit on our honeymoon. I hope I will make you very happy Nina while I am there and unfortunately I will have to leave you there in Italy and return to America without you. You must bear with me and have faith and courage to wait until I prepare documents for your entry in to America. They say it will take almost four months for your documents to be ready. You can take an airplane or a ship to America whichever one you prefer. We will have difficulties speaking to each other while we are alone. I believe if we try hard enough we can understand each other.

I wish you and everyone there luck and happiness and I will see you very soon.

Give my regards to everyone.

Love and Kisses,

George

I laughed when Dad mentioned he just wanted a small wedding. He had many surprises in store for him, but at least that one was a little entertaining!

January 25, 1951

Dear George,

With my great joy I am answering soon your nice letter. I am pleased to hear your good news and to know everyone is all right there. We are all fine here. Well George I have understand everything in your letter. I am very happy because you will be with me next month. I only made me a little sad because I can not come back with you in America. Well George I won't mind about that because I will be a little late after you in America. George you know well I had always my great trust on you and I will do everything I can and I am very pleased to say everyone of my family are very pleased because you will stay one month in Italy. I will be everyday with you and Domenico. He is very happy about our decision. Well George you have said nothing about the last photo I have sent you. I hope you will like that one.

I think you will prepare soon the documents necessary for you to get married here. Because when you get everything right we won't spoil your time here. Well George you will excuse me if I will ask you a little favor if you could get in America the white wedding dress because here there is not much good.

> Well George I must close this my letter. All the happiness to see you soon in Italy. I will send all my best regards to everyone and all regards from my family.
>
> All my love and kisses to you from Nina.
>
> All the best and good luck from Domenico

Later that month, my father gathered all his letters and put them in a manila envelope for safekeeping. He'd written each letter in long hand and then typed them before mailing them to Italy, leaving him with a complete record of his love story.

No one ever read them again until I did 62 years later.

I'd found my father's and grandmother's letters amazing. My father wrote from his heart in every letter.

In the end, my grandmother struggled with what she had done. From what my mother said, she had something she wanted to tell her but never got the chance. My grandfather did a great job fooling my father up to the end. I'm sure the war made him very nervous that his plans would go up in smoke. But, in the end, he kept my father convinced that Nina loved him very much. I still had so many questions. How I wished I could have just one more day with my dad.

* * *

It had been 62 years since my father wrote his last letter in 1951. I was anxious to share my discoveries with my family.

So, as Easter was drawing near, I invited my family over to celebrate. The fancy tablecloths and napkins came out, along with the china and crystal. As always, to ensure everything was perfect, I set the table the day before for the nine of us: my mom, my two brothers, my two sons, and Mark's parents. Mom was bringing string beans and our favorite cheese pie. Mark was making a ham. I made the sweet potatoes.

I was also excited to tell my brothers, George and Alan, about the book I was writing and our father's lovely letters. As the family arrived, we sat around pouring drinks and chatting. I told my brothers about the letters and how our father had done everything right, unlike what I had initially thought.

I told them how concerned Dad was with the 15-year age difference between my parents. How he asked in his letter's repeatedly if his Nina was sure she wanted to marry a man so much older. Then I told them about my grandmother's deception. They were shocked but didn't seem to experience near the emotion that I had felt. Neither George, who is two years younger nor Alan, who is ten years younger, had any interest in reading the letters. I couldn't really understand, but that was their choice. In my opinion, I had done my dad wrong, but I guess that was just me. I was coming to grips with my parents' reality and true story enlightened part of my journey, not theirs.

At some point, George had made an effort to know more about Dad. He asked Dad about the war and why he went back for Mom. Dad told him, "I thought I was going to die in the battle of Anzio and promised God that if I survived, I would go back and somehow help your mother and her family." Dad had nothing more to offer my brother on the subject, and I guess my brother was satisfied with his answer.

Alan formed a special bond with Dad. He still lived at home when Dad was dying and helped care for him. I guess I was the only one who suffered guilt because I didn't try and get to know my dad better.

We shifted to the dining room to enjoy our meal. I continued talking about Dad and his letters and how I felt closer to him than I had my whole life. Mom sat quietly, not adding anything to the conversation.

George seemed the most interested. As I watched him, I could see the wheels turning. He was sitting directly across from my mother and staring at her. He hesitated for an instant, then blurted out what he'd been thinking, "Mom, why did you sometimes call Dad an Old Goat?"

The table got very quiet. Mom looked down at her lap and didn't answer.

George didn't want to let it go. "Adela, you remember Mom calling Dad an Old Goat, don't you?"

I didn't know what to say. I had always been the peacekeeper in our family.

"Well, vaguely," I said. I just wanted to pacify him and not have our holiday destroyed. I'd always been good at shoving most of the bad under the rug and forgetting things my brother keenly remembered.

My mother mumbled, "No, I didn't."

Then my brother raised his voice, "Yes, you did."

She wasn't going to admit it. George got up and left quickly without finishing his food and Mom left soon after in tears and somewhat shaken. They left before I served dessert, and the rest of us no longer wanted to eat it either. I felt sorry for mom; I always hated to see her hurt. I guess my brother was experiencing more emotion about what I shared than I'd originally thought.

Upon reflection, Mom probably always did think of Dad as an old man. Although my father tried to do everything right as he contemplated marriage during those four years, his biggest fear of being too old for my mom had been realized.

A few days later, I went over to my Mom's to talk to her about the next part of the book. I had finished the chapter about Dad's young life and was pleased with the book's progress. Unfortunately, the next part of the book would be more difficult. I had no more letters. The trauma mom suffered in her youth was easy for her to talk about, like they were burned into her memory. Also, the stories her mother had told her were vivid memories, almost like she'd lived those early years with her. But her memories of when she was 17 and Dad had arrived in Italy seemed dim in comparison. I guess at that time, it was challenging to wrap her head around what was happening to her.

She struggled with the details as she described Dad's arrival in Italy. The drama and handwringing were absent, and there were no more tears. She was detached and emotionless, offering more information only when I pushed her. Her stories were rich with details when she talked about her early years with her mother and during the war. Now, I had to pull everything out of her, which wasn't easy.

I studied her as she spoke. I realized that this part of the story was mostly about Dad, and she was no longer at the center. Even when the magazines and the newspapers descended on them, most reporters talked to my father in English. When I read the media articles, they quoted only my father, even the ones in Italian. My mom was shy then, not the confident woman I'd always known. Now, mom could stand in front of a crowd in a restaurant and sing in Italian or talk to anyone who would listen to her story. I started thinking about the change in her and went looking for the scrapbook with all the pictures and articles. The early images revealed a shy, timid girl, but as the pictures in the timeline progressed, even over that short span of months, the magazine covers showed a more confident woman.

What would my mom be like today if she hadn't had that eight months of fame when the newspapers and magazine reporters wouldn't leave them alone? It was an interesting question. I had never understood how such a poor little girl who came from nothing could turn into someone who craved being the center of attention. But, as I contemplated my parents' lives, I was beginning to understand more and more how their experiences had changed both of them.

PART THREE

NINETEEN

After years of expectations, hopes, and plotting, it was time to prepare for a wedding.

I can only imagine my father's state of mind. So many people had put him down and judged him for his commitment. He had come too far to give up on his dream now. His letters showed me he'd had many doubts, but it would have been like winning the lottery if he was right about his little Nina. I see now why he had to try.

On the other hand, my mom had no clue what was really going on or how it even came about. She had no idea that her mother had started a false correspondence or that her father had continued it. She'd been told repeatedly over the years that the "American Soldier" was coming for her. Still, the story was so unbelievable to her that it just seemed like a mysterious fairytale that she never thought would become reality. So even as her future spouse organized all the finishing details of his journey, all she was told was that he was coming, and so she clung to her denial.

Dad went to the travel agency in preparation for his trip. There, he learned he needed to be married before he could arrange to have Mom return with him. He would need to go to Italy, marry her, and return alone while the paperwork was processed in Washington, DC. To Dad, I'm sure this didn't sound like something that would be easy to accomplish, but I think he felt this was the path that God had chosen for him, and he would overcome every obstacle. He decided he wasn't going by ship as it would take too long, and there was the Korean War to consider. He bought a plane ticket for February.

He booked Trans World Airlines from Logan Airport, Suffolk County, Massachusetts, to Rome. His plane left on February 8th, flying first to New York, Paris, Switzerland, and finally to Rome, all in just twenty hours of flying time. From there, he took the train to Cava de' Tirreni. The trip would decimate his savings, but after four years of writing to his sweetheart, he was sure he was making the right decision.

I can't help but get teary-eyed when I think of the sacrifices Dad made while having no idea what he was getting himself into. He always had the best of intentions for himself and my mother. While preparing to get his bride, he'd even read books on marriage and family. How many men read books and put that kind of effort into their preparation? I was in awe of that discovery and knew he meant well and wanted to be a good father and husband.

Departure day arrived. Dad packed the white wedding

dress for his bride with care. My Uncle Rene drove Dad to Logan Airport for his flight. Maybe his brother had to calm him, telling him how wonderful his life would be when he brought his wife home and how the family would welcome her with love.

The flight was costly, nearly $400.00, which was a lot of money in those days. He also had saved money for passage home with my mother, another $400.00. With all the income he would lose being in Italy for eight months and then the money he spent there, he could've paid cash for a car and a sizable down payment on a house. I don't think my mother's family ever realized the sacrifices my father made to go and get my mother.

I'm sure Dad enjoyed his roomy seat and the stylish flight crew dressed in crisp blue and white uniforms, waiting on him with drinks and food as they flew above the sparkling blue of the Atlantic. When he arrived in Rome, he boarded a train for Cava de' Tirreni.

February 9th, 1951, Mom and her family walked the hour trek to Cava de' Tirreni's train station to welcome my father. It was evening, and Dad was expected to arrive at 10:00 p.m. It was late, so only a few family members were in attendance. Uncle Joseph's fiancée had stayed home with Mom's sisters.

As they walked, Mom felt shy, scared, and unsure of what to think about the commotion. In her mind, she couldn't let go of the denial she'd held onto, repeatedly thinking, "He's not really going to come for me."

And yet, as they walked to the train station to meet him, how could it not be real? So, then she worried about how she looked compared to the girls in America. They were all so glamorous, and all she had to wear was an old wool dress that once belonged to her mother.

In fact, everything she had on had belonged to her mother, except her coat. Her aunt Cecilia promised she would find a way to make Nina presentable. She sold some sheets so she could buy material to make a new coat. She labored day and night until she was pleased with it, a black-and-white plaid with large black buttons. Mom loved her new coat and hoped it made her look pretty.

She didn't understand how her family could be so excited about a man who probably would not show up. My mother didn't know that her parents had ensured the American soldier would return by writing him deceitful letters. She knew nothing about the words of love between this man and the person he thought was her. She could barely remember this soldier she met when she was nine. She knew nothing about the many sacrifices Dad made to come for her.

I'm sure my grandmother often thought about the day my father would finally arrive in their small village. It's such a shame she didn't live to see him again. The deceit was wrong, but I'd grown to understand the passion behind her need to save her children by paving the way for the whole family to emigrate from poor, war-torn Italy to the perceived bounty of the United States.

Dad arrived on time at the old Cava train station. He

carried an armful of gifts for the family and a glamorous wedding gown for my mom. All the family kissed and hugged him except for my mother, who lingered in the background. With her dark hair, big brown eyes, and fair skin, she looked like a pixie in her new black and white coat. Dad appeared so handsome in his new clothes, with his blonde hair and blue eyes. My mother must have been in awe and maybe even scared. She had never had a boyfriend, and here was a man intending to marry her. There is a good chance she felt like a little peasant girl meeting her prince. I would love to know what she really thought, but no matter how much I pushed, she would never share her whole reaction, only her mantra that she didn't believe he was coming and her worry about her clothes.

My father would've immediately sensed something was wrong. He'd probably hoped Nina would run to him; instead, she was almost hiding. He tried to communicate by speaking a little French, Italian, and English with hand signals, but it was challenging. It was an hour-long walk to my mother's step-grandmother's house, where my dad would stay.

I can only imagine how strange Dad must have felt to be with these people he didn't know. In the dark, it must have been a very long walk on those old cobblestone roads. I doubt anyone was talking much. Domenico was there but really didn't speak much English. He'd written the letters with the help of a dictionary.

Dad must have felt fear and apprehension as his

intuition kicked in. As I write, I feel like I am right there with him, watching her and wondering what's happening. Her watching him and not knowing what to make of everything. This is how a couple with an arranged marriage would feel; only Dad didn't know he had an arranged marriage. He thought they were in love.

George didn't have a clue about the avalanche of attention that awaited him that morning in the sleepy little town he remembered. Photographers were already at the door the following morning, wanting photos of Nina and George together. I asked my mother how the media heard about my father's arrival, but she didn't know. What she did know was that they came from all over. Photographers were there from Germany, France, and several other countries. The media said the wedding would be filmed and their story would be published all over Europe. Two of Italy's major magazines, La Settimana Incom and Tempo, were already there. When Life Magazine pulled the story off the wire, the magazine dispatched a photographer and reporter on the next train. Overnight, the couple were celebrities.

It's always been a nagging question as to how the media found out about my father going to Italy to get my mother. I thought it was my grandfather who contacted the media, but he couldn't read or write. So, Domenico might have initiated it on behalf of my grandfather to ensure there was too much publicity to back out.

With this question on my mind, I texted my cousin Alessandro in Italy, the son of my Zia Amelia, asking if he knew how the media got a hold of the story. He guessed that the paperwork for my mother was submitted to the US Embassy, and either with encouragement or on their own, someone at the embassy leaked the story to the press. But as the Italian media was the first to show up, that explanation had some holes. They would have to know the exact date of my father's arrival. Somehow, the police knew as well because they were there to push back the crowd when the media showed up at my mother's step-grandmother's house, where my father was staying. I doubted I would ever find the true answer because anyone who would have known was no longer alive.

I can't help but wonder if Dad would've still gone through with it if their faces weren't being plastered in magazines and newspapers worldwide. I'm sure Dad just went through the motions, not knowing what else to do. This is one of the main reasons I wondered if Grandfather and Domenico contacted the media about the American soldier returning for his bride. They had to make sure all their hard work would come to fruition. They easily could have spread the word of Dad's arrival through the town, getting everyone excited for the big day because the townspeople lined the streets with flags the day after he arrived. I can't imagine that either embassy had anything to do with that.

After a few days, Dad settled into Italian life, soaking up all the attention, whether he wanted to or not. My father probably had never been so spoiled. He was celebrated and looked up to like never before. But the girl he had come to collect as his bride was keeping her distance.

Dad certainly would've asked questions. The only person who spoke any English who was close to the situation was Domenico, so that's who my father would have gone to with his questions. Why is my bride avoiding me? Where is the girl who said she loved me? A couple of weeks later, Domenico told my mother that Dad was upset that she had no affection for him. He was considering backing out of the whole thing. Domenico told her he smoothed it over by saying she was shy, kept away from boys, and didn't know how to act with a man.

At some point, Domenico must have told Dad the truth about the letters. I just can't imagine it was happening any other way. Dad probably figured Domenico was complicit in the deceit. At any time, as he had been translating the correspondence, Domenico could've made it clear to Dad that it wasn't really Nina writing the letters. Unfortunately, Domenico never took that opportunity. So did Domenico try to temper his response, or just dump the whole story in my dad's lap?

Everyone had warned him, but he hadn't listened. His savings were almost gone. Over and over, everyone told him he was being foolish, and he had ignored them. He would be a laughingstock if he went home without Nina and admitted to the truth.

I guess my father decided he should spend time courting my mother because that's what he did. He took her shopping and bought them matching sweaters. She took him to the tailor, where he had a suit made for the wedding. They needed to get to know each other, and she was still shy. It would've been evident that, unlike what he had been told in the letters, she had never tried to learn English. Slowly and painstakingly, they planned their marriage and their life together. Bit by bit, using his Italian-English dictionary, my parents began to communicate. Dad decided to go along with his new fate. I don't know that he had much choice at that point.

Mom and Dad posing for the camera with letters Mom never read

Taking a walk in the countryside

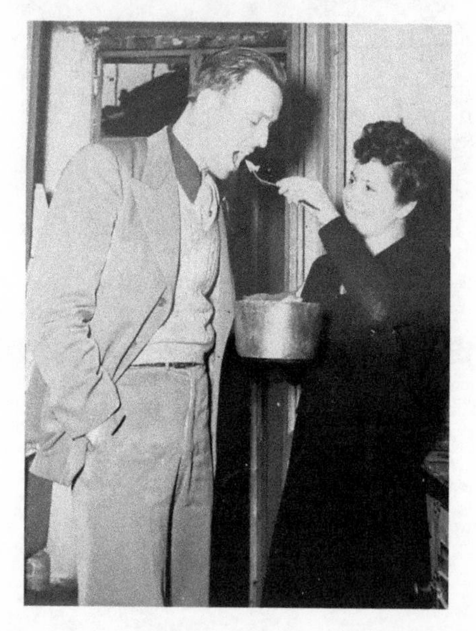

Nina enjoying cooking for her husband to be

Nina wearing the locket with her mother's picture

I'm sure Grandfather and Domenico spent many nights talking and plotting to make sure everything went how they wanted it to. They succeeded, and it probably went even better than they had planned. But what was in it for Domenico? Maybe Domenico had feelings for my grandmother and just wanted to help her. We will never know for sure.

My Mom was young, beautiful, and innocent. Once Dad got used to the idea, he was probably ok with it, even though I'm sure he never would've come if he'd known the truth. My grandfather approached my dad through Domenico and asked if he'd take him to America, where he could get a better job to provide for his family. Dad promised my grandfather that he would arrange for him to come one day. Which, of course, had been my grandparents' plan all along.

My grandfather also stressed to my father that he couldn't leave Italy without his bride. This would be a hardship for my father because he needed to return to work. It seemed he had no choice and wired his father in America, asking him for money so he could stay as long as it took to get my mother's paperwork done.

The night before the wedding, my mom confessed to her brother that she was scared and didn't want to go through with it. However, he insisted that she must, as everything was already arranged, and their father would be angry. Besides, he knew their mother had worked so hard for Nina to marry the American soldier.

Mom recalled her mother on her deathbed begging her to stay and tend to her sisters. She sat in silence, not knowing what to do. In the end, her father was unyielding. He gave her no choice but to go through with it. My mother never knew her father's involvement or the lengths he'd taken to ensure this big day would happen. Grandfather was the only one with a motive to contact the media, and the media made it very difficult for either of my parents to back out.

Almost seven weeks after my father's arrival, the wedding day arrived. The church was crowded with photographers, reporters, citizens of Cava, the mayor, and everyone that was anyone was there. The crowd was difficult to handle, and security had to be everywhere. The church was flooded with the unaccustomed lights of cameras flashing.

Nina and her Father walking towards the church

The Happy Couple

Nina and George exchanging rings

Nina and George reciting vows

Nina and George in courtyard outside of church

Nina and George walking from the church to the reception

My mother looked beautiful in her silk wedding dress, even though it was a little big. She looked like a princess, but when I pressed her to see if she felt like one, she focused on wondering why it was so big. It was stitched and pinned to fit her with her tiny waist. It had long sleeves and a train that stretched out behind her. Surely, she felt beautiful. My father looked so handsome in his new Italian suit. The two made a striking couple, and the cameras and media loved them.

Those closest to Nina had a hard time keeping their emotions in check. But for my mom, the most important people weren't there. Her father had ordered her four sisters to stay home because they didn't have proper clothing.

After the wedding, the couple, surrounded by friends and relatives, paused in the church courtyard to pose for more photographs. They looked happy in the pictures, and I hope they were. I know my mom was torn, loving all the attention but missing her mother and sisters. I will never know what my dad was thinking. I saw a film clip where he stepped a little away from her and lit a cigarette. Was the cigarette to calm his nerves?

Townspeople and peasants from near and far threw flowers and confetti at George and Nina as they boarded a horse and buggy. The bridal procession toured the nearby village of Passiano. Among those in attendance was Commendatre Guidi Avelliano, mayor of Cava. Thousands of people lined the streets, cheering and clapping hands all along the way. The procession ended in the town's social hall, where a banquet was spread for family and friends.

Despite what their father instructed them, Nina's sisters Amelia, Carmelina, Cristina, and Angelina, respectively 12, 9, 5, and 3, tried desperately to enter the social hall but were turned away by the police. The four sisters walked home hand in hand, holding back tears. The vast crowd frightened them. They had never seen so many people. I can't imagine how difficult this would've been for my aunts. They'd lost their mother and were about to lose their sister, who they called Mom. So those little girls walked home hand in hand in their shabby clothes and tear-stained faces.

My mother's frustration toward her father overshadowed the whole day. He had forced her to marry, wouldn't let her visit her mother's grave before the wedding, and had banned her sisters. Of course, she was pleased that all the flowers from the wedding were tucked into a wagon and brought to her mother's grave, but I don't believe that appeased her seething anger.

During the banquet, Mom was subjected to a barrage of questions from friends and reporters: "Are you happy?" "When do you leave for America?" There were countless other questions. She did not answer but only smiled. My parents escaped by taking the horse and buggy to Pompeii, where they were to spend their honeymoon.

Taking the horse and buggy to Pompeii for a honeymoon

Returning from Pompeii, they were asked to go to Rome to be screen-tested for a movie about their courtship and marriage. They spent seventeen days in Rome, consumed with screen tests and script development. The couple lodged in a Roman hotel.

Rome was full of many firsts for my mother. She had never stayed in a hotel, never seen an actual bathtub, and never used bottled shampoo. At home, she washed once a week in a barrel and put aside a small bucket of water for cleaning later. She was usually the first to go in the barrel because she was the cleanest, and then they all had to share the same water. For shampoo, like her mother, she made a concoction of boiled ashes, lemons, and flowers that she would wash her hair with once a week. When she saw the hotel's marble bathtub, she couldn't wait for her bath. As she disrobed and climbed into the tub, she noticed the ceiling painted with beautiful artwork of angels and people. One stared straight at her, making her uncomfortable, adding to an experience she would never forget.

Sergio Corbucci, an Italian filmmaker, penned a script. During their stay in Rome, the production company snapped hundreds of pictures of the couple, making Mom feel like a movie star. The Pope wanted to meet the couple, and a meeting was set up. Unfortunately, the driver hired to take them to the Vatican never showed up. My father was very disappointed. At the end of seventeen days, George and Nina were sent back to Cava as the filmmakers needed to raise money.

Unfortunately, the film was never shot. Sergio Corbucci was yet to be successful in 1951, but he went on to become famous for his Spaghetti Westerns in the 1960s, including Django. My mother brought the movie script with her to America. I think she hoped she would meet someone famous who could produce it. Some of the script was in English, but most was in Italian. I read what I could and realized that it was all a fabrication and that the true story wasn't there. Even faced with fame and fortune, my father wasn't willing to reveal the truth of how he'd been duped.

Nina and George continued waiting for Nina's paperwork to be processed so she could come to America. They had to go to Naples several times to transport documents to the American Embassy. The state department needed to approve her paperwork before she could sail to America with my father.

My parents were both staying with my mother's step-grandmother. After a month or more, my mother didn't feel well, bleeding so profusely that the family sent for the doctor, believing she had a miscarriage. When the doctor examined Nina, he found she was just having a bad period and was still a virgin. No one had explained the facts of life to her. She'd been afraid to let my father touch her. Of course, my grandmother had lied to my father years ago, insisting in letters that she'd explained everything about sex to her daughter. Now, Dad feared frightening his new bride, with whom he could hardly communicate. At this point, my dad must've been very frustrated with all the lies he had been told.

Upon realizing this, Nina's aunt explained everything to her and insisted that once Nina had sex, she should wipe herself with a clean rag to show her mother-in-law that she'd been a virgin.

About four months after they were married, my dad finally tried to consummate the marriage. When I asked my mother about her first time, she only said she didn't love my father, which made it difficult. Our conversation was awkward, discussing such a private topic, and she was unwilling to share many details, only that it was painful. She did as she was told and saved her blood-stained rag to take to America as was the custom.

Dad had a lot of time on his hands. However, he relished the company of Mom's Uncle Antonio and went with him most mornings. They'd hitch up a wagon and go to Salerno for supplies. Since the family owned a grocery store, Antonio needed to visit the wholesale warehouse to purchase flour, rice, beans, and bread. Two friends of Antonio's lived above the family's store, and the men included Dad when they played cards. Dad loved to play cards and made friends easily, which was different from his norm.

My father's love for playing cards was another thing I never knew about him. I love games, and to think I could've shared that with my dad was another little stab to my soul. But my mother hated playing cards, so it appears my dad just let it go. Italians are primarily extroverts, always laughing, singing, and dancing. Dad was a hero to them, and they accepted him just the way he was. He didn't have to make much conversation, not knowing the language, and no one noticed he was a bit shy.

To Mom, even though she didn't love him, Dad must've been her Prince Charming. As the newspapers described him, he was handsome, bringing her hope of a new life. She had felt just like Cinderella, as the newspapers portrayed. Her life was still brimming with chores, cooking, cleaning, and taking care of her sisters as it had been ever since her mother had taken ill over three years ago, but now there was a promise of something more. Of course, she would never admit this. Later in life, her sisters would repeatedly ask her why she had left them. How could she say that she wanted to? Over time, I think the mantra she told them, that she'd been a victim and didn't want to leave them, became a part of her reality.

This was probably one of the best times in my parents'

lives. Dad was amazed at how everyone just wanted to be in his company. So many were thrilled just to get a glimpse of him. I again studied the many pictures of Mom and Dad. On the cover of Tempo magazine, she looked so confident. What happened to the scared little girl? The constant attention from the media had utterly changed her in only a few short months. Dad was still very shy; I don't know if the attention changed him at all.

Since their wedding, my parents were constantly invited to dinner. Many influential families in Cava sought the pair out to spend time with them. Their social calendar was always full.

Dad also tried painstakingly teaching Mom English since she hadn't learned any during those years that her mother and later Domenico and her father had written to my dad. Mom had not been motivated, thinking my father would never come for her. I'm sure my grandmother thought that he would want her little Nina if she could just get him to Italy. So, grandmother lied and lied in order to make it all happen.

The newspapers said my father was concerned with how the Italians viewed him. They saw him as a knight in shining armor and a war hero. Everyone, including the Farano family, had difficulty believing he wasn't a hero in America, where he lived in New Bedford. Italian women pressed studio portraits into his hands and pleaded with him to get them published in American papers where they might find husbands. Italians were convinced he lived in a country where milk and honey flowed freely. He tried to explain real life in the United States but was constantly interrupted with questions about skyscrapers, fancy cars, and movie stars. Nevertheless, he remained optimistic that my mother would adjust to her new life in America.

Mom's family adored Dad. He'd become very attached to all of them. Five-year-old Cristina was especially fond of Dad. She followed him around, hanging on to his leg at times. They often went to the grocery store, hand in hand, where Dad would buy her cherries. Cristina was hoping the couple would take her with them to America. The sisters were all hoping for that, but it would be twenty years before they would see their big sister again. The festive time was ending, and soon the couple would be leaving.

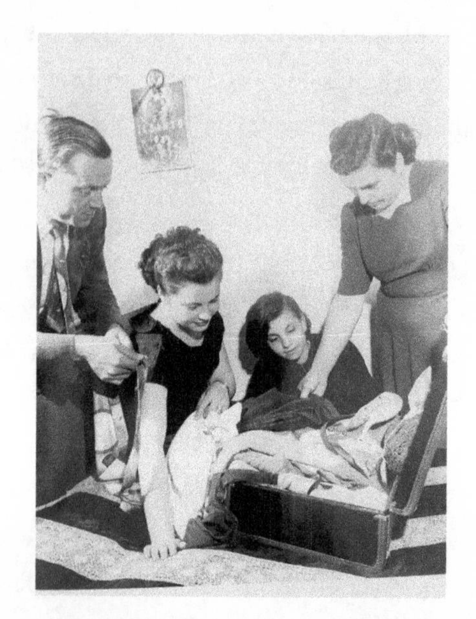

Packing for the trip to America

TWENTY

My parents departed Italy on September 18, 1951, on the Greek passenger ship Nea Hellas. Numbness consumed Mom as she stood at the rail, thinking about the distance that would soon separate her from her family. Mom was sick with worry for her four sisters, but her father had given her no choice but to go with the American. Looking out across the water, she worried that her 12-year-old sister, Amelia, would be overwhelmed by all her new responsibilities. Now, it would be up to Amelia to draw the water from the well; my mom feared she might fall in. Her youngest sister, Angelina, would now live with her aunt.

She didn't cry as she told me this part of the story, and I wondered if she'd been excited enough about her new adventure to erase some of her worries. Since her mother got sick when she was 14, she'd been taking care of her family. She washed, cleaned, and cooked constantly. But, to me, it seemed like Cinderella, rescued by her Prince, to live a better life.

As she stood on the deck of the Nea Hellas, she realized her new husband had disappeared. She panicked among so many strangers and started to cry. As she wiped her tears, she scanned the crowd for him. Standing several feet away, he was watching her.

What was he thinking? All the excitement was over; reality was setting in. Was he worried he'd made a mistake? What I'd been discovering about my father thus far was that he always kept his promises. I'm sure he knew she was his destiny, and he would try to make the most of it, but he must've had reservations. I wonder if he thought of the many women he'd dated and wondered if one of them would've been a better choice.

Mom was seasick during the entire voyage. The newlyweds slept in separate cabins. Since every cabin had two sets of bunk beds for four people, only families could stay in the same cabin. Dad didn't especially mind, as the ship had an award-winning Greek restaurant and bakery, plus he made friends to play cards with. Poor Mom felt abandoned during the entire voyage. She complained to the Ships doctor about her absent husband, but he could do nothing but feel sorry for her. She also befriended the family in the cabin next door, who also pitied her. After asking her about the voyage, I googled the Nea Hellas. I found the cabins were tiny. As she said, there were two sets of bunk beds with very little room in between and no chair. Three strangers would've been staying in that room with my mother. How could she complain about my dad eating in the dining room and playing cards with friends? What in the world would he have done in that tiny little room where he had nowhere even to sit? They could barely even communicate with each other. But she was very young and probably scared.

I suspect her immaturity in the early part of their marriage influenced why she saw herself as the only victim and never understood how my father was affected by the situation. Over time, I believe that feeling of victimhood morphed into her role in their relationship, a role that she never let go of. Perhaps if she had read his letters early in their marriage, she would've understood that he was just as much of a victim as she was, and she would have softened toward him, but she never did, and she never changed her opinion.

The Nea Hellas steered into New York Harbor on October 2, 1951, sixteen days after leaving Italy. The two stood at the rail as Dad pointed out the Statue of Liberty. Dad told her people could walk up to the torch, but she didn't believe him.

At the dock, George's parents, his brother Rene, and sister-in-law Francis were waiting to pick them up. Mom's dark eyes darted around. Everything looked so much newer, bigger, brighter, and louder. They stopped for coffee at Dad's cousin's house in Union City, N.J., then drove to New Bedford, MA.

Mom's eyes were glued to the window and the wonders that passed by. She had never seen wooden houses before, and the wide roads were six times the size of Passiano's main cobblestone road. And all the cars! There were only three cars in Passiano, and only the wealthiest families had them. In America, there seemed to be no end to them. When they pulled into the driveway of my grandparents' house, Mom was impressed by the neat green shingle cottage. In the kitchen, she opened the refrigerator and gasped at all the fresh food inside. She was amazed to see the television and afraid to touch its screen. The whole family gathered at the Fortin house to welcome Nina. The local newspaper following the couple documented that George felt anxious and wanted everyone to leave so he could have her to himself, take her for a ride in his car, and maybe for some ice cream.

Nina admiring Dad's car

Nina learning how to turn on the TV

Nina in front of her mother-in-laws home admiring the neighborhood

She went outside to see Dad's car and loved the chrome and red radiator cap. She told Dad that she wanted to learn how to drive. She even fell in love with Grandmother's dinette set with its gleaming chrome legs. At the time, she spoke very few words of English, but she learned to say "so nice" and must've said "so nice" a hundred times. The town planned a party for my parents. Everyone was so thrilled to meet my dad's little darling. Of course, the media loved them in New Bedford as well. There was article upon article printed about them in numerous American newspapers.

The couple settled in, living with my grandparents. Dad went back to work in the mill as a weaver, and Mom watched a lot of television, trying to learn English. Television turned out to be a skillful teacher, with Hopalong Cassidy, The Cisco Kid, and I Love Lucy as her role models.

Mom and Dad rented a house on Lafayette Street the following year, and Mom got a job in a garment factory. She loved to sew but wasn't crazy about sewing in the factory. She'd thought Dad had money and she wouldn't have to work. He was honest in his letters, but of course, she hadn't read them, and even her parents ignored how hard he said he worked. Unfortunately, Dad making her go to work in a factory was something she complained about for the rest of her life. I tried to explain to her that Dad had spent everything he had on going to get her, but she refused to understand.

One day, she made a nightgown from some fabric her mother-in-law gave her. She attached white lace to the edges and was very proud of it. She put it on that Friday night and waited for her husband to return. When he arrived home, she sat on his lap and kissed him. He was tired after his long day of working on his damaged feet and pushed her off and told her that if he wanted her, he would come to her. I've heard this story many times, and it always upsets me. If that was her main complaint in over 70 years, Dad couldn't have done much else to criticize. Mom tends to hold on to stuff way longer than she should, which causes pain to herself and those around her. I've tried numerous times to get her just to let go of stuff and be more positive. Many times, those conversations ended with her being irritated with me.

In March, Mom became pregnant with me and was frightened because she didn't know the first thing about how the baby would maneuver through the birth canal. With everything her family had gone through, nobody had told her about the birth process. Nature took over anyway, and I was born on November 18, 1953. I was named Adela Christina Fortin after my grandmother.

In 1954, my parents purchased a new house for about nine thousand dollars: two bedrooms, a single bath, and 768 square feet. They loved their new little place. Dad painted shutters, and Mom made curtains. Soon after they bought their house, my grandfather, Giovanni, was able to immigrate from Italy to America and live with my parents. He left his little girls behind in the care of Joseph to make way for them all to come to America.

Mom prepared to become an American citizen and took the oath on March 18, 1955. Soon, she became pregnant again, and George Junior was born on February 4, 1956. Already, their little house was too crowded. Dad was having trouble finding his father-in-law work.

Giovanni questioned his daughter, "What am I doing here? If I had known your husband had no money, I would never have let you marry him or come here."

Mom's stomach churned. She felt like slapping her father because she had never wanted to leave her sisters. But they were both here now, and she resolved that it must have been their fate. They would make the best of it. After all, her children would have a better life here. I know my mom struggled to get along with her father. She felt he always drank too much and was sure he had cheated on her mother. But, I think she kept the peace for the sake of her sisters. My grandfather was a fantastic carpenter. He could make almost anything out of wood. Most of what money my grandfather made he sent to his family in Italy. But my mother told me that every time she looked at her father, she saw her mother's tears.

Uncle Leo, my father's brother, had moved to California years earlier and encouraged my parents to follow. He bragged to my father that there were many more opportunities there. Since Dad had always entertained fantasies of the good life on the West Coast, he hatched a plan.

TWENTY-ONE

My parents started planning to move cross-country to California. They sold their little house and moved back in with Dad's parents. In August 1956, Dad and his father-in-law started the long drive to California to find a place to settle while the rest of us waited at home. Dad and Grandfather slept in the car each night to save money during their long journey. It couldn't have been a very relaxing trip.

This was a challenging time for Dad. Not only did he have to worry about finding work, but he also had to search for a job for his father-in-law. As I had learned, Dad's word was binding; he would help the Farano family to the best of his abilities. He also fretted about where his family was going to live. It was not easy for my father to impose upon my Uncle Leo. He yearned for a job and home as soon as possible.

There were six letters from September 18, 1956, to October 27, 1956, until my mom, brother, and I flew over in November. I'm sure my grandmother read the letters to my mother as she could not read English.

September 18, 1956

Dear Nina and Mom,

Pop and I have been here three days now and miss you all. I filled out an application at North American Aviation and now I am waiting until they need me. As for Pop we found a cabinet place that needed a good man and Pop was just the man they needed. But when I told him he couldn't speak English he said he couldn't hire him. They were going to pay about $2.32 an hour. Tomorrow we will speak with a man at the Carpenters' Local Union who might be able to place him in a cabinet shop with Italians, and who knows, I might work with him, and we could travel together. Because if he works in one place and I work in another place 20 miles away or on a different shift, that will not do unless he can travel with someone here, and that is hard.

Rachel and Leo are doing the best they can to help us find work. There is an Italian Club near L.A. It might be a good idea if Pop joined up. Then he could speak Italian with them and find out more about work of his type.

I'm getting a little familiar now with this place. When you use the Santa Ana Freeway there is nothing to it. As long as I stay to the right of the road. It has been in the 90's since we arrived here but it is due to slacken off a bit soon.

We had a wonderful trip across the States. But

I don't advise you, Mom, to come here by car with my wife and kids. Some stretches through the desert are almost 50 miles long without anything from one place to another except a gas station, motel and a few houses. And traveling in the desert in mid afternoon is awfully hot. I'm as brown as a Mexican now. We were in the mountains too in Nevada and the roads were curves and hills. It was dangerous. We saw accidents that happened in the mountains. A trailer truck jack-knifed, a car went over the cliff and another trailer run off the road and it's load of sacks was burning up. Pop was good all the way up but after the accidents he was a little nervous. He kept telling me to take it easy and watch the speed limits.

The houses here are pretty nice and they are roomy. The kitchens are beautiful But I still miss my little house, maybe because I worked so much around it to make it look beautiful. The bathrooms are really nice here. Moving the refrigerator and the heavy parlor set here would be throwing money away. Because Leo got his refrigerator at wholesale and it's almost twice as big as ours and it has the latest features. Maybe if we sold our parlor set and refrigerator we could get back most of our money although a lot of people still bring their old furniture here from back east.

Nina, don't forget your father's Alien registration card with his picture and number on it, because he has to have it to go to work here. He will have his social security card soon.

Nina and Mom, how are the kids? I miss them very much and I miss you very much. It makes it much harder for me when you're not here. But who knows maybe we will be all together soon. After two weeks, if we don't get anything we are going back to New Bedford and try to find work in Connecticut.

The weather is wonderful for outside work. There is outside work year round because it never gets too cold. I am wasting a lot of time trying to get Nina's father a job first but I have my little family to think about too.

Take good care of yourself , Nina, and don't overwork yourself. I know you because you are always trying to do too much when you could leave some work for the next day.

And don't worry about me everybody is trying to help us.

God bless you Mom, Pop, Nina, and children. I love you very much, Nina

Your father gives his regards.

P.S. If you get mail from Italy send it to him because he is worrying about them over there because your brother has all the load on his shoulders to take care of your sisters.

Dad continued to stress and worry. He wasn't sure he had made the right decision but was determined to try his best to find jobs for himself and his father-in-law. It amazed me that he started immediately trying to find work for the two of them without even taking time to recuperate from his journey. We are so very spoiled today and don't realize it.

September 31, 1956

Dear Nina and Mom,

We're getting along fine here. Your father received his social security card. He is not working yet. He might start next week with me. And when he starts we may be able to buy a house together. We saw a house and we both liked it. It had a beautiful big front yard and it is on a corner. Not far from where Leo lives. For most of these houses I have to make $100.00 a week in order to buy one but if your father buys it with me we'll be all right. All he wants to do is send about $10.00 a week to Italy and the rest of his pay, he wants to put on the house. But I want him to put some in the bank so he can have his house later on and send for your sisters.

Nina, try to bring everything you can like the lawn mower, rack, shovel, little hand tools and all those little things because we need them and we'll only have to buy them here. The washing machine will be alright to bring here too.

We are getting to like it here more and more every day. The people here are all so nice. Your father came with me at the place where I work. He stayed all morning and then I brought him back home at noon. And besides he goes to the California High School now. He wants to learn English. He can say a lot of words now.

Nina, be careful for yourself don't try to do too much at once when you're packing to move. Do a little at a time. Because if you do to much you will get run down. I wish Pop was here he could get a job as a carpenter. They get $3.00 an hour and they are building so many houses here all over. Maybe I can get in the Carpenters' Union and make that much too. But I don't know too much about carpenter work. I didn't know too much about cabinet work either and I am in a cabinet shop. It cost $150.00 to get in the Carpenters' Union but after you're in they find you plenty of work. They work winter and summer on houses. There are no slack periods in winter here like there is in the Northeast. There is so much work here it is fascinating. And all the traffic on the Santa Ana Freeway in the morning at 8:00 a.m. The cars are bumper to bumper going to Los Angeles. But if I could get a good job in Los Angeles with your father I don't think I should mind that. Where Leo works there are a lot of industries and he will look around for something for us while I am still working at this place. I like it here and it is so close to Leo's home but I've got to make more money if I want to buy a good house. There are a lot of good jobs that don't require any experience but some are far about 20 or 30 miles or more and that probably would not pay us.

It gets dark here now about 5 o'clock. We turned our clocks back one hour. All this week, the temperature at about noon will be in the 90's. What nice weather for October. We are feeling better now your father and I. We are eating very good at Rachel's. She puts out some nice meals. And I always have an appetite to eat. It must be the California air. Nina, Adela and Junior I am dying to see them. Adela must talk so much about me now. I hope God brings us together soon.

Give our regards to the family. All my love to you Nina and the children.

Love, George and Pop

My grandfather had been taking English classes at the local high school. One night my father went to the high school to pick him up. He discovered his father-in-law on the curb. Grandfather had decided it was too hard to learn English and didn't want to attend school any longer. He was embarrassed to tell my father. I'm sure his learning was hampered by the fact he couldn't read or write Italian, much less English.

As Mom prepared for the move at home, Dad continued to struggle to find grandfather work. Grandfather thought he should return to Connecticut, where there were more Italians, which must've frustrated Dad.

In a letter dated Oct. 10, 1956, Dad had finally found work for Grandfather with two other Italians making $1.50 an hour. Dad was applying for other jobs, and at that time, he had his application in at the B.F. Goodrich Company, where he would eventually work for the next 19 years.

At the end of the letter, he had sweet sentiments for his family, "Hurry up, Nina and come out here. I think you'll like it very much. The kids look big in their pictures, especially Junior. Boy am I proud of them! I hope everything goes fine and I get another job soon with more money!"

In a letter a few days later, he confirmed that Grandfather was a new man now that he was finally working. He was able to send some money to Joseph in Italy. Dad quit the job he had been working at the trailer place and joined Grandfather at his job.

They had put a binder down on a house, which Dad was very excited about and hoped that Nina wouldn't be disappointed.

October 27, 1956

Dear Mom and Nina,

We are very happy to know that Nina and the children will leave Sunday. I think it is best that way to come by plane. Because if you come by car it will take at least two weeks. I came in five days because we didn't waste time sleeping and eating along the road. And when we got here we were really tired you have nice roads and with the map and booklet with the route you can't go wrong. But here in Arizona and Nevada it is rough going thru the mountains. But it is only for a while. If you should decide to come by car you will have to take it easy and gas up often in some spots because gas stations are further apart in some places. But I don't think you have too much to worry about. And check your oil every 500 miles.

You know, Mom, I made about over 500 miles a day. And that is too much for us and the poor car. If you make 250 miles a day you will be doing good.I hope you make a good decision one way or the other. We would like to have you here with us. Well Mom, you know what to do now it is up to you.

I have

$603.21 in bank I will give Nina $250.00

$547.00 cash Down payment $350.00

$1,150.21 total Furniture movers $536.00

Total $1,136.00

I am sending Nina $250.00 come by plane or car. Cabins or Motels for two people is $7—$5 or less. I forgot how much it cost me for the whole trip. About $150.00. It might cost you less or more. And there is so much to see by car. You will meet a lot of traffic at times. When you are driving don't let Nina or the kids distract you. With Pop we didn't talk much and it was fine that way. You have to watch the roads all the time. Watch the route numbers. I took the wrong roads a few times. One time I went 35 miles on the wrong road. And I had to come 35 miles back on my route again. I lost two hours doing that.

We are happier now than we were two weeks ago. I had so much on my mind about Pop getting work here, about selling the house in New Bedford, and buying one here. And trying to put two and two together. And not trying to put one thing ahead of another. Now things are going much smoother. We go to the Escrow Office

Tuesday night and if everything goes O.K. they give us the keys for the house and we move in. When we move in we will let you know how we are progressing. Pop wants to buy a bed. And when you arrive we will arrange to buy the other things we need.

So keep your fingers crossed that everything goes OK. I talked to the Escrow Officer on the phone and he said that you will have to sign some papers for the house. But I will let you know about that as soon as I know definitely.

God Bless you all and keep you.

Your loving husband George, and your father.

Kiss the kids for us. Our love to Mom and Pop

We came by plane soon after Dad's last letter. Unfortunately, the escrow had fallen through, and we rented a place for six months until we bought a lovely house within walking distance of Uncle Leo's. Brand new, it sat on a nice lot, all 1,288 square feet. Dad and Mom were very content with their new home and enjoyed fixing it up. They took a lot of pride in their house as the outside and inside were meticulous.

Dad always kept his promises, so as soon as we were settled, he started the paperwork to bring Mom's sisters to America. But the process stalled when Mom's next oldest sister, Amelia, decided to marry a local boy in Cava. The sisters were growing up and seemed to have little interest in moving to America.

Dad was on a mission to get a better job to care for his family. So he took little three-year-old me with him to the B.F. Goodrich factory to fill out another application. While he filled out the paperwork, the office girls watched me. Apparently, I was his lucky charm because he was offered a position on the night shift. Tire building was a physically challenging job, but it was steady work that paid relatively well. He built tires, standing at a machine all night. His injured feet hurt standing for so many hours, but Dad never missed work, picking up overtime whenever he could and never complaining. Working nights meant that I rarely saw him. Mom told me he worked nights so he wouldn't have to be with us, but I knew that wasn't true; at least, I chose not to believe it.

Grandpa lived in Los Angeles during the week, where he had a job building furniture. Dad would pick him up and bring him home for the weekends. He sent most of his money home to his family in Italy. Grandpa was a master woodworker and kept all his tools in our garage. He spoke broken English, but he and Dad seemed to get along fine. Saturdays and Sundays, my dad would limp out and help him create the furniture they were making for our home. They'd made the built-in table in my mom's pink kitchen, new living room furniture, and a fancy oblong dining room table.

We were by no means rich, but Dad had it in his mind that he wanted a beautiful piece of art for our house, so he tried his hand at painting. Since he couldn't afford to buy one, he started his own. He bought canvas and pulled it tight on a board. Then, copying from a book, he drew the Last Supper. I thought it looked amazingly like the original. I was in awe. He attempted to fill in his drawing with oil paint but never finished it.

TWENTY-TWO

Mom made many friends in the neighborhood whom she socialized with often. Every year, the community took turns hosting a New Year's Eve Party. In 1963, when I was 10 years old, it was my parents' turn to throw the party. While my parents sometimes had a few friends over for dinner or hosted family holidays, this was the only party I can remember my parents ever having. But it was terrific. Dad moved all the machines and tools to the rear of the garage, then tacked paper on the walls, transforming the garage into a beautiful, festive room. They hung balloons and streamers from the ceiling. My most vivid memory of the evening was Mom singing Al Di La for everyone to enjoy. She sang so beautifully and had no problem singing in front of a crowd. I envied her ease in front of people. At the time, I was in awe of my beautiful mother and wondered why I couldn't be that brave. After her song, my brother and I were rushed off to bed, but we could still hear laughing and singing as we drifted off to sleep.

A few months later, Mom's friend Alice, a pleasant, red-haired lady from down the street, came over. They sat at our kitchen table, drinking coffee and gossiping about the neighborhood. I didn't want Mom complaining about me, so I walked swiftly to my room, hoping not to attract any attention. The previous week, she'd embarrassed me, making me stand in front of Alice and spell the words I'd missed on my recent spelling test. Then, just out of sight, I stopped to listen to their conversation.

"Oh, Nina! I brought you this book," Alice said. A book? I'd never seen my mom read anything."

"It's all the rage," Alice continued, digging around in her purse. "Here it is, Peyton Place. Have you read it?"

"No, I'm so busy," my mother answered.

"You must make time for this one. It's actually banned in some places; it's so scandalous."

Mom took the book as if she would read it, but I knew better.

Later, after Alice had left, I spotted Peyton Place lying on the counter. I didn't know what scandalous meant, but I wanted to find out. The current book I was reading would have to wait. I grabbed the book and headed for my room. I was in for an awakening.

"Indian summer is like a woman. Ripe, hotly passionate, but fickle, she comes and goes as she pleases so that one is never sure whether she will come at all, nor for how long she will stay," the book began.

I had so many questions. What did hotly passionate

mean? Was my mom hotly passionate? I had heard people call her sexy; maybe that was what it meant. But I didn't know what sexy meant either. This was like nothing I had ever read before. As a ten-year-old this book wasn't meant for me, but how else would I learn about life? I kept reading. I could only understand half of the story, but half was enough for me.

The men in this book liked breasts, although I didn't know why. My friend Shari constantly rubbed her chest, hoping her breasts would grow. She knew they were as she could feel some bumps there. I didn't have any bumps. In this book, breasts seemed pretty important, so I hoped mine would grow. I wondered what I would look like when I grew up. I was undecided as to whether I wanted big breasts.

I skimmed the pages I couldn't understand. Then I came across Norman peeking through the bushes at a couple undressing each other and doing strange things. Norman was shocked and backed away from the bushes, and ran home. I felt like Norman as I quickly shut the book and stuck it under the bed in fear of what I had just read. I hoped God wouldn't be mad at me for reading such things. It seemed grown-ups had lots of secrets I knew nothing about. Had my parents done stuff like that? My mom was now pregnant, and from conversations with Shari, I had a vague idea that had something to do with making babies. I certainly didn't want to grow up if that was expected of me. Maybe I just wouldn't have any kids. I wished I could talk to my parents about all this, but that wasn't the kind of thing we talked about.

Now, as an adult, I think about my dad asking for the

birds and the bees to be explained to my mother and how they never were. Did he ever think about making sure I understood those things? Or was he just too closed up to consider it at that point? And how could Mom let me learn all these things on my own? Hadn't her own experience taught her anything?

Back then, Mom wasn't handling her pregnancy very well. Our family friend, Aunt Helen, came over to help Mom while she was ill. I was supposed to go to a birthday party that afternoon and was so excited. Aunt Helen made me a hamburger for lunch. I'd developed an aversion to meat, which she was unaware of. I tried to eat it but gagged and couldn't finish my meal. The adults yelled at me and told me I wouldn't be going to the birthday party. I'm sure my refusal was so hard for my mother to understand; she had actually suffered starvation, but of course, I didn't see the whole picture at that age. I ran in tears to my fort, questioning why life had to be so hard when I really tried to be good.

My fort was my retreat from trouble, and I used it often. My dad had let me have the cardboard boxes from our new washer and dryer. I can still recall the musty scent of the boxes mixed with the sweet smell of the grass and eucalyptus bark. My blue blanket hanging over the opening shaded me from the sun, outlined through the fibers. I would sit and wonder about God. Where was he? I wanted him to explain things to me. Sure, he must be watching somewhere; I'd lie down on the musty blanket and pillow and contemplate life. So many tears escaped my eyes on those lonely days. I felt like no one truly knew me or cared to know me. Sometimes, I felt like screaming, "I'm here, and I'm worthwhile. Know me, speak to me, hear me". But I was just a little girl and didn't know how to make such feelings known, even if anyone would have listened.

TWENTY-THREE

Two years later, in 1965, we moved to a new house in Diamond Bar, and I started Junior High in Walnut, California. Grandpa had moved back to Italy the year before, which made life for my father a little easier since he would no longer have to drive Grandfather back and forth to Los Angeles every weekend. My younger brother Alan was two years old, and my parents were in awe of this curly-haired bundle of joy. Alan gave me a new purpose, and I enjoyed caring for him whenever Mom allowed me to.

Being in a new school meant I could start over, or that was what I hoped. These new kids didn't know me. So why couldn't I be different? I had high hopes as I walked down the halls of my new school. That year, I aimed to try and make friends, but I couldn't get past my fear that no one would like me. Shari had liked me, but I doubted I would ever see her again, which left a hole in my life. I had to change, but instead of coming out of my shell, I retreated further inside my fears and low self-esteem. The loneliness I had always felt when I was younger was still there and wouldn't be going away anytime soon.

When I became a parent myself, it became clear to me that all parents struggle to know how to raise their children and balance their frustration with understanding how and when to discipline. By the time I had children, the expectations of parenting had changed drastically from when I was a child. The standards of the 50s and 60s, coupled with the trauma both my parents had experienced, created a situation that left me frequently feeling lonely and misunderstood. We have more understanding of many things now than when my parents were raising me. Layered on top of all those issues were cultural differences. As a child, things always seemed unfair.

That Thanksgiving, my mom invited some friends from the same part of Italy that she was from. They came for the day as they drove over an hour from Encino. Their daughter Louise and I gravitated to each other because we were the same age. We decided to take my brother George's bike out for a joy ride. We left him screaming after us in the driveway as we headed down the hill with a burst of energy. We didn't get very far before we crashed. Louise barely got hurt, but I went flying over the handlebars. I broke my arm and cracked open my chin. Blood was everywhere as my dad scooped me up in his arms and put me in the car with Mom close behind. I remember watching my father from my emergency room bed as he stood in the doorway. He was sobbing as he watched me. I'd never seen him have such an outpouring of emotion. Of course, I always knew he cared but never saw much tenderness from him. Those tears I watched him shed meant the world to me; even as a child, I knew they were an expression of his love.

Things settled down after my accident, and Mom got a job across the street, cleaning model homes. She loved socializing, and people coming through the models were easy targets. She ended up being the reason why several families bought homes in our neighborhood. That experience prompted her to apply for her Real Estate license several years later. The man who sold us our house became a good friend of the family and helped my mom study. This was a challenging task for Mom.

By this time, Mom spoke English really well. She just had trouble reading and writing it. To pass her Real Estate exam, she had her doctor write a note requesting more time for the test. They said because of her thalassemia, which she had been diagnosed with as a child in Italy, she tired easily. That extra time gave her just what she needed to pass the exam. As a realtor, she compensated by having her clients fill out their deposit receipts and paperwork.

She absolutely loved selling Real Estate. She was the happiest I had ever seen her. Going to work gave her confidence and purpose. She made lots of friends, and her clients absolutely loved her. Mom made enough money to buy her car and help Dad with some household expenses. In later years, she helped him pay off the house. She was very successful, especially considering what she had to overcome.

TWENTY-FOUR

I was 18, a freshman in college, living in the dorm at Southern California College in Newport Beach, when my mom approached me with the idea of taking me to Italy. It sounded exciting, and I loved the idea of seeing where my roots started. My relationship with my mom at this point was good. She was pleased with herself and what she had accomplished in real estate. She couldn't wait to see her family again and was very excited about our trip. It would have been nice if she could have taken Dad, but they were already at the point where she was embarrassed to go anywhere with him.

Mom booked our flight for June 10, 1972. We would be gone for six weeks. I was a little nervous about being gone so long in a country where I didn't speak the language, but Mom reassured me it would be fine. It was a very long flight to Rome. My mom is five foot with short dark hair, big brown eyes, and lovely legs, which she always showed off in short skirts. I was five foot five with longer, lovely legs, long blonde hair, and large blue eyes like my dad. We didn't look like mother and daughter; we looked like two friends on holiday. That may be why Italian men had no problem approaching me and flirting. I received my first marriage proposal at Leonardo da Vinci International Airport in Rome from a dark-haired, beautiful boy who followed me around the airport. Apparently, Italians still considered America the land of milk and honey and were willing to marry a stranger to get there.

Zio Mateo and Zia Cristina picked us up from the airport and drove us to Naples for my first night in Italy. Besides all the looks I was getting from Italian boys, the first thing I noticed was the crazy drivers. They would just honk and go! I was holding on for dear life as my Zio drove us around. My Zio and Zia had a beautiful apartment in the heart of Naples. We went to dinner that night at a wonderful pizzeria. They used a salty fish paste in their pizza that I loved. My blond hair and blue eyes drew attention everywhere we went. My relatives decided they would have to keep a close eye on me.

We drove to Cava de Terrini the next day. It was rural and like nothing I had ever seen. The timelessness of Italy struck me. I didn't believe much had changed since my mother left twenty years before. Unlike America's rapid progress, change came slowly in Italy. Churches and icons have been there for centuries, not just decades. The countryside was dotted with olive trees, fig trees, and many beautiful gardens. Walking the dusty cobblestone streets, my sandaled feet were quickly dirty, and I was always looking for a place to wash them.

I was eager to get to my grandfather's house as I missed him and hadn't seen him in many years. We climbed five flights of stairs to reach his flat. It was small but clean, with pasta sauce cooking on the stove. I had to hurry and wash up as the water would be shut off at 2:00 p.m. They had been rationing water for years, but at least my mom and her siblings didn't have to go to the well with buckets like they used to.

Grandfather was very protective and hardly took his eyes off me. He had a soft spot for me, and I could sense his pride when he looked at me. He'd grown much older but still strode rapidly like he always had. There was no leaving him behind as he followed me around, keeping a close eye when we walked the town, maybe just like he had watched my mother when she was being saved for my dad.

I marveled at the village. How many people had come and gone along those cobblestone roads? How many stories, how many steps? I thought about my mother there, all those years ago, walking to the well or running for the trees' safety during the war. Then my father walked those same paths. I could imagine the first time my parents had laid eyes on each other, the pretty little girl and the handsome American soldier. My mother so long ago, and then twenty years later, the same person, yet someone else entirely. I looked at her in her short skirt with pantyhose and white high-heeled sandals. She had short dark hair and a large smile, oozing with the confidence she didn't have when she was young. If there hadn't been a war and if she hadn't been shielded from other young people to be saved for the American soldier, she might have been less shy. The same person with the same history, but she seemed to have morphed into someone else totally. It gave me hope that, at some point, I would do the same, leaving my insecure self by the wayside to grow into someone new.

After my mom's twenty-year absence, the townspeople were delighted to have her back. Handmade posters, with pictures of my mom and I, hung from the trees and buildings proclaiming their angel had returned. A story and photos were published in the local paper. I found myself an instant celebrity, which would have been more fun if I could have understood what people were saying.

We had many dinner invitations, and I met so many people I couldn't communicate with. They were all so thrilled to see us. My mom glowed with all the attention like she must have had 20 years before.

I thought of my grandmother as we walked the cobblestone streets in Cava. Mom pointed out the store that Mama Lucia used to own. I'd heard the name as a child. She used to sell my grandmother's fine needlepoint and embroidery. Mom had spent many hours there with her mother and sisters. We also owned a book about her, which included the story of my parent's wedding.

Several days later, while waiting for the bus to take us to the ferry to the Island of Capri, by chance, my mom spotted Mama Lucia in person. She ran to her in tears. Mama Lucia was on her way to church, as was her custom. I watched them hug from across the street. Unfortunately, she didn't have much time; the bus was approaching. I yelled at my mom to hurry. She walked quickly back, stopping for one last wave at Mama Lucia. She was emotional as she told me how glad she was that she had the opportunity to embrace and chat with the dear woman.

As the bus bumped along on the way to Capri, my mother told me the story of Lucia Apicella, Mama Lucia. She was a kind woman to my grandmother, our family, and everyone she encountered. After the war, she had witnessed a scene where children were kicking the skull of a German soldier. That night, she dreamed of dead soldiers begging her to return them to their mothers. So, after the war in 1946, Lucia began her quest to find as many sons to return to their mothers as she could. Most of the soldiers she returned were German, which sparked controversy and backlash. No matter what anyone said to her or who got in her way, she always replied to them, "sono tutti figli di una madre." They're all sons of a mother. She walked along the hillsides each day in the early morning hours, scanning the ground for remains. Any bones she found, she cleaned and placed in zinc boxes, sometimes traveling to dangerous areas to pick up the remains.

She would take the remains to the church of San Giacomo, where my mom saw her from the bus stop. She still went daily to pray for the fallen soldiers, always calling them her sons. Mama Lucia, from this beautiful little town where my mother was born, became an international figure. She gained acclaim and awards for her tireless efforts. There were several books and articles published about Mama Lucia. Mom has a couple of her books on a shelf, and her wedding is featured in both. Mama Lucia's faith and passion may have even inspired my grandmother. I'm sure she helped my grandmother endure those difficult years of suffering during and after the war. Thinking about Mama Lucia, I wonder how she would have felt about my grandmother deceiving the son of a mother. I'm sure this is something my grandmother never shared with her.

We arrived in Capri. The blue, blue water and the rugged green coastline were stunning and totally unlike the California beaches of home. We enjoyed a wonderful day at the beach. I teased my Zio Mateo as he was afraid to go in the water. Try as I might, I couldn't get him to go in. He was in good company since my mother wouldn't either. The sun had worn me out as we got ready to go home. Grandfather helped me and carried some of my things as we headed for the bus stop. Back at his house, I complained of a headache. My mom said that someone had put a spell on me, probably out of jealousy. My mom must have been remembering the superstitions she'd grown up with.

That evening, Zio Mateo told my mother that his brother wished to marry me. I'd met him a few days before, and my mother had told me he was engaged. It turned out he broke off his engagement in hopes of marrying me and going to America. I was furious and quickly said no. Things hadn't changed that much in twenty years. I remember reading a newspaper article that said women were putting their names and phone numbers in my father's pockets in hopes that he could find a husband in America for them. He tried to explain to them that most Americans weren't wealthy, but they wouldn't believe him. I'm sure Zio Mateo's brother wouldn't have believed me either, but we didn't speak the same language, and I don't think I saw him again.

The next morning, we went to the cemetery. My mom cried as she stood next to the wall that held many boxes of bones. Her mother's bones set in the wall had a light above it that my Zia Amelia paid for. I had always loved cemeteries; they had an amazing feeling of peace. My grandmother suffered so much as she had tried to protect her children during the war. I can't imagine not having enough food to feed her children. As I watched my mother, I realized again she had never gotten over losing her mother at the tender age of 15.

That afternoon, we had another home to visit, one of my mother's cousins. It was a shame I couldn't understand what these people were saying. It was frustrating as I wanted to experience everything. The food was excellent and so, so much. They served us 7-course meals, and my mother told me I would insult them if I didn't eat everything. Sometimes, after a meal, I would retire to a couch or bed to take a nap as I was bored listening to everyone speaking a language I couldn't understand. It just sounded like noise to me. I would quickly find myself asleep until my mother or grandfather woke me up to go home. I gained 20 pounds on that trip, but my mother didn't seem to gain any. Everyone wanted my mother to come to their house for a meal. Journalists followed us and recognized us everywhere because of the posters and word of mouth. As the trip was coming to an end, my mother became more emotional, knowing she would soon have to leave.

The trip was long, and I was glad when it came time to go home. Of course, my mother shed many tears as she told her sisters and family goodbye. It was a trip I will never forget, as I got to experience just a little bit of what my mother must have experienced 20 years prior.

Mom with her siblings she hasn't seen in 20 years

TWENTY-FIVE

Mom went to Italy several more times after that and was always treated like a celebrity. The last time she was there was after Dad had passed, and she received a plaque from the mayor for all her sacrifices. The occasion was filmed and put on television and in the local movie theatre in Cava de' Tirreni. Her sacrifice was coming to America, which she did to help her family. The video is on the internet and shows Mom tearfully talking about what she had to endure coming to America. Marrying Dad wasn't supposed to be a sacrifice. It upsets me whenever I notice that plaque proudly hanging on the wall in my mother's family room. What about the sacrifices Dad made? He worked so hard, often doing double shifts or working two jobs to save enough money to travel halfway across the world to retrieve the women he thought he loved, only to be duped. Knowing Dad, he was probably happy for Mom and the attention she got on her trips. Dad was used to being in the background of Mom's life. Maybe he even felt guilty for taking her away from her family. He never seemed angry at her, but it was evident that she wasn't happy with him.

* * *

As a result of my mom's career, my brother George and I both become real estate agents. I don't think Mom wanted me to become a real estate agent. She told me that my father said I would never pass the exam. At the time, I was very hurt, but when I thought about it, I realized Dad was probably trying to make her feel better about her accomplishments. Her comment only made me more determined to pass that exam. So I did, on the first try, in 1979 when I was 26. This was something very positive for me. George and I both had long, successful careers in real estate.

Dad had retired in his early 70s after many years of hard work standing on his damaged feet. He wore his slippers everywhere after that, even on his long walks around the neighborhood. Mom was working at a nearby real estate office, and Dad stayed home and cooked, baked, and gardened. I remember him buying an Italian cookbook and trying all kinds of new dishes. I liked his eggplant the best. He whistled a lot in those days. I always loved hearing him whistle because it meant he was happy. During his retirement, Dad would often visit his brothers. Uncle Leo now had a Truck Supply store in Azusa, and Uncle Armond had moved to California from Massachusetts to help Leo in the shop. The three brothers would often go gambling at the casino nearby. He also joined a bingo group, making some new friends. It seemed Dad really enjoyed gambling or just playing games.

When Mom made enough money, she bought a time-share and went to Puerto Vallarta with friends every year. Dad was never invited. But they had found some happiness separately. She did what she wanted, and he never complained. I think he knew that if he couldn't make her happy, they each had to find their own happiness. He loved her even though she chose not to see it. My brothers and I agree that he must have loved her from what we saw.

He was really having fun with his bingo buddies and his brothers. I was glad for him as I had never seen my father take much enjoyment out of life. Mom had made friends with some of her clients and the people in her office. She went to conventions, workshops, and meetings and loved every minute. It wasn't ideal, but it worked.

My parents each had complex challenges later in life. My dad was diagnosed with prostate cancer when he was 72. It was slow-growing, and the doctor said he would probably die of old age before cancer. However, it went into his bones many years later when he was 84. In early 2003, Mom took Dad to the hospital for tests. She dropped him off and then parked the car. As she crossed the street, a distracted young man hit her; she flew up and over the vehicle. Upon hearing what happened, Dad kept repeating, "My Nina, oh no, my little Nina." Dad was devastated, and his illness was forgotten as he worried about Mom for the following weeks.

My brother, Alan, took care of Dad in Diamond Bar. I brought Mom home from the hospital to my house in San Diego. Dad was heartbroken and couldn't worry about anything but his Nina. When Mom was finally well enough to go home, the two of them seemed very close. I'm sure Mom felt vulnerable for the first time in a long time, and Dad was so glad to have her home after coming so close to losing her. They needed each other, and now she was his caretaker. He died in 2005 at the age of 86, and I'd never seen my parents more connected. It seemed he had his little Nina back when he was at the end of his life.

Now that Mom is old and frail, she always talks about how handsome Dad was. The walls in her home are covered with dozens of pictures taken by Life Magazine photographers 70 years ago. You can't visit Mom without looking at her photos and listening to her stories. She claims Dad is still with her and still naps on his favorite couch in the living room because she often finds the pillows in disarray. I'm glad she takes comfort in feeling that he is near.

TWENTY-SIX

I cherish the images I now have of my father as a young man. He was so different than the man I grew up with. I can picture him playing with his dog and listening to music as he took a drive in his car. I loved the letter where he was sitting on the beach thinking about my mother, how the ocean separated them, and his longing for her. That night, he went home and wrote her another love letter.

I can picture him with his family playing crazy eights and laughing and enjoying themselves. How much fun would I have had with Dad if he had shared his love of cards with me? Dad also loved to cook, so I always think of him when I come across one of his favorite foods. He made the best bread pudding, which he doused with evaporated milk. He used evaporated milk in his coffee as well. I also love it that way. One morning, years after he died, I woke up smelling that old familiar smell of evaporated milk in coffee. I was convinced my husband was up and had made it for me until I saw him next to me, fast asleep. It left me feeling Dad was near, glad I was writing the book and discovering who he truly was.

My mother really was a lovely woman. My early memories were of her always singing. She never lost her beautiful voice. She sang old Italian songs Al di La with Jerry Vale and many others with Dean Martin, Frank Sinatra, and Tony Bennet. I can now picture her walking through the cobblestone streets carrying a bucket of water, singing in her lovely Italian. Mom was always happy when she sang, and she often sang when I was young. It just seemed she kept that joy all to herself. But she had her demons, and I don't think they were ever far from her.

I spent my childhood wondering why my dad brought my mother from Italy and why he was the way he was. Why our family was the way they were. I've solved many of the puzzles of my family. I've kept the promise to my mother by writing her story. I hope I've made both of my parents proud. I searched through time for any hint of what my father suffered in the war and afterward. I remember looking at Dad's discharge papers and reading them repeatedly, hoping that there were more clues somehow hidden there. His discharge papers identified him as Alderic George Fortin instead of George Alderic Fortin, switching his first and middle name and never fixing it. Dad risked his life for his country, and they didn't even get his name right. It was like Dad was always in the shadows of his life and not right out in the center of it where he should've been. I was glad to be able to tell the true story of my father's interesting life.

Unfortunately, my mother won't be able to see this labor of love being published. Her health started going downhill in 2023, and she died on November 28, 2023, at 89 years old.

Without all the stories my mother embraced, this book could never have happened. Her passionate desire to see her memories in print motivated me to search through my dad and her beginnings. As this book explores, there was more, so much more. Some of which she never wanted to bring to light. She lived in the past, clutching to the short-lived fame she had in 1951. Trying to do the story justice meant the whole story needed to be told.

When I started writing this book, my mother was very enthusiastic. She spent many hours translating her mother's letters, answering questions, and sharing her childhood memories with me. Initially, it was a straightforward story, which I titled "The American Soldier and the Passiano Cinderella." In 2021, however, I refined the perspective of the book to a memoir of discovery, and I told my mother that I had to tell the truth about our dysfunctional family. She wasn't thrilled but didn't object. However, when I changed the working title of the book to "My Father's Letters," she no longer cared if I finished it. She wanted the book to be about her; she wanted it to be all hers. Her dismissal hurt me greatly, but if I only wrote what she wanted, I would dishonor my father and miss the core drama of the story. I couldn't do it! After her death, my publisher and I decided to change the title to "Whispers Of Betrayal: Love Letters That Changed Everything." I'm sure my mother would have hated that title, but it fits what my grandparents did and does the story justice.

She had always refused to acknowledge my father's letters had touched me deeply. How could she understand since she had never read them and wasn't interested in reading them? She translated her mother's letters for me, never reading any of my father's letters, refusing to believe the betrayal orchestrated by her parents.

The letters provided me with the motivation to throw myself into this project with passion and enthusiasm. The secrets I found gave me the confidence to go forward because I knew we had an amazing story. Rewording the story into a memoir gave me an avenue to work through my sizable degree of regret. The letters revealed that I'd treated my father unjustly, blaming him for our dysfunctional family. I wanted to make it right. I didn't take away from my mother's story; that was never my intention. All her stories are here, even if she had refused to believe it.

I wanted her to be proud of what I had done with our family story. But she just didn't understand. No longer did she tell people her daughter was writing a book. In fact, she told friends and family that I didn't want her in my book and that the book wasn't about her at all.

Maybe she had a feeling that 2023 would be her last year on this planet. Unbeknownst to me, she was on a mission to get her very own book published. A book about her, with her name and picture on the cover. She shared the fabrication about her exclusion from my book with my cousin in Italy, and he joined her cause, putting a team together to get her book published. He asked a friend of theirs, a journalist, to write my mother's book. He agreed and jumped right in and started interviewing her by phone.

I was saddened that my book wasn't enough for my mother since, after all, I'd started the whole project at her request. Why couldn't she trust me just this once? Would she never believe in me? I'd strived to create a book that others would want to read, a book full of surprises and truths that deserved to be told. I'd spent ten years researching, writing draft after draft, and developing my writing skills to produce a candid book about my journey of discovery into the lives of both my parents. The more I researched and wrote, the more I was able to see just how interesting this story was.

While I was crushed and confused by my mother's rejection, I could see that the book my cousin was putting together was a wonderful gift to my mother. She would finally have her lifelong dream realized. She would have a book mostly about her. Her book was titled NINA: The True Story of the American Dream.

I was happy my mother would have what she always wanted. Her book was self-published in August of 2023. It was a small book, about 128 pages, with lots of pictures. In the book, my mother shares her wisdom about moving to America. She shares the pluses and minuses of having been forced to be here with a man she never loved. I was glad to see she never blamed my father; she just thought the war had damaged him to the point he was incapable of loving her.

Although she always said she never felt loved and thought Dad had pushed her away, my brothers and I always believed he loved her very much. She was the one who never seemed to love him. After reading my father's letters, I could see where he may have felt guilty for taking her away from Italy and her family. I think he had resigned himself to letting her do anything she wanted; he never complained.

They released my mother's book during a celebration of the 80th Anniversary of "Operation Avalanche," which honored the Allied landing in Salerno on September 14, 1943. I thanked my cousin and was grateful for the book.

On the day of the celebration, a full presentation had been arranged to honor my mother, including a platform with posters featuring my mother's book cover and showcasing a video of her in her home that a camera crew had taken a week before. Several people from her little town of Cava de'Tirreni shared memories from the platform. Mom was able to take it all in via Skype. Two hundred and fifty chairs were set up, and every chair was filled. My mother felt like a celebrity once again. I put aside my own emotions and was very happy for her. It was one of her happiest moments. A hundred books were sold. She had a piece of that fame back that she had been searching for most of her life.

It was soon after those glorious days that my mother's health took a turn for the worse.

It was almost like she had known her days were numbered the way she manifested those last moments of fame, finally getting the book about her that she had always wanted. I was at peace with that, just wanting her to be happy.

In the days that followed, she got very sick and had to be admitted to the hospital. Watching her share her stories with everyone who entered her hospital room gave me hope. I wanted her to stay alive as long as she could. It seemed she had manifested that book just in the nick of time as she would hold it up for others to see with a big smile on her face.

The time had come for her to go into hospice. We set her hospital bed up in our living room. She was scared but had no pain. I tried to soothe her as much as I could, reminding her of the time her jugular vein had broken over 65 years ago, and she told me she'd floated above her body and felt at peace to the point she didn't want to return until her mom's spirit told her she must return for her children. Those words seemed to calm her. I reminded her of how much she loved and missed her mother, and now she would see her again. I put her mother's picture near her so she could see it, hoping she would get some rest.

I didn't leave her side for eight days, trying to care for her every need. On November 28th, 2023, she took her last breath. Her loneliness and depression were now gone. Her terror of dying was over. My whole life, she had been very hard to please. In her passing, I felt she could finally know me, see how much I loved her, and wanted to please her. She could have the clarity to be impressed by my accomplishments and how I never gave up on getting her stories into print and her legacy. Through my tears, I feel her and know she's near, and yes, she's proud. May she now be at peace.

I'll always be grateful my mother gave me my grandmother in her stories, whom I'd never met. Her life was unhappy, but now I can see her so clearly in my mind, like I really knew her. My poor grandmother how she struggled to keep her family safe. I now think of her often. I can picture her standing with her hair in a bun and the big iron key around her neck, clutching it to her chest.

I still wonder if my children have inherited any of the trauma of their grandparents, great-grandparents, or even great-great-grandparents. The current generation seems so spoiled compared to all I've learned about our previous generations. It would be nice if the lessons of those before us were passed down in our cells. We are a product of our genes and generations of trauma, war, and global conflict. Our genes probably know something about fear, and they have a lot to be afraid of. Those genes may have built some resilience in me and taught me how to live, change, and appreciate the lives lived before me. Within their story lay my own story, and writing it felt like I had filled an aching emptiness with answers instead of only questions.

I'll always cherish the way I got to know my parents as young people struggling to find their way in this world. They didn't always make the best choices, but I believe they did the best they could with the cards they were dealt. They forced me to grow and change into who I am, and I'm proud of the life I have and how they were a part of it. Dad and I now have a special connection and always will. When I picture his face in his later years, I see the pain in those blue eyes that look so much like my own. I now know more about why that pain was there. There are still questions I would love to ask him, but I hope he knows I've solved most of the puzzles of his life and our family. I would love to go to him one more time, wrap my arms around him, and tell him I understand. I understand so much now.

What a gift my parents have given me with this story that I know I was meant to write

Mom, Dad, and I at my wedding in 2003

ACKNOWLEDGMENTS

I have to start by thanking my awesome husband, Mark, for reading all my many drafts, praising me, and pushing me when I needed it.

No writer could ask for a more devoted and wonderful writing coach and editor than Shannon Cullip. Your friendship, dedication, and wisdom carried me through. You were always there for me, no matter what time I called or what I needed. I am forever grateful.

My appreciation and gratitude extend to my super friends Rosalind Miller, Christie King, Grace Vanderwerf, Ken Scott, and Aleya Annaton for loving me and believing in me enough to help edit and advise over and over again.

Thank you to my daughter, Kate Edgecombe, for reading, advising, and being there for whatever I might need.

Thank you to my cousin Trish Sargent for filling me in on my father's early life. You are always there when I need you.

Thank you, Author Gary Brozek, who believed in me and my memoir and spent hours explaining what I needed to do.

Thank you, Author Jinsey Willett, for editing, advising, and giving the most wonderful review.

I am deeply appreciative of my publisher Armin Lear and Maryann Karinch. Maryann believed in me and my manuscript and kept on top of all the essential details. She provided wonderful support in every way throughout the process and had lots of patience with this first time Author. Also, Vincent Lupiano for loving and believing in the story and for superb editing.

Finally, Thank you to all the many, many, friends and relatives who read my book. Some of you loved it, and some told me I needed to make changes. I love you all and appreciate your support and encouragement. I am so blessed to have so many wonderful people in my life who gave of their time. I can't thank you all enough.

Printed in the USA
CPSIA information can be obtained
at www.ICGtesting.com
CBHW030443140524
8337CB00004B/7